Interdomain Multicast Solutions Guide

Cisco Systems, Inc.

Brian Adams

Ed Cheng

Tina Fox

Andy Kessler

Mark Manzanares

Bryan Mclaughlin

Jim Rushton

Beverly Tai

Kevin Tran

Cisco Press

Cisco Press
201 West 103rd Street
Indianapolis, IN 46290 USA

Interdomain Multicast Solutions Guide

Cisco Systems, Inc.

Copyright© 2002 Cisco Systems, Inc.

Published by:
Cisco Press
201 West 103rd Street
Indianapolis, IN 46290 USA

All rights reserved. No part of this book may be reproduced or transmitted in any form or by any means, electronic or mechanical, including photocopying, recording, or by any information storage and retrieval system, without written permission from the publisher, except for the inclusion of brief quotations in a review.

Printed in the United States of America 1 2 3 4 5 6 7 8 9 0

First Printing June 2002

Library of Congress Cataloging-in-Publication Number: 2002100661

ISBN: 1-58705-083-8

Warning and Disclaimer

This book is designed to provide information about selected topics for the CCIE Exam for the Routing & Switching track. Every effort has been made to make this book as complete and as accurate as possible, but no warranty or fitness is implied.

The information is provided on an "as is" basis. The authors, Cisco Press, and Cisco Systems, Inc. shall have neither liability nor responsibility to any person or entity with respect to any loss or damages arising from the information contained in this book or from the use of the discs or programs that may accompany it.

The opinions expressed in this book belong to the authors and are not necessarily those of Cisco Systems, Inc.

Feedback Information

At Cisco Press, our goal is to create in-depth technical books of the highest quality and value. Each book is crafted with care and precision, undergoing rigorous development that involves the unique expertise of members from the professional technical community.

Readers' feedback is a natural continuation of this process. If you have any comments regarding how we could improve the quality of this book, or otherwise alter it to better suit your needs, you can contact us through e-mail at feedback@ciscopress.com. Please make sure to include the book title and ISBN in your message.

We greatly appreciate your assistance.

Trademark Acknowledgments

All terms mentioned in this book that are known to be trademarks or service marks have been appropriately capitalized. Cisco Press or Cisco Systems, Inc. cannot attest to the accuracy of this information. Use of a term in this book should not be regarded as affecting the validity of any trademark or service mark.

Publisher	John Wait
Editor-In-Chief	John Kane
Cisco Systems Program Management	Michael Hakkert
	Tom Geitner
Production Manager	Patrick Kanouse
Development Editor	Dayna Isley
Project Editor	Marc Fowler
Copy Editor	Marcia Ellett
Technical Editors	Kevin C. Almeroth, Ph.D.
	Jon Crowcroft, Ph.D.
Team Coordinator	Tammi Ross
Book Designer	Gina Rexrode
Cover Designer	Louisa Klucznik
Compositor	Mark Shirar
Indexer	Tim Wright

CISCO SYSTEMS

Corporate Headquarters
Cisco Systems, Inc.
170 West Tasman Drive
San Jose, CA 95134-1706
USA
http://www.cisco.com
Tel: 408 526-4000
    800 553-NETS (6387)
Fax: 408 526-4100

European Headquarters
Cisco Systems Europe
11 Rue Camille Desmoulins
92782 Issy-les-Moulineaux
Cedex 9
France
http://www-europe.cisco.com
Tel: 33 1 58 04 60 00
Fax: 33 1 58 04 61 00

Americas Headquarters
Cisco Systems, Inc.
170 West Tasman Drive
San Jose, CA 95134-1706
USA
http://www.cisco.com
Tel: 408 526-7660
Fax: 408 527-0883

Asia Pacific Headquarters
Cisco Systems Australia,
Pty., Ltd
Level 17, 99 Walker Street
North Sydney
NSW 2059 Australia
http://www.cisco.com
Tel: +61 2 8448 7100
Fax: +61 2 9957 4350

Cisco Systems has more than 200 offices in the following countries. Addresses, phone numbers, and fax numbers are listed on the Cisco Web site at www.cisco.com/go/offices

Argentina • Australia • Austria • Belgium • Brazil • Bulgaria • Canada • Chile • China • Colombia • Costa Rica • Croatia • Czech Republic • Denmark • Dubai, UAE • Finland • France • Germany • Greece • Hong Kong • Hungary • India • Indonesia • Ireland Israel • Italy • Japan • Korea • Luxembourg • Malaysia • Mexico • The Netherlands • New Zealand • Norway • Peru • Philippines Poland • Portugal • Puerto Rico • Romania • Russia • Saudi Arabia • Scotland • Singapore • Slovakia • Slovenia • South Africa • Spain Sweden • Switzerland • Taiwan • Thailand • Turkey • Ukraine • United Kingdom • United States • Venezuela • Vietnam • Zimbabwe

Copyright © 2000, Cisco Systems, Inc. All rights reserved. Access Registrar, AccessPath, Are You Ready, ATM Director, Browse with Me, CCDA, CCDE, CCDP, CCIE, CCNA, CCNP, CCSI, CD-PAC, CiscoLink, the Cisco NetWorks logo, the Cisco Powered Network logo, Cisco Systems Networking Academy, Fast Step, FireRunner, Follow Me Browsing, FormShare, GigaStack, IGX, Intelligence in the Optical Core, Internet Quotient, IP/VC, iQ Breakthrough, iQ Expertise, iQ FastTrack, iQuick Study, iQ Readiness Scorecard, The iQ Logo, Kernel Proxy, MGX, Natural Network Viewer, Network Registrar, the Networkers logo, Packet, PIX, Point and Click Internetworking, Policy Builder, RateMUX, ReyMaster, ReyView, ScriptShare, Secure Script, Shop with Me, SlideCast, SMARTnet, SVX, TrafficDirector, TransPath, VlanDirector, Voice LAN, Wavelength Router, Workgroup Director, and Workgroup Stack are trademarks of Cisco Systems, Inc.; Changing the Way We Work, Live, Play, and Learn, Empowering the Internet Generation, are service marks of Cisco Systems, Inc.; and Aironet, ASIST, BPX, Catalyst, Cisco, the Cisco Certified Internetwork Expert Logo, Cisco IOS, the Cisco IOS logo, Cisco Press, Cisco Systems, Cisco Systems Capital, the Cisco Systems logo, Collision Free, Enterprise/Solver, EtherChannel, EtherSwitch, FastHub, FastLink, FastPAD, IOS, IP/TV, IPX, LightStream, LightSwitch, MICA, NetRanger, Post-Routing, Pre-Routing, Registrar, StrataView Plus, Stratm, SwitchProbe, TeleRouter, are registered trademarks of Cisco Systems, Inc. or its affiliates in the U.S. and certain other countries.

All other brands, names, or trademarks mentioned in this document or Web site are the property of their respective owners. The use of the word partner does not imply a partnership relationship between Cisco and any other company. (0010R)

About the Authors

Brian Adams is a technical editor (emphasis on dial and IP technologies) for the Knowledge Management and Delivery Group (IOS Technologies) at Cisco Systems. He received his B.A. in Communications from Seton Hall University. Brian was formerly a newspaper reporter and an editor of a small, weekly newspaper. He also published a small horror story and has two unpublished novels (and is now working on his third unpublishable novel).

Ed Cheng has a B.S. in Computer Science from the University of California at Davis (1998) and is currently a systems test engineer for the End-to-End System Test ISP solutions team at Cisco Systems. Ed's responsibilities include designing and building lab environments representative of customer topologies based on Tier 1 and 2 ISPs.

Tina Fox is currently the Integration Solutions program manager for the Knowledge Management and Delivery Group (IOS Technologies) at Cisco Systems and has been with the company for more than five years. She attended the University of California at Los Angeles for both her undergraduate degree and graduate studies, and completed a Certificate in Data and Telecommunications at the University of California at Irvine.

Andy Kessler has been a network professional for the past 15 years. He received his B.S. in Computer Science from the State University of New York at Buffalo and his M.S. in Telecommunications from the University of Colorado. Currently, Andy is a senior test engineer with the End-to-End System Test group at Cisco Systems. For the past several years, he has worked closely with customers (with requirements for real-time market data applications in the financial industry) on designing networks for IP multicast.

Mark Manzanares has a BSCE (Computer Engineering) from Santa Clara University (1997) and is currently a lead engineer and technical lead for the End-to-End System Test ISP solutions team at Cisco Systems. Mark designs and supports large-scale projects for ISP/SP customers, such as MPLS environments with VPN, TE, Remote Access, QoS/CoS, and content distribution networks.

Bryan Mclaughlin (CCIE# 2502) has worked in networking since 1989 and has been with Cisco Systems since 1995. He began working in multicast in late 1996. He is currently a technical marketing engineer with ITD Product Marketing at Cisco Systems and is a frequent presenter at NetWorkers. Bryan is happily married to Michelle and has a baby daughter, Sacha.

Jim Rushton has worked with enterprise networking technology, in various capacities, for more than 15 years. He is currently a Cisco Systems technical writer in the Irvine, California office, assigned to Knowledge Management and Delivery Group (IOS Technologies).

Beverly Tai is a technical writer for Cisco Systems in the Knowledge Management and Delivery Group (IOS Technologies), working on Cisco IOS software documentation. She writes mainly IP Multicast feature and solutions documentation. She received a B.S. in Engineering from the University of California, Los Angeles, in 1993 and an M.S. in Engineering from the University of California, Davis, in 1999.

Kevin Tran (CCIE #4990) has been with Cisco Systems for 10 years. He currently works in the End-to-End System Test Group. Kevin's responsibilities include deploying and testing multicast and QoS solutions.

About the Technical Reviewers

Kevin C. Almeroth earned his Ph.D. in Computer Science from the Georgia Institute of Technology in 1997. He is currently an associate professor at the University of California in Santa Barbara (UCSB) where his main research interests include computer networks and protocols, multicast communication, large-scale multimedia systems, and performance evaluation. At UCSB, Dr. Almeroth is a founding member of the Media Arts and Technology Program (MATP), Associate Director of the Center for Information Technology and Society (CITS), and on the Executive Committee for the University of California Digital Media Innovation (DiMI) program.

In the research community, Dr. Almeroth is on the Editorial Board of IEEE Network, has co-chaired NGC 2000, Global Internet 2001, NOSSDAV 2002, and MMNS 2002; has served as tutorial chair for several conferences, and has been on the program committee of numerous conferences. Dr. Almeroth is serving as the chair of the Internet2 Working Group on Multicast and is a member of the IETF Multicast Directorate (MADDOGS). He is also serving on the advisory boards of several startups including Occam Networks, NCast, Hidden Footprint, and the Santa Barbara Technology Incubator. He has been a member of both the ACM and IEEE since 1993.

Jon Crowcroft has been the Marconi Professor of Communications Systems in the Computer Lab at Cambridge University since October 2001, almost exactly 100 years after Guglielmo Marconi's "groundbreaking" first transatlantic wireless call. Prior to that, Dr. Crowcroft was a professor in the Department of Computer Science at University College London (UCL). He graduated in Physics from Trinity College, Cambridge University in 1979, earned an MSC in Computing from UCL in 1981, and a PhD from UCL in 1993.

Dr. Crowcroft is a member of the ACM and the British Computer Society, a fellow of the IEE and the royal academy of engineering, and a Senior Member the IEEE. He is also on the editorial team for Computer Networks, IEEE Networks, Internet Protocol Journal, Cluster Computing, and Mobile Applications and Networks. He is involved in two COST actions for the UK: 264 on Group Communication, which has an NGC 2001 Workshop, and 263 on Quality of Future Internet Services, which also has an annual QofIS 2001 Workshop, as well as Cabernet. He's currently on the Internet Architecture Board and is on the program committee for ACM SIGCOMM 2002, IEEE Infocom 2002, Networks 2002, NGC2002, NOSSDAV 2002, IWQoS 2002, QofIS 2002, PfHSN 2002, and PV 2002.

Acknowledgments

This project was truly a collaborative effort. Many people contributed their time, effort, and expertise in creating the material presented in this book.

Many thanks to Andy Kessler for his invaluable contributions to this book; without his help and direction, it is unlikely that this project would have been completed. We love you, Andy!

Many thanks, also, to Brian Mclaughlin for his contribution to this book during the developmental edit review cycle. Without Bryan's support, this book would never have been completed in time to meet publication deadlines. We love you too, Bryan!

Thanks to Mark Manzanares and Ed Cheng for setting up the test lab environment and providing all the configuration files, to Beverly Tai for gathering all the pieces and making it into a book, to Brian Adams for editing this material (twice!), and to Scott Miller for his help with all of the illustrations.

Thanks to Jim Rushton for putting the command summary together, to Toerless Eckert for his contributions to the theoretical content in this book and for his skills in reviewing this material, and to Tina Fox and Bob Anstey for presenting the idea for this book to Cisco Press and pushing this project along.

Thanks to all of our reviewers: Greg Shepherd, John Zwiebel, Shobana Gubbi, and Vinay Anand. Last but not least, thanks to every member of the IP Multicast Solutions documentation team, whose participation anchored this project in the first place: Andy Kessler, Steve Weber, Mark Manzanares, Kevin Tran, Yao-Hua Teng, Ed Cheng, Tina Fox, Beverly Tai, Dan Alvarez, Toerless Eckert, and Bryan Mclaughlin.

Contents at a Glance

Introduction xiv

Part I **Introduction 3**

Chapter 1 IP Multicast Technology Overview 5

Part II **Interdomain Multicast with MSDP 35**

Chapter 2 Implementing Interdomain Multicast Using MSDP 37

Chapter 3 ISP1 Device Characteristics and Configuration Files 91

Chapter 4 ISP2 Device Characteristics and Configuration Files 151

Chapter 5 ISP3 and ISP4 Device Characteristics and Configuration Files 195

Part III **Interdomain Multicast with SSM 235**

Chapter 6 Implementing Interdomain Multicast Using SSM 237

Chapter 7 Device Characteristics and Configuration Files for Implementing Interdomain Multicast Using SSM 255

Appendix A IP Multicast Command Summary 273

Index 299

Contents

Introduction   xiv

Part I   **Introduction**   3

Chapter 1   IP Multicast Technology Overview   5

IP Multicast   5

Multicast Group Concept   6

IP Multicast Addresses   7
  IP Class D Addresses   7
  Layer 2 Multicast Addresses   9

Intradomain Multicast Protocols   11
  Internet Group Management Protocol (IGMP)   11
  Multicast in the Layer 2 Switching Environment   16
  Multicast Distribution Trees   19
  Multicast Forwarding   22
  Protocol Independent Multicast (PIM)   24
  Bidirectional PIM (Bidir-PIM)   26
  Pragmatic General Multicast (PGM)   27

Interdomain Multicast Protocols   27
  Multiprotocol Border Gateway Protocol (MBGP)   27
  Multicast Source Discovery Protocol (MSDP)   28
  Source Specific Multicast (SSM)   32

Summary   32

Related Documents   33

Part II   **Interdomain Multicast with MSDP**   35

Chapter 2   Implementing Interdomain Multicast Using MSDP   37

Strategy for Implementing Interdomain Multicast   38
  Phase 1: Establishing an Overall Intradomain Multicast Strategy   40
  Phase 2: Establishing an Overall Interdomain Multicast Strategy   42
  Phase 3: Establishing an Implementation Strategy for Connecting Customers into Infrastructure   48

Implementing Interdomain Multicast Using MSDP   49
  ISP2 Scenario   49
  ISP1 Scenario   59
  ISP3 and ISP4 Scenarios   75

Summary   88

Related Documents   88

Chapter 3   ISP1 Device Characteristics and Configuration Files   91

    ISP1BB1   93
        Device Characteristics for ISP1BB1   93
        Configuration File for ISP1BB1   94

    ISP1BB2   97
        Device Characteristics for ISP1BB2   98
        Configuration File for ISP1BB2   99

    ISP1BB3   102
        Device Characteristics for ISP1BB3   103
        Configuration File for ISP1BB3   104

    ISP1BB4   108
        Device Characteristics for ISP1BB4   108
        Configuration File for ISP1BB4   109

    ISP1BB5   113
        Device Characteristics for ISP1BB5   113
        Configuration File for ISP1BB5   114

    ISP1BB6   119
        Device Characteristics for ISP1BB6   119
        Configuration File for ISP1BB6   120

    ISP1BB7   123
        Device Characteristics for ISP1BB7   124
        Configuration File for ISP1BB7   124

    ISP1DA1   128
        Device Characteristics for ISP1DA1   129
        Configuration File for ISP1DA1   129

    ISP1DA2   133
        Device Characteristics for ISP1DA2   133
        Configuration File for ISP1DA2   134

    ISP1DA3   138
        Device Characteristics for ISP1DA3   138
        Configuration File for ISP1DA3   139

    ISP1AC1   142
        Device Characteristics for ISP1AC1   143
        Configuration File for ISP1AC1   144

    ISP1AC2   146
        Device Characteristics for ISP1AC2   147
        Configuration File for ISP1AC2   148

Chapter 4   ISP2 Device Characteristics and Configuration Files   151

    ISP2BB1   153
        Device Characteristics for ISP2BB1   153
        Configuration File for ISP2BB1   154

    ISP2BB2   160
        Device Characteristics for ISP2BB2   160
        Configuration File for ISP2BB2   161

    ISP2BB3   167
        Device Characteristics for ISP2BB3   168
        Configuration File for ISP2BB3   168

    ISP2BB4   174
        Device Characteristics for ISP2BB4   175
        Configuration File for ISP2BB4   175

    ISP2BB5 for Solutions Using MSDP   179
        Device Characteristics for ISP2BB5   180
        Configuration File for ISP2BB5   180

    ISP2BB6   184
        Device Characteristics for ISP2BB6   185
        Configuration File for ISP2BB6   186

    ISP2BB7 for Solutions Using MSDP   189
        Device Characteristics for ISP2BB7   189
        Configuration File for ISP2BB7   190

Chapter 5   ISP3 and ISP4 Device Characteristics and Configuration Files   195

    ISP3BB3   197
        Device Characteristics for ISP3BB3   197
        Configuration File for ISP3BB3   198

    ISP3BB4   203
        Device Characteristics for ISP3BB4   203
        Configuration File for ISP3BB4   204

    ISP3BB6   208
        Device Characteristics for ISP3BB6   209
        Configuration File for ISP3BB6   209

    ISP3BB7   215
        Device Characteristics for ISP3BB7   215
        Configuration File for ISP3BB7   216

    ISP4BB3   221
        Device Characteristics for ISP4BB3   222
        Configuration File for ISP4BB3   222

ISP4BB4   229
  Device Characteristics for ISP4BB4   229
  Configuration File for ISP4BB4   230

Part III   **Interdomain Multicast with SSM   235**

Chapter 6   Implementing Interdomain Multicast Using SSM   237

Initial Interdomain Network Topology   238

Understanding SSM   238
  Differences between SSM and ISM   239
  SSM IP Address Range   239
  SSM Operations   240

Possible Solutions for Implementing SSM   241
  Solution 1: IGMPv3 Host Signaling   241
  Solution 2: IGMP v3lite Host Signaling   241
  Solution 3: URD Host Signaling   242

Proposed Solution: URD Host Signaling   242
  Strategy   243
  Network Topology   243
  Benefits   244
  Ramifications   245
  How URD Host Signalling Works   247

Implementing URD Host Signaling   249
  Prerequisite   249
  Implementation Process Steps   249

Summary   253

Related Documents   253

Chapter 7   Device Characteristics and Configuration Files for Implementing Interdomain Multicast Using SSM   255

ISP1AC1   256
  Device Characteristics for ISP1AC1   257
  Configuration File for ISP1AC1   258

ISP2BB3   260
  Device Characteristics for ISP2BB3   261
  Configuration File for ISP2BB3   262

ISP1BB3   266
  Device Characteristics for ISP1BB3   267
  Configuration File for ISP1BB3   267

Appendix A IP Multicast Command Summary 273

    address-family ipv4 Command 273

    debug ip igmp Command 274

    debug ip mrouting Command 274

    debug ip urd Command 274

    ip cgmp Command 275

    ip igmp v3lite Command 275

    ip igmp version Command 275

    ip mrm Command 276

    ip mrm manager Command 276

    ip mroute-cache Command 276

    ip msdp cache-sa-state Command 277

    ip msdp originator-id Command 277

    ip msdp peer Command 277

    ip msdp redistribute Command 278

    ip msdp sa-filter in Command 278

    ip msdp sa-filter out Command 279

    ip multicast boundary Command 280

    ip multicast multipath Command 280

    ip multicast-routing Command 280

    ip pim Command 281

    ip pim accept-register Command 281

    ip pim accept-rp Command 282

    ip pim bsr-border Command 282

    ip pim rp-address Command 282

    ip pim send-rp-announce Command 283

    ip pim send-rp-discovery Command 284

    ip pim spt-threshold Command 284

    ip pim ssm Command 284

    ip urd Command 285

manager Command 285

match nlri Command 285

neighbor activate Command 286

neighbor default-originate Command 286

neighbor peer-group (creating) Command 287

neighbor remote-as Command 287

neighbor route-map Command 288

network (BGP) Command 288

receivers Command 289

redistribute (IP) Command 290

senders Command 293

set nlri Command 293

show ip bgp ipv4 multicast summary Command 294

show ip bgp neighbors Command 294

show ip igmp groups Command 295

show ip mbgp summary Command 295

show ip mroute Command 295

show ip msdp peer Command 296

show ip msdp sa-cache Command 296

Index 299

Introduction

The objective of this book is to assist network architects and operators in designing and implementing Cisco IP multicast into their production networks by providing verified end-to-end network design and configuration examples. This book targets competent, proficient, and expert users. The solutions presented in this book are intended primarily for network administrators and operations teams working for service providers that provide IP multicast services to their customers. The solutions are also useful for enterprise customers who want to establish IP multicast services within their own network environment.

Organization

This book is organized into four parts, as follows:

- Part 1 provides a brief summary and review of IP multicast.
- Part II provides interdomain multicast solutions using Protocol Independent Multicast Sparse Mode (PIM-SM), Multiprotocol Border Gateway Protocol (MBGP), and Multicast Source Discover Protocol (MSDP). The solutions described in Part II are based on a network topology consisting of four different Internet service providers (ISPs). The interdomain multicast implementation for each ISP is presented separately, with emphasis on the following three implementations:
    — intradomain multicast
    — interdomain multicast
    — connecting customers to an ISP infrastructure
- Part III provides interdomain multicast solutions using Source Specific Multicast (SSM). The solutions described in Part III are an extension of the interdomain multicast solutions presented in Part II of this book and focus mainly on implementing SSM using URL Rendezvous Directory (URD).
- Part IV is a command summary appendix consisting of all of the multicast commands discussed in this book.

Evolution of Interdomain Multicast Solutions

Before approaching the interdomain multicast solutions presented in this book, it helps to have some context about how interdomain multicast solutions evolved from 1992 to the present day (2002). Please note that this section is intended as an informal summary, and not a comprehensive historical survey.

Figure I-1 *Multicast Deployment Timeline*

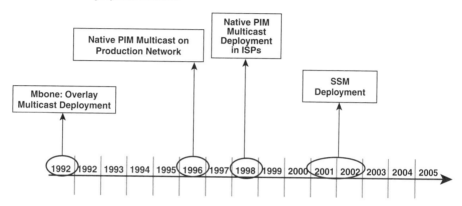

In 1986, Steve Deering created the first practical implementation of multicast when he was a student at Stanford University. He wanted to create a mechanism by which multicast data could flow between IP subnetworks. His initial solution consisted of two protocols: Internet Group Message Protocol (IGMP) and Distance Vector Multicast Routing Protocol (DVMRP). IGMP enabled individual hosts to join or leave a multicast group by interacting with a multicast-enabled router. IGMP is discussed in detail in Chapter 1, "IP Multicast Technology Overview." DVMRP is a dense mode protocol and works on the "flood and prune" principle. DVMRP enabled multicast routers to share information about how nodes were connecting to multicast sources. Internet Group Message Protocol Version 1 (IGMPv1) and DVMRP were used to establish the first practical application of multicast, the Multicast Backbone (MBone), in 1992.

The MBone was (and still is) an overlay network comprised of tunnels using DVMRP to connect various isolated "islands" of multicast-enabled nodes. It was successful as a bootstrap multicast network but, because of the inherent limitations of DVMRP (for example, the 32-hop limit) and the fact that tunnels were used, the MBONE could never be considered a true multicast solution.

To move beyond the limitations imposed by DVMRP (and move toward native multicast deployment), various developers associated with the IETF developed other protocols, the most successful of which was Protocol Independent Multicast Sparse Mode (PIM-SM). PIM was designed to operate with any unicast routing implementations and to leverage existing unicast routing protocol table information (this approach is in contrast to DVMRP, which maintained its own multicast routing table). PIM-SM distributes information about active sources by forwarding data packets on the shared tree; PIM uses rendezvous points (RPs) on the shared tree to accomplish this. PIM-SM has become the model by which both intradomain and interdomain multicast is deployed.

Because PIM-SM no longer maintains a separate multicast routing table, there is the possibility within non-congruent networks (meaning networks where multicast is not uniformly deployed) for Reverse Path Forwarding (RPF) failure.

The requirement to support non-congruent networks led to the development of Multiprotocol Border Gateway Protocol (MBGP). With MBGP, multiprotocol extensions were added to the Border Gateway Protocol (BGP). MBGP (as described in RFC 2858) uses standard BGP characteristics to keep additional Routing Information Bases (RIBs) for protocols other than IPv4 unicast. One of these additional RIBs is the multicast RIB (MRIB), which allows non-congruent unicast and multicast routing to exist and still perform a successful RPF check. Using MBGP allowed ISPs to create a true interdomain multicast network.

Challenges in Deploying Interdomain Multicast

This brings our historical discussion to the late 20th century. Interdomain multicast still poses the following significant deployment challenges:

- Addressing
- Third-Party Dependency

Addressing

The first problem network architects and engineers must face when planning to deploy interdomain multicast is to decide what kind of addressing to use. RFC 1112, "Host Extensions for IP Multicasting," specifies the extensions that IANA has reserved for multicast deployment—specifically 224.0.0.0 to 239.255.255.255 Class D range of addresses. The initial solution for determining which group address to use was to use Session Description Protocol (SDP), as described in RFC 2327 and Session Announcement Protocol (SAP), as described in RFC 2974. By listening to the announcements, a host could assume any addresses not advertised as being used. However, this process was random and not particularly scalable. It also relied on "polite behavior" (meaning there was no enforcement) to prevent sources from broadcasting to the same group and disrupting service. Network architects and engineers needed a solution that would provide a guaranteed unique group address.

Introduced in October 1999, GLOP provided what was intended to be a temporary solution to the need for a guaranteed unique group address. GLOP was initially an experimental RFC (RFC 2770), but it eventually evolved into a best current practice (RFC 3180). GLOP uses the unique autonomous system (AS) number of the source domain to create globally unique groups. It creates a unique number by using the prefix 233 and a 16-bit/2-byte AS number to create the middle two octets as follows:

      233.AS.AS.xxx.

The last octet is assignable by the AS owner as a unique group address. Because only a maximum of 255 globally unique groups can be identified per AS, GLOP provides a functional stop gap but not a scalable solution.

The following table provides a partial listing of the current groups IANA has allocated for use, such as the link local range used by routing protocols; the highlighted entries are those specific to interdomain multicast.

Table I-1   *Class D Address Ranges Allocated by IANA*

Range	Allocated Block
224.0.0.0–224.0.0.255 (224.0.0/24)	Local Network Control Block
224.0.1.0–224.0.1.255 (224.0.1/24)	Internetwork Control Block
224.0.2.0–224.0.255.0	AD-HOC Block
224.1.0.0–224.1.255.255 (224.1/16)	ST Multicast Groups [RFC 1190]
224.2.0.0–224.2.255.255 (224.2/16)	SDP/SAP Block
224.3.0.0–224.251.255.255	Reserved [IANA]
224.252.0.0–224.255.255.255	DIS Transient Groups [IANA]
225.0.0.0–231.255.255.255	Reserved [IANA]
232.0.0.0–232.255.255.255 (232/8)	SSM
233.0.0.0–233.255.255.255 (233/8)	GLOP Block [RFC 3180]
234.0.0.0–238.255.255.255	Reserved [IANA]
239.0.0.0–239.255.255.255 (239/8)	Administratively Scoped [IANA, RFC 2365]

Third-Party Dependency

The next problem with deploying interdomain multicast is third-party dependency. With PIM-SM, there can only be one active RP per multicast group. If all domains are owned and operated by the same ISP, having one RP could be a workable solution. If not, it becomes a question of who owns and operates the RP. Each ISP ideally should have control over its own RP.

The first deployed solution addressing the problems associated with interdomain multicast was to create a new protocol: Multicast Source Discovery Protocol (MSDP). MSDP enabled multiple RPs to exist in the same multicast group by sharing knowledge of the active sources with other MSDP peers so that RPs could be aware of all active sources. MSDP was meant to be a transitional solution until a global system could be created.

Then the idea was posed that a group could be rooted at a domain, instead of a router, if group allocation could be coordinated within the Internet. Border Gateway Multicast Protocol (BGMP) was discussed as a possible method to create these shared interdomain trees. BGMP would allow there to be a bi-directional tree across the Internet so that multicast domains could communicate over the Internet. BGMP could act as an exterior gateway protocol (EGP) and PIM-SM or another protocol could act as the IGMP in the intradomain multicast network. Under this scenario, BGMP would choose a "domain" to be the root of a global tree. These domains were also to run the protocol Multicast Address-Set Claim (MASC). MASC used the concept of leasing group addresses and then reclaiming them after the expiration of the lease period. MASC offered aggregation of group addresses because the allocation scheme was hierarchical, parent to child. A significant obstacle to MASC was the issue of reclaiming group addresses. If a portion of the allocated group was in use and the group had expired its lease time, applications were required to handle this change of address possibly in mid-operation. Before a satisfactory solution could be worked out, Source Specific Multicast (SSM) was developed. SSM offers a simpler solution.

A Simpler Solution

internet Group Message Protocol Version 3(IGMPv3) enables receiving hosts to include or exclude specific sources for the group being "joined to." This allows for the joining of an (S,G) channel rather than a (*,G) group. The traffic for one (S,G) channel consists of IP datagrams with an IP unicast source address S and a multicast group address G as the destination IP address. Because interdomain unicast addresses are unique, even if the same G is used by more than one mulitcast source, there is no overlap in delivery. The channel remains unique due to the inclusion of the unique S source address. There are no address conflicts and all trees are optimally routed.

SSM requires the existence of sources to be communicated to receivers in and out of band method (for example, through a web page), not through the multicast network itself as in regular PIM-SM through the RP and shared tree. IANA has allocated the 232/8 range of addresses for sole use by SSM.

IGMPv3 has not yet been standardized, and it may take some time before its ubiquitous deployment occurs and all applications are IGMPv3-capable. The large number of hosts with Internet access makes this a formidable task. IGMP v3lite and URD are both interim solutions that mitigate this obstacle. Of these two, URD is the easiest solution to implement as it requires no software updates on the IP host receiver.

SSM is being successfully used over the Internet today. For example, IGMPv3, IGMP v3lite, and URD were all successfully demonstrated by Cisco at the LINX multicast conference in London in November 2000 using content from the University of Oregon. As both MSDP and SSM are independent solutions and can be deployed on their own, both the SSM model and the ISM model are expected to co-exist together in interdomain multicast deployment for the foreseeable future. The solutions in this book, therefore, demonstrate both MSDP and SSM utilizing URD.

Command Syntax Conventions

The conventions used to present command syntax in this book are the same conventions used in the Cisco IOS Command Reference. The Command Reference describes these conventions as follows:

- Vertical bars (|) separate alternative, mutually exclusive elements.
- Square brackets [ ] indicate optional elements.
- Braces { } indicate a required choice.
- Braces within brackets [{ }] indicate a required choice within an optional element.
- **Boldface** indicates commands and keywords that are entered literally as shown. In actual configuration examples and output (not general command syntax), boldface indicates commands that are manually input by the user (such as a **show** command).
- *Italics* indicate arguments for which you supply actual values.

Icons Used in This Book

Throughout the book, you will see the following icons used for networking devices:

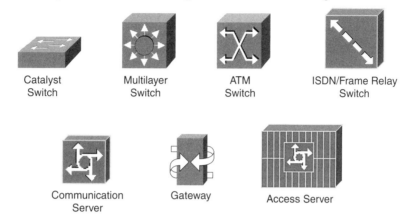

Throughout the book, you will see the following icons used for peripherals and other devices:

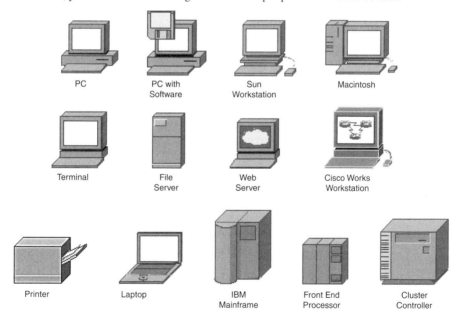

Throughout the book, you will see the following icons used for networks and network connections:

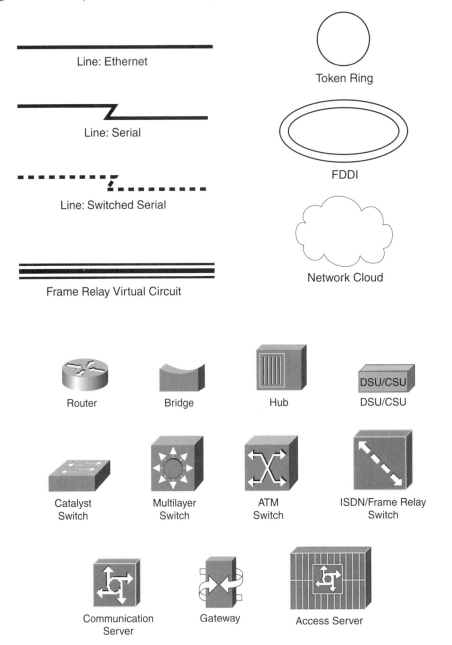

PART I

Introduction

Chapter 1 IP Multicast Technology Overview

CHAPTER 1

IP Multicast Technology Overview

Traditional IP communication allows a host to send packets to a single host (unicast transmission) or to all hosts (broadcast transmission). IP multicast provides a third possibility: it allows a host to send packets to a subset of all hosts as a group transmission. This overview provides a brief summary of IP multicast to set the stage for the solutions presented later in this book. This chapter discusses general topics such as multicast group concept, IP multicast addresses, and Layer 2 multicast addresses. It reviews intradomain multicast protocols, such as Internet Group Management Protocol (IGMP), Cisco Group Management Protocol (CGMP), Protocol Independent Multicast (PIM), and Pragmatic General Multicast (PGM). This chapter also covers interdomain protocols, such as Multiprotocol Border Gateway Protocol (MBGP), Multicast Source Directory Protocol (MSDP), and Source Specific Multicast (SSM).

This chapter is intended as a general "refresher" on IP multicast, not a tutorial. You need to be familiar with TCP/IP, Border Gateway Protocol (BGP), and networking in general. Please refer to Beau Williamson's book, "Developing IP Multicast Networks, Volume 1" (Cisco Press, 1999) if you need more information about any of the topics presented in this overview.

IP Multicast

IP multicast is a bandwidth-conserving technology that reduces traffic by simultaneously delivering a single stream of information to potentially thousands of corporate recipients and homes. Applications that take advantage of multicast include video conferencing, corporate communications, distance learning, and distribution of software, stock quotes, and news.

IP multicast uses a minimum of network bandwidth and delivers application source traffic to multiple receivers without burdening the source or the receivers. Cisco routers enabled with Protocol Independent Multicast (PIM) and other supporting multicast protocols replicate multicast packets in the network at the point where paths diverge, resulting in the most efficient delivery of data to multiple receivers.

Many alternatives to IP multicast require the source to send more than one copy of the data. Some, such as application-level multicast, require the source to send an individual copy to each receiver. Even low-bandwidth applications can benefit from using Cisco IP multicast when there are thousands of receivers. High-bandwidth applications, such as MPEG video, might require a large portion of the available network bandwidth for a single stream. In these applications, IP multicast is the only way to send to more than one receiver simultaneously. Figure 1-1 shows how IP multicast is used to deliver data from one source to many interested recipients.

Figure 1-1 *Multicast Transmission to Many Receivers*

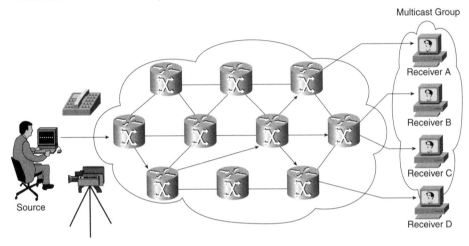

In the example shown in Figure 1-1, the receivers (the designated multicast group) are interested in receiving a video data stream from the source. The receivers indicate their interest by sending an IGMP Host Report to the routers in the network. The routers are responsible for delivering the data from the source to the receivers. The routers use PIM to dynamically create a multicast distribution tree. The video data stream is delivered to only the network segments that are in the path between the source and the receivers. This process is further explained in the following sections.

Multicast Group Concept

Multicast is based on the concept of a group. A multicast group is a group of receivers that expresses an interest in receiving a particular data stream. This group has no physical or geographical boundaries; the hosts can be located anywhere on the Internet or on any private internetwork. Hosts that are interested in receiving data that is flowing to a particular group must join the group using IGMP. (IGMP is discussed later in this chapter.)

IP Multicast Addresses

IP multicast addresses specify a "set" of IP hosts that have joined a group and are interested in receiving multicast traffic designated for that particular group. IPv4 multicast address conventions are described in the following sections.

IP Class D Addresses

The Internet Assigned Numbers Authority (IANA) controls the assignment of IP multicast addresses. IANA has assigned the IPv4 Class D address space to IP multicast. All IP multicast group addresses fall in the range from 224.0.0.0 through 239.255.255.255.

NOTE The Class D address range is used only for the group address or destination address of IP multicast traffic. The source address for multicast datagrams is always the unicast source address.

IP addresses reserved for IP multicast are defined in RFC 1112, "Host Extensions for IP Multicasting." You can find more information about reserved IP multicast addresses at the following location:

www.iana.org/assignments/multicast-addresses

NOTE You can find all RFCs at www.isi.edu/in-notes/rfc*xxx*.txt, where *xxx* is the number of the RFC. If you do not know the number of the RFC, you can find it by doing a topic search at www.rfc-editor.org/rfcsearch.html.

Reserved Link Local Addresses

The IANA has reserved addresses in the range 224.0.0.0/24 to be used by network protocols on a local network segment. Packets with link-local destination addresses are typically sent with a time-to-live (TTL) of 1 and are not forwarded by a router.

Network protocols use these addresses for automatic router discovery and to communicate important routing information. For example, Open Shortest Path First (OSPF) uses the IP addresses 224.0.0.5 and 224.0.0.6 to exchange link-state information. Table 1-1 lists some well-known link-local IP addresses.

Table 1-1 *Examples of Link-Local Addresses*

IP Address	Usage
224.0.0.1	All systems on this subnet
224.0.0.2	All routers on this subnet
224.0.0.5	OSPF routers
224.0.0.6	OSPF designated routers
224.0.0.12	Dynamic Host Configuration Protocol (DHCP) server/relay agent

Globally Scoped Addresses

Addresses in the range from 224.0.1.0 through 238.255.255.255 are called *globally scoped addresses*. These addresses are used to multicast data between organizations and across the Internet.

Some of these addresses have been reserved for use by multicast applications through IANA. For example, IP address 224.0.1.1 is reserved for Network Time Protocol (NTP).

Source Specific Multicast (SSM) Addresses

Addresses in the 232.0.0.0/8 range are reserved for SSM. SSM is an extension of the PIM protocol that allows for an efficient data delivery mechanism in one-to-many communications. SSM is described later in this chapter.

GLOP Addresses

RFC 3180, "GLOP Addressing in 233/8," proposes that the 233.0.0.0/8 address range be reserved for statically defined addresses by organizations that already have an autonomous system (AS) number reserved. This practice is called *GLOP addressing*. The domain's AS number is embedded into the second and third octets of the 233.0.0.0/8 address range. For example, AS 62010 is written in hexadecimal format as F23A. Separating the two octets F2 and 3A results in 242 and 58 in decimal format. These values result in a subnet of 233.242.58.0/24 that would be globally reserved for AS 62010.

Limited Scope Addresses

Addresses in the 239.0.0.0/8 range are called *limited scope* addresses or *administratively scoped* addresses. These addresses are described in RFC 2365, "Administratively Scoped IP Multicast," to be constrained to a local group or organization. Companies, universities, or other organizations can use limited scope addresses to have local multicast applications that will not be forwarded outside their domain. Routers are typically configured with filters to prevent multicast traffic in this address range from flowing outside of an AS or any user-defined domain. Within an autonomous system or domain, the limited scope address range can be further subdivided so that local multicast boundaries can be defined. This subdivision is called *address scoping* and allows for address reuse between these smaller domains.

Table 1-2 gives a summary of the multicast address ranges discussed in this chapter:

Table 1-2 *Multicast Address Range Assignments*

Description	Range
Reserved Link Local Addresses	224.0.0.0/24
Globally Scoped Addresses:	224.0.1.0 to 238.255.255.255
Source Specific Multicast	232.0.0.0/8
GLOP Addresses	233.0.0.0/8
Limited Scope Addresses	239.0.0.0/8

Layer 2 Multicast Addresses

Historically, network interface cards (NICs) on a LAN segment could receive only packets destined for their burned-in MAC address or the broadcast MAC address. In IP multicast, several hosts need to be able to receive a single data stream with a common destination MAC address. Some means had to be devised so that multiple hosts could receive the same packet and still be able to differentiate between several multicast groups.

One method to accomplish this is to map IP multicast Class D addresses directly to a MAC address. Today, using this method, NICs can receive packets destined for many different MAC addresses—their own unicast, broadcast, and a range of multicast addresses.

The IEEE LAN specifications made provisions for the transmission of broadcast and multicast packets. In the 802.3 standard, bit 0 of the first octet indicates a broadcast or multicast frame. Figure 1-2 shows the location of the broadcast or multicast bit in an Ethernet frame.

Figure 1-2 *IEEE 802.3 MAC Address Format*

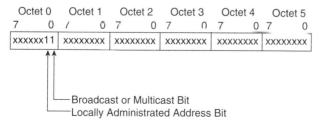

This bit indicates that the frame is destined for a group of hosts or all hosts on the network (in the case of the broadcast address, 0xFFFF.FFFF.FFFF).

IP multicast makes use of this capability to send IP packets to a group of hosts on a LAN segment.

Ethernet MAC Address Mapping

The IANA owns a block of Ethernet MAC addresses that start with 01:00:5E in hexadecimal format. Half of this block, from 0100.5E00.0000 through 0100.5E7F.FFFF, is allocated for multicast addresses.

This allocation allows for 23 bits in the Ethernet address to correspond to the IP multicast group address. The mapping places the lower 23 bits of the IP multicast group address into these available 23 bits in the Ethernet address (see Figure 1-3).

Figure 1-3 *IP Multicast to Ethernet or FDDI MAC Address Mapping*

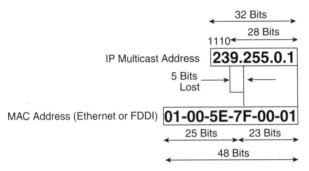

Because the upper 5 bits of the IP multicast address are dropped in this mapping, the resulting address is not unique. In fact, 32 different multicast group IDs map to the same Ethernet address (see Figure 1-4). Network administrators should consider this fact when assigning IP multicast addresses. For example, 224.1.1.1 and 225.1.1.1 map to the same multicast MAC address on a Layer 2 switch. If one user subscribed to Group A (as designated by 224.1.1.1) and another user subscribed to Group B (as designated by 225.1.1.1), they would both receive both A and B streams. This situation limits the effectiveness of this multicast deployment.

Figure 1-4 *MAC Address Ambiguities*

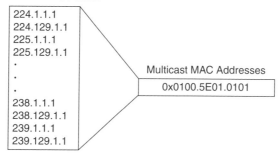

Intradomain Multicast Protocols

Intradomain multicasting protocols are used inside of a multicast domain to support multicasting. This section presents the following topics:

- Internet Group Management Protocol (IGMP)
- Multicast in the Layer 2 Switching Environment
- Multicast Distribution Trees
- Multicast Forwarding
- Protocol Independent Multicast (PIM)
- Bidirectional PIM (Bidir-PIM)
- Pragmatic General Multicast (PGM)

Internet Group Management Protocol (IGMP)

IGMP is used to dynamically register individual hosts in a multicast group on a particular LAN. Hosts identify group memberships by sending IGMP messages to their local multicast router. Under IGMP, routers listen to IGMP messages and periodically send out queries to discover which groups are active or inactive on a particular subnet.

IGMP versions are described in the following sections.

IGMP Version 1

RFC 1112, "Host Extensions for IP Multicasting," describes the specification for IGMP Version 1 (IGMPv1). A diagram of the packet format for an IGMPv1 message is shown in Figure 1-5.

Figure 1-5 *IGMPv1 Message Format*

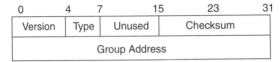

In Version 1, only the following two types of IGMP messages exist:

- Membership query
- Membership report

Hosts send IGMP membership reports corresponding to a particular multicast group to indicate that they are interested in joining that group. The TCP/IP stack running on a host automatically sends the IGMP membership report when an application opens a multicast socket. The router periodically sends an IGMP membership query to verify that at least one host on the subnet is still interested in receiving traffic directed to that group. When there is no reply to three consecutive IGMP membership queries, the router times out the group and stops forwarding traffic directed toward that group.

IGMP Version 2

IGMPv1 has been superseded by IGMP Version 2 (IGMPv2), which is now the current standard. IGMPv2 is backward-compatible with IGMPv1. RFC 2236, "Internet Group Management Protocol, Version 2," describes the specification for IGMPv2. A diagram of the packet format for an IGMPv2 message is shown in Figure 1-6.

Figure 1-6 *IGMPv2 Message Format*

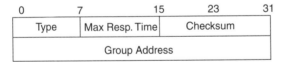

In Version 2, the following four types of IGMP messages exist:

- Membership query
- Version 1 membership report
- Version 2 membership report
- Leave group

IGMP Version 2 works basically the same way as Version 1. The main difference is that there is a leave group message. With this message, the hosts can actively communicate to the local multicast router that they intend to leave the group. The router then sends out a group-specific query and determines if any remaining hosts are interested in receiving the traffic. If there are no replies, the router times out the group and stops forwarding the traffic. The addition of the leave group message in IGMP Version 2 greatly reduces the leave latency compared to IGMP Version 1. Unwanted and unnecessary traffic can be stopped much sooner.

IGMP Version 3

IGMP Version 3 (IGMPv3) is the next step in the evolution of IGMP. IGMPv3 adds support for *source filtering*, which enables a multicast receiver host to signal to a router the groups from which it wants to receive multicast traffic and from which sources this traffic is expected. This membership information enables Cisco IOS software to forward traffic from only those sources requested by the receivers.

IGMPv3 is an emerging standard. The latest versions of Windows, Macintosh, and UNIX operating systems all support IGMPv3. At the time of this writing, application developers were in the process of porting their applications to the IGMPv3 API.

A diagram of the query packet format for an IGMPv3 message is shown in Figure 1-7.

Figure 1-7 *IGMPv3 Query Message Format*

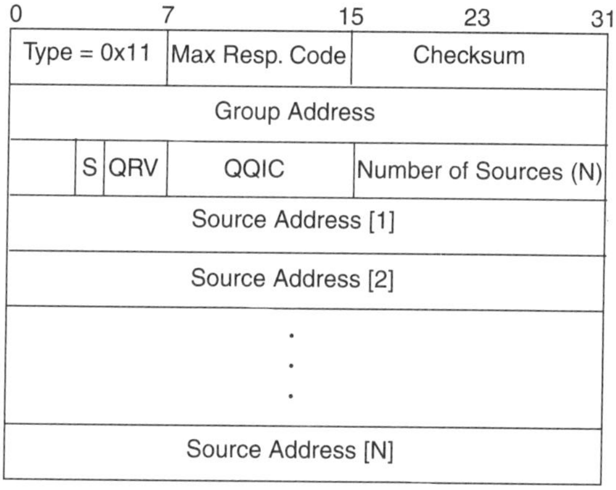

0	7	15	23	31
Type = 0x11	Max Resp. Code		Checksum	
Group Address					
	S	QRV	QQIC	Number of Sources (N)
Source Address [1]				
Source Address [2]				
. . .				
Source Address [N]				

Table 1-3 describes the significant fields in an IGMPv3 query message.

Table 1-3 *IGMPv3 Query Message Field Descriptions*

Field	Description
Type = 0×11	IGMP query.
Max resp. code	Maximum response code (in seconds). This field specifies the maximum time allowed before sending a responding report.
Checksum	The checksum is the 16-bit one's complement of the one's complement sum of the whole IGMP message (the entire IP payload). For computing the checksum, the Checksum field is set to zero. When receiving packets, the checksum must be verified before processing a packet.*
Group address	This multicast group address is 0.0.0.0 for general queries.
S	This S flag indicates that processing by routers is being suppressed.
QRV	Querier Robustness Value. This Querier Robustness Value affects timers and the number of retries.
QQIC	Querier's Query Interval Code. This field specifies the Query Interval used by the querier.
Number of sources [N]	This represents the number of sources present in the query. This number is nonzero for a group-and-source query.
Source address [1...N]	Address of the source(s).

* The checksum information was excerpted from the IETF Internet Draft "Internet Group Management Protocol, Version 3," which you can find at www.ietf.org/internet-drafts/draft-ietf-idmr-igmp-v3-09.txt

A diagram of the report packet format for an IGMPv3 message is shown in Figure 1-8.

Figure 1-8 *IGMPv3 Report Message Format*

```
0        7        15       23       31      0        7        15       23       31
+--------+--------+--------+--------+       +--------+--------+--------+--------+
|Type=0x22| Reserved |    Checksum   |      |Record Type|Aux. Data Length| # of Sources (N)|
+--------+--------+--------+--------+       +--------+--------+--------+--------+
|   Reserved    | # of Group Sources (M)|   |         Group Address           |
+--------+--------+--------+--------+       +--------+--------+--------+--------+
|         Group Record [1]          |      |        Source Address [1]         |
+--------+--------+--------+--------+       |        Source Address [2]         |
|         Group Record [2]          |      |               .                   |
+--------+--------+--------+--------+       |               .                   |
|               .                   |      |               .                   |
|               .                   |      |        Source Address [N]         |
+--------+--------+--------+--------+       +--------+--------+--------+--------+
|         Group Record [M]          |      |         Auxilliary Data           |
+--------+--------+--------+--------+       +--------+--------+--------+--------+
```

Table 1-4 describes the significant fields in an IGMPv3 report message.

Table 1-4 *IGMPv3 Report Message Field Descriptions*

Field	Description
# of group records [M]	Number of group records present in the report.
Group record [1...M]	Block of fields containing information regarding the sender's membership with a single multicast group on the interface from which the report was sent.
Record type	The group record type (for example, MODE_IS_INCLUDE, MODE_IS EXCLUDE).
# of sources [N]	Number of sources present in the record.
Source address [1...N]	Address of the source.

In IGMPv3, the following types of IGMP messages exist:

- Version 3 membership query
- Version 3 membership report

IGMPv3 supports applications that explicitly signal sources from which they want to receive traffic. With IGMPv3, receivers signal membership to a multicast host group in the following two modes:

- **INCLUDE mode**—In this mode, the receiver announces membership to a host group and provides a list of source addresses (the INCLUDE list) from which it wants to receive traffic.

- **EXCLUDE mode**——In this mode, the receiver announces membership to a multicast group and provides a list of source addresses (the EXCLUDE list) from which it does not want to receive traffic. The host will receive traffic only from sources whose IP addresses are not listed in the EXCLUDE list. To receive traffic from all sources, which is the behavior of IGMPv2, a host uses EXCLUDE mode membership with an empty EXCLUDE list.

The current specification for IGMPv3 can be found in the Internet Engineering Task Force (IETF) draft titled "Internet Group Management Protocol, Version 3" on the IETF web site (www.ietf.org). One of the major applications of IGMPv3 is SSM, which is described later in this chapter.

Multicast in the Layer 2 Switching Environment

The default behavior for a Layer 2 switch is to forward all multicast traffic to every port on the switch that belongs to the destination LAN. This behavior reduces the efficiency of the switch, whose purpose is to limit traffic to the ports that need to receive the data.

The following three methods efficiently handle IP multicast in a Layer 2 switching environment:

- **Cisco Group Management Protocol (CGMP)**—CGMP is used on subnets that include end users or receiver clients.
- **IGMP Snooping**—IGMP Snooping is used on subnets that include end users or receiver clients.
- **Router-Port Group Management Protocol (RGMP)**—RGMP is used on routed segments that contain only routers, such as in a collapsed backbone.

The following sections describe these three methods.

Cisco Group Management Protocol (CGMP)

CGMP is a Cisco-developed protocol that allows Catalyst switches to leverage IGMP information on Cisco routers to make Layer 2 forwarding decisions. You must configure CGMP on the multicast routers and the Layer 2 switches. The result is that, with CGMP, IP multicast traffic is delivered only to those Catalyst switch ports that are attached to interested receivers. All other ports that have not explicitly requested the traffic will not receive it unless these ports are connected to a multicast router. Multicast router ports must receive every IP multicast data packet.

The basic operation of CGMP is shown in Figure 1-9. When a host joins a multicast group (part A in the figure), it multicasts an unsolicited IGMP membership report message to the target group (224.1.2.3, in this example). The IGMP report is passed through the switch to the router for normal IGMP processing. The router (which must have CGMP enabled on this interface) receives the IGMP report and processes the report as it normally would, but also creates a CGMP join message and sends it to the switch (part B in Figure 1-9).

Figure 1-9 *Basic CGMP Operation*

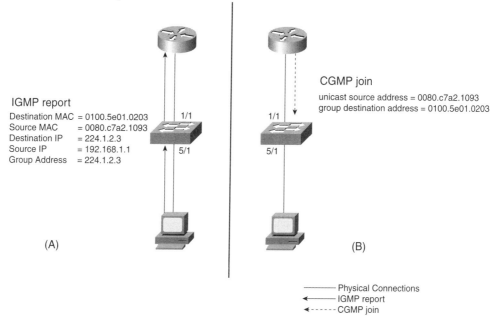

The switch receives this CGMP join message and adds the port to its content-addressable memory (CAM) table for that multicast group. All subsequent traffic directed to this multicast group will be forwarded out the port for that host. The Layer 2 switches were designed so that several destination MAC addresses could be assigned to a single physical port. This allows switches to be connected in a hierarchy and allows many multicast destination addresses to be forwarded out a single port. The router port is also added to the entry for the multicast group. Multicast routers must listen to all multicast traffic for every group because the IGMP control messages are also sent as multicast traffic. With CGMP, the switch must listen to only CGMP join and CGMP leave messages from the router. The rest of the multicast traffic is forwarded using the CAM table with the new entries created by CGMP.

IGMP Snooping

IGMP Snooping is an IP multicast constraining mechanism that runs on a Layer 2 LAN switch. IGMP Snooping requires the LAN switch to examine, or "snoop," some Layer 3 information (IGMP join/leave messages) in the IGMP packets sent between the hosts and the router. When the switch hears the IGMP host report from a host for a particular multicast group, the switch adds that host's port number to the associated multicast table entry. When the switch hears the IGMP leave group message from a host, the switch removes the table entry of the host.

Because IGMP control messages are sent as multicast packets, they are indistinguishable from multicast data at Layer 2. A switch running IGMP Snooping must examine every multicast data packet to determine if it contains any pertinent IGMP control information. IGMP Snooping implemented on a low-end switch with a slow CPU could have a severe performance impact when data is sent at high rates. The solution is to implement IGMP Snooping on high-end switches with special application-specific integrated circuits (ASICs) that can perform the IGMP checks in hardware. CGMP is a better option for low-end switches without special hardware.

Router-Port Group Management Protocol (RGMP)

CGMP and IGMP Snooping are IP multicast constraining mechanisms designed to work on routed network segments that have active receivers. They both depend on IGMP control messages that are sent between the hosts and the routers to determine which switch ports are connected to interested receivers.

Switched Ethernet backbone network segments typically consist of several routers connected to a switch without any hosts on that segment. Because routers do not generate IGMP host reports, CGMP and IGMP Snooping cannot constrain the multicast traffic, which will be flooded to every port on the VLAN. Routers instead generate PIM messages to join and prune multicast traffic flows at a Layer 3 level. PIM is explained later in this chapter.

RGMP is an IP multicast constraining mechanism for router-only network segments. RGMP must be enabled on the routers and on the Layer 2 switches. A multicast router indicates that it is interested in receiving a data flow by sending an RGMP join message for a particular group (part A in Figure 1-10). The switch adds the appropriate port to its forwarding table for that multicast group, similar to the way it handles a CGMP join message. IP multicast data flows are forwarded only to the interested router ports (part B in Figure 1-10). When the router is no longer interested in that data flow, it sends an RGMP leave message and the switch removes the forwarding entry. The current specification for RGMP can be found in the Internet Engineering Task Force (IETF) draft titled "Router-port Group Management Protocol" on the IETF web site (www.ietf.org).

Figure 1-10 *Basic RGMP Operation*

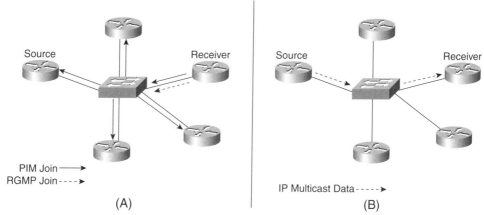

Multicast Distribution Trees

To deliver traffic to all receivers, multicast-capable routers create distribution trees that control the path that IP multicast traffic takes through the network. The two basic types of multicast distribution trees are source trees and shared trees, which are described in the following sections.

Source Trees

The simplest form of a multicast distribution tree is a source tree with its root at the source and branches forming a spanning tree through the network to the receivers. Because this tree uses the shortest path through the network, it is also referred to as a shortest path tree (SPT).

Figure 1-11 shows an example of an SPT for group 224.1.1.1 rooted at the source, Host A, and connecting two receivers, Hosts B and C.

Figure 1-11 *Host A Source Tree*

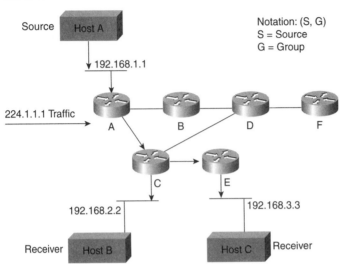

The special notation of (S, G), pronounced "S comma G," enumerates an SPT where S is the source IP address and G is the multicast group address. Using this notation, the SPT for the example shown in Figure 1-11 would be (192.168.1.1, 224.1.1.1).

The (S, G) notation implies that a separate SPT exists for each individual source sending to each group, which is correct. For example, if Host B is also sending traffic to group 224.1.1.1 and Hosts A and C are receivers, a separate (S, G) SPT would exist with a notation of (192.168.2.2, 224.1.1.1).

Shared Trees

Unlike source trees that have their root at the source, shared trees use a single common root placed at a chosen point in the network. This shared root is called a rendezvous point (RP).

Figure 1-12 shows a shared tree for the group 224.2.2.2 with the root located at Router D. This shared tree is uni-directional. Source traffic is sent toward the RP on a source tree. The traffic is then forwarded down the shared tree from the RP to reach all of the receivers (unless the receiver is located between the source and the RP, in which case it will be serviced directly).

Figure 1-12 *Shared Distribution Tree*

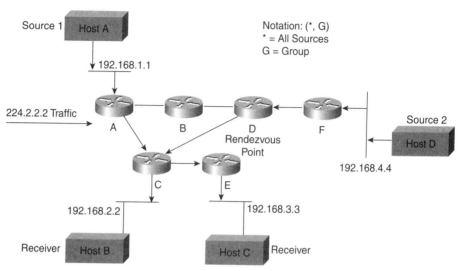

In this example, multicast traffic from the sources, Hosts A and D, travels to the root (Router D) and then down the shared tree to the two receivers, Hosts B and C. Because all sources in the multicast group use a common shared tree, a wildcard notation written as (*, G), pronounced "star comma G," represents the tree. In this case, * means all sources, and G represents the multicast group. Therefore, the shared tree shown in Figure 1-12 would be written as (*, 224.2.2.2).

Source Trees Versus Shared Trees

Both source trees and shared trees are loop-free. Messages are replicated only where the trees branch.

Members of multicast groups can join or leave at any time; therefore, the distribution trees must be dynamically updated. When all the active receivers on a particular branch stop requesting traffic for a particular multicast group, the routers prune that branch from the distribution tree and stop forwarding traffic down that branch. If one receiver on that branch becomes active and requests the multicast traffic, the router dynamically modifies the distribution tree and starts forwarding traffic again.

Source trees have the advantage of creating the optimal path between the source and the receivers. This advantage guarantees the minimum amount of network latency for forwarding multicast traffic. However, this optimization comes at a cost: The routers must maintain path information for each source. In a network that has thousands of sources and thousands of groups, this overhead can quickly become a resource drain on the routers. Memory consumption from the size of the multicast routing table is a factor that network designers must take into consideration.

Shared trees have the advantage of requiring the minimum amount of state in each router. This advantage lowers the overall memory requirements for a network that allows only shared trees. The disadvantage of shared trees is that under certain circumstances the paths between the source and receivers might not be the optimal paths, which might introduce some latency in packet delivery. For example, in Figure 1-12, the shortest path between Host A (source 1) and Host B (a receiver) would be Router A and Router C. Because Router D is being used as the root for a shared tree, the traffic must traverse Routers A, B, D and then C. Network designers must carefully consider the placement of the RP when implementing a shared tree-only environment.

Multicast Forwarding

In unicast routing, traffic is routed through the network along a single path from the source to the destination host. A unicast router does not consider the source address; it considers only the destination address and how to forward the traffic toward that destination. The router scans through its routing table for the destination address and forwards a single copy of the unicast packet out the correct interface in the direction of the destination.

In multicast forwarding, the source sends traffic to an arbitrary group of hosts that are represented by a multicast group address. The multicast router must determine which direction is the upstream direction (toward the source) and which one is the downstream direction (or directions). If there are multiple downstream paths, the router replicates the packet and forwards it down the appropriate downstream paths (best unicast route metric), which is not necessarily all paths. Forwarding multicast traffic away from the source rather than to the receiver is called Reverse Path Forwarding (RPF). RPF is described in the following section.

Reverse Path Forwarding (RPF)

PIM uses the unicast routing information to create a distribution tree along the reverse path from the receivers toward the source. The multicast routers then forward packets along the distribution tree from the source to the receivers. RPF is a key concept in multicast forwarding. It enables routers to correctly forward multicast traffic down the distribution tree. RPF makes use of the existing unicast routing table to determine the upstream and downstream neighbors. A router will forward a multicast packet only if it is received on the upstream interface. This RPF check helps to guarantee that the distribution tree will be loop-free.

RPF Check

When a multicast packet arrives at a router, the router performs an RPF check on the packet. If the RPF check succeeds, the packet is forwarded. Otherwise, it is dropped.

For traffic flowing down a source tree, the RPF check procedure works as follows:

1 The router looks up the source address in the unicast routing table to determine if the packet has arrived on the interface that is on the reverse path back to the source.

2 If the packet has arrived on the interface leading back to the source, the RPF check succeeds and the packet is forwarded.

3 If the RPF check in Step 2 fails, the packet is dropped.

Figure 1-13 shows an example of an unsuccessful RPF check.

Figure 1-13 *RPF Check Fails*

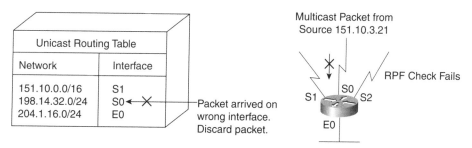

As Figure 1-13 illustrates, a multicast packet from source 151.10.3.21 is received on serial interface 0 (S0). A check of the unicast routing table shows that serial interface 1 (S1) is the interface this router would use to forward unicast data to 151.10.3.21. Because the packet has arrived on interface S0, the packet is discarded.

Figure 1-14 shows an example of a successful RPF check.

Figure 1-14 *RPF Check Succeeds*

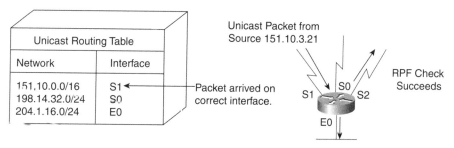

In this example, the multicast packet has arrived on interface S1. The router refers to the unicast routing table and finds that interface S1 is the correct interface. The RPF check passes and the packet is forwarded.

Protocol Independent Multicast (PIM)

PIM is IP routing protocol-independent and can leverage whichever unicast routing protocols are used to populate the unicast routing table, including Enhanced Interior Gateway Routing Protocol (EIGRP), Open Shortest Path First (OSPF), Border Gateway Protocol (BGP), and static routes. PIM uses this unicast routing information to perform the multicast forwarding function. Although PIM is called a multicast routing protocol, it actually uses the unicast routing table to perform the RPF check function instead of building up a completely independent multicast routing table. Unlike other routing protocols, PIM does not send and receive routing updates between routers.

PIM forwarding modes are described in the following sections:

- PIM Dense Mode (PIM-DM)
- PIM Sparse Mode (PIM-SM)

PIM Dense Mode (PIM-DM)

PIM-DM uses a push model to flood multicast traffic to every corner of the network. This push model is a brute force method for delivering data to the receivers. This method would be efficient in deployments in which there are active receivers on every subnet in the network.

PIM-DM initially floods multicast traffic throughout the network. Routers that have no downstream neighbors prune back the unwanted traffic. This process repeats every 3 minutes.

Routers accumulate state information by receiving data streams through the flood-and-prune mechanism. These data streams contain the source and group information so that downstream routers can build up their multicast forwarding tables. PIM-DM supports only source trees, that is (S, G) entries, and cannot be used to build a shared distribution tree.

PIM Sparse Mode (PIM-SM)

PIM-SM uses a pull model to deliver multicast traffic. Only network segments with active receivers that explicitly request the data receive the traffic.

PIM-SM distributes information about active sources by forwarding data packets on the shared tree. Because PIM-SM uses shared trees (at least, initially), it requires the use of an RP. The RP must be administratively configured in the network.

Sources register with the RP and data is forwarded down the shared tree to the receivers. The edge routers learn about a particular source when they receive data packets on the shared tree from that source through the RP. The edge router sends PIM (S,G) join messages toward that source. Each router along the reverse path compares the unicast routing metric of the RP address to the metric of the source address. If the metric for the source address is better, the router will forward a PIM (S,G) join toward the source. If the metric for the RP is the same or better, the PIM (S,G) join is sent in the same direction as the RP. In this case, the shared tree and the source tree are considered congruent.

Figure 1-15 shows a standard PIM-SM unidirectional shared tree. The router closest to the source registers with the RP (Part A in Figure 1-15) and then creates a source tree (S,G) between the source and the RP (Part B in Figure 1-15). Data is forwarded down the shared tree (*,G) toward the receiver from the RP.

Figure 1-15 *Unidirectional Shared Tree and Source Tree*

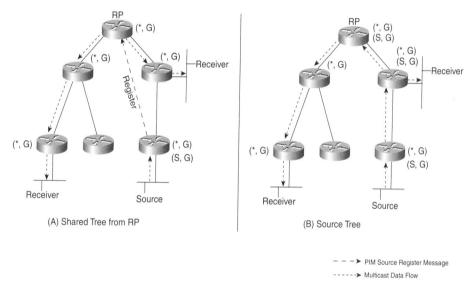

If the shared tree is not an optimal path between the source and the receiver, the routers dynamically create a source tree and stop traffic from flowing down the shared tree. This behavior is the default behavior in Cisco IOS software. Network administrators can force traffic to stay on the shared tree by using the Cisco IOS command **ip pim spt-threshold infinity**.

PIM-SM was originally described in RFC 2362, "Protocol Independent Multicast-Sparse Mode (PIM-SM): Protocol Specification." This RFC is being revised and is currently in draft form. The current draft specification, "Protocol Independent Multicast-Sparse Mode (PIM-SM): Protocol Specification (Revised)," can be found on the IETF Web site (www.ietf.org).

PIM-SM scales well to a network of any size, including those with WAN links. The explicit join mechanism will prevent unwanted traffic from flooding the WAN links.

Bidirectional PIM (Bidir-PIM)

Bidirectional PIM (bidir-PIM) is an enhancement of the PIM protocol that was designed for efficient many-to-many communications within an individual PIM domain. Multicast groups in bidirectional mode can scale to an arbitrary number of sources with only a minimal amount of additional overhead.

The shared trees that are created in PIM Sparse Mode are unidirectional. A source tree must be created to bring the data stream to the RP (the root of the shared tree), and then it can be forwarded down the branches to the receivers. Source data cannot flow up the shared tree toward the RP; this would be considered a bidirectional-shared tree.

In bi-directional mode, traffic is routed along a bidirectional shared tree that is rooted at the RP for the group. In bidir-PIM, the RP's IP address acts as the key to having all routers establish a loop-free spanning tree topology rooted in that IP address. This IP address need not be a router address, but can be any unassigned IP address on a network that is reachable throughout the PIM domain.

Figure 1-16 shows a bidirectional shared tree. Data from the source can flow up the shared tree (*,G) toward the RP and down the shared tree to the receiver. There is no registration process and no source tree (S,G) created.

Figure 1-16 *Bi-directional Shared Tree*

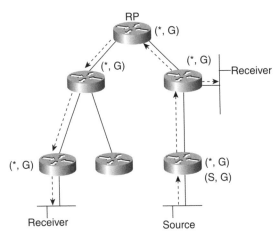

Bidir-PIM is derived from the mechanisms of PIM sparse mode (PIM-SM) and shares many of the shared tree operations. Bidir-PIM also has unconditional source traffic forwarding toward the RP upstream on the shared tree, but no registering process for sources as in PIM-SM. These modifications are necessary and sufficient to allow traffic forwarding in all routers based solely on the (*, G) multicast routing entries. This feature eliminates any source-specific state and allows scaling capability to an arbitrary number of sources.

The current specification of bidir-PIM can be found in the IETF draft titled, "Bi-directional Protocol Independent Multicast (BIDIR-PIM)" on the IETF Web site (www.ietf.org).

Pragmatic General Multicast (PGM)

PGM is a reliable multicast transport protocol for applications that require ordered, duplicate-free, multicast data delivery from multiple sources to multiple receivers. PGM guarantees that a receiver in a multicast group either receives all data packets from transmissions and retransmissions, or can detect unrecoverable data packet loss.

The PGM reliable transport protocol is implemented on the sources and on the receivers. The source maintains a transmit window of outgoing data packets and resends individual packets when it receives a negative acknowledgment (NAK). The network elements (such as routers) assist in suppressing an implosion of NAKs (when a data packet is dropped) and in efficient forwarding of the re-sent data to only the networks that need it.

PGM is intended as a solution for multicast applications with basic reliability requirements. PGM is better than best effort delivery but is not 100 percent reliable. The specification for PGM is network-layer-independent. The Cisco implementation of the PGM Router Assist feature supports PGM over IP.

You can find the current specification for PGM in RFC 3208, "PGM Reliable Transport Protocol Specification."

Interdomain Multicast Protocols

Interdomain multicast protocols are used between multicast domains. ISPs also use these protocols to forward multicast traffic on the Internet. This section discusses the following protocols:

- Multiprotocol Border Gateway Protocol (MBGP)
- Multicast Source Discovery Protocol (MSDP)
- Source Specific Multicast (SSM)

Multiprotocol Border Gateway Protocol (MBGP)

MBGP provides a method for providers to distinguish which route prefixes they will use for performing multicast RPF checks. The RPF check is a fundamental mechanism that routers use to determine the paths that multicast forwarding trees will follow and to successfully deliver multicast content from sources to receivers. Refer to the RPF Check section earlier in this chapter for more information.

MBGP is described in RFC 2858, "Multiprotocol Extensions for BGP-4." Because MBGP is an extension of BGP, it contains the administrative machinery that providers and customers require in their interdomain routing environment, including all the inter-AS tools to filter and control routing (for example, route maps). Any network utilizing internal BGP (iBGP) or external BGP (eBGP) can use MBGP to apply the multiple policy control knobs familiar in BGP to specify the routing policy (and thereby the forwarding policy) for multicast.

Two path attributes, MP_REACH_NLRI and MP_UNREACH_NLRI, were introduced in BGP4. These new attributes create a simple way to carry two sets of routing information—one for unicast routing and one for multicast routing. The routes associated with multicast routing are used for RPF checking at interdomain borders.

The main advantage of MBGP is that an internetwork can support non-congruent unicast and multicast topologies. When the unicast and multicast topologies are congruent, MBGP can support different policies for each. Separate BGP routing tables are maintained for the Unicast Routing Information Base (U-RIB) and the Multicast Routing Information Base (M-RIB). The M-RIB is derived from the unicast routing table with the multicast policies applied. RPF checks and PIM forwarding events are performed based on the information in the M-RIB. MBGP provides a scalable policy-based interdomain routing protocol.

Multicast Source Discovery Protocol (MSDP)

In the PIM-SM model, multicast sources must register with their local RP. Actually, the router closest to a source registers with the RP, but the key point to note is that the RP "knows" about all the sources for any particular group. The RP also needs to know if there are interested receivers and where they are located downstream. The designated router for each receiver network is responsible for sending joins toward the RP.

RPs in one domain have no way of knowing about sources located in other domains. MSDP is a mechanism that allows RPs to share information about active sources. RPs know about the receivers in their local domain. When RPs in remote domains hear about the active sources, they can pass on that information to their local receivers. Multicast data can then be forwarded between the domains. A useful feature of MSDP is that it allows each domain to maintain an independent RP that does not rely on other domains, but it does enable RPs to forward traffic between domains. PIM-SM is used to forward the traffic between the multicast domains.

The RP in each domain establishes an MSDP peering session using a TCP connection with the RPs in other domains or with border routers leading to the other domains. When the RP learns about a new multicast source within its own domain (through the normal PIM register mechanism), the RP encapsulates the first data packet in a Source-Active (SA) message and sends the SA to all MSDP peers. Each receiving peer uses a modified RPF check to forward the SA until the SA reaches every MSDP router in the interconnected networks—theoretically the entire multicast Internet. If the receiving MSDP peer is an RP, and the RP has a (*, G) entry for the group in the SA (there is an interested receiver), the RP creates (S, G) state for the source and joins to the shortest path tree for the source. The encapsulated data is decapsulated and forwarded down the shared tree of that RP. When the last hop router (the router closest to the receiver) receives the multicast packet, it may join the shortest path tree to the source. The MSDP speaker periodically sends SAs that include all sources within the RP's domain.

MSDP was developed for peering between Internet service providers (ISPs). ISPs did not want to rely on an RP maintained by a competing ISP to provide service to their customers. MSDP allows each ISP to have its own local RP and still forward and receive multicast traffic to the Internet. Figure 1-17 shows how data would flow between a source in domain A to a receiver in domain E.

Figure 1-17 *MSDP Example: MSDP Shares Source Information Between RPs in Each Domain*

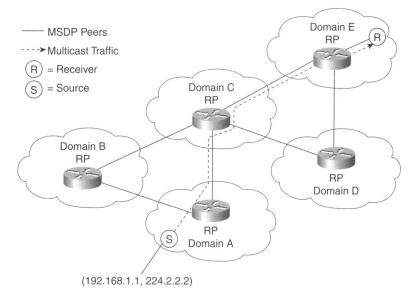

Anycast RP

Anycast RP is an extremely useful application of MSDP's ability to allow multiple RPs to exist in a PIM-SM network. Allowing more than 1 RP to be active at the same time creates not only a fault tolerant RP method but also a load-sharing mechanism. Anycast RP allows 2 or more RPs to share the load for source registration and to act as hot backup routers for each other. MSDP is the key protocol that makes Anycast RP possible. With Anycast RP, the same unicast address is configured on each RP; this address should be configured as a host address (that is, with a 32-bit mask), and should be configured only on a loopback interface not used for anything other than Anycast RP.

All the leaf routers are configured so that the host IP address used by Anycast routers is the IP address assigned to be the RP. IP routing automatically selects the topologically closest RP for each source and receiver. Because some sources might choose one physical RP and some receivers a different physical RP, the rendezvous process for PIM-SM cannot operate as designed. With the addition of MSDP and its ability to exchange source-active information, the RP's ability to operate as designed (which is to have knowledge of all active sources) is restored. In the event of a network failure, the speed of RP failover to a backup RP is determined by the speed of the Internal Gateway Protocol (IGP) convergence. Therefore, Anycast RP is an extremely robust method of configuring the RP function within PIM-SM.

The RPs are used only to set up the initial connection between sources and receivers. After the last hop routers join the shortest path tree, the RP is no longer necessary.

Anycast RP Overview

Originally developed for interdomain multicast applications, MSDP used for Anycast RP is an intradomain feature that provides redundancy and load-sharing capabilities. Enterprise customers typically use Anycast RP for configuring a PIM-SM network to meet fault tolerance requirements within a single multicast domain.

In Anycast RP, two or more RPs are configured with the same IP address on loopback interfaces. The Anycast RP loopback address should be configured with a 32-bit mask, making it a host address. All the downstream routers should be configured to know that the Anycast RP loopback address is the IP address of their local RP. IP routing automatically selects the topologically closest RP for each source and receiver. Assuming that the sources are evenly spaced around the network, an equal number of sources will register with each RP. That is, the process of registering the sources will be shared equally by all the RPs in the network.

Because a source may register with one RP and receivers may join to a different RP, a method is needed for the RPs to exchange information about active sources. This information exchange is done with MSDP.

In Anycast RP, all the RPs are configured to be MSDP peers of each other. When a source registers with one RP, an SA message is sent to the other RPs informing them that there is an active source for a particular multicast group. The result is that each RP knows about the active sources in the area of the other RPs. If any of the RPs were to fail, IP routing would converge and one of the RPs would become the active RP in more than one area. New sources would register with the backup RP. Receivers would join toward the new RP and connectivity would be maintained.

Anycast RP Example

The main purpose of an Anycast RP implementation is for the downstream multicast routers to see just one address for an RP. The example given in Figure 1-18 shows how the loopback 0 interface of the RPs (RP1 and RP2) is configured with the same 10.0.0.1 IP address. If this 10.0.0.1 address is configured on all RPs as the address for the loopback 0 interface and configured as the RP address, IP routing will converge on the closest RP. This address must be a host route—note the 255.255.255.255 subnet mask.

Figure 1-18 *Anycast RP Configuration*

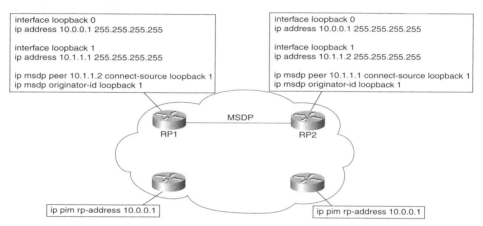

The downstream routers must be informed about the 10.0.0.1 RP address. In Figure 1-18, the routers are configured statically with the **ip pim rp-address 10.0.0.1** global configuration command. You can also accomplish this configuration using the Auto-RP or bootstrap router (BSR) features.

The RPs in Figure 1-18 must also share source information using MSDP. In this example, the loopback 1 interface of the RPs (RP1 and RP2) is configured for MSDP peering. The MSDP peering address must be different than the Anycast RP address.

Many routing protocols choose the highest IP address on loopback interfaces for the Router ID. A problem can arise if the router selects the Anycast RP address for the Router ID. You can avoid this problem by manually setting the Router ID on the RPs to the same address as the MSDP peering address (for example, the loopback 1 address in Figure 1-18). In OSPF, you configure the Router ID using the **router-id** router configuration command. In BGP, you configure the Router ID using the **bgp router-id** router configuration command. In many BGP topologies, the MSDP peering address and the BGP peering address must be the same to pass the RPF check. You can set the BGP peering address using the **neighbor update-source** router configuration command.

The Anycast RP example in the previous paragraphs used IP addresses from RFC 1918. These IP addresses are normally blocked at interdomain borders and are not accessible to other ISPs. You must use valid IP addresses if you want the RPs to be reachable from other domains.

Source Specific Multicast (SSM)

SSM is an extension of the PIM protocol that allows for an efficient data delivery mechanism in one-to-many communications. SSM enables a receiving client, once it has learned about a particular multicast source through a directory service, to receive content directly from the source, rather than receiving it using a shared RP.

SSM removes the requirement of MSDP to discover the active sources in other PIM domains. An out-of-band service at the application level, such as a Web server, can perform source discovery. SSM also removes the requirement to have an RP.

In traditional multicast implementations, applications must join to an IP multicast group address because traffic is distributed to an entire IP multicast group. If two applications with different sources and receivers use the same IP multicast group address, receivers of both applications will receive traffic from the senders of both the applications. Even though the receivers, if programmed appropriately, can filter out the unwanted traffic, this situation would likely generate noticeable levels of unwanted network traffic.

In an SSM-enhanced multicast network, the router closest to the receiver will see a request from the receiving application to join to a particular multicast source. The receiver application can signal its intention to join a particular source by using the INCLUDE mode in IGMPv3. The INCLUDE mode is described in the IGMP Version 3 section earlier in this chapter.

The multicast router can now send the request directly to the source rather than send the request to a common RP (as in PIM sparse mode). At this point, the source can send data directly to the receiver using the shortest path. In SSM, multicast traffic routing is entirely accomplished with source trees. There are no shared trees so an RP is not required.

SSM's ability to explicitly include and exclude particular sources allows for a limited amount of security. Traffic from a source to a group that is not explicitly listed on the INCLUDE list will not be forwarded to uninterested receivers.

SSM also solves IP multicast address collision issues associated with one-to-many applications. An address collision can occur when two organization use the same multicast destination address (group address) for different applications. Routers running in SSM mode route data streams based on the full (S, G) address. Assuming that a source has a unique IP address to send on the Internet, any (S, G) from this source would be unique.

Summary

In this chapter, you reviewed general multicast topics such as the multicast group concept, IP multicast addresses, and Layer 2 multicast addresses. You learned about intradomain multicast protocols such as Internet Group Management Protocol (IGMP), Cisco Group Management Protocol (CGMP), Protocol Independent Multicast (PIM), and Pragmatic General Multicast (PGM). You also reviewed interdomain protocols such as Multiprotocol Border Gateway Protocol (MBGP), Multicast Source Directory Protocol (MSDP), and Source Specific Multicast (SSM).

Related Documents

- Williamson, Beau, *Developing IP Multicast Networks*, Indianapolis: Cisco Press, 2000
- Multicast Quick-Start Configuration Guide (No author—Cisco Documentation) (www.cisco.com/warp/customer/105/48.html)
- Bi-directional Protocol Independent Multicast (BIDIR-PIM), IETF Internet-Draft, M. Handley, I. Kouvelas, T. Speakman, L. Vicisano
- Internet Group Management Protocol, Version 3, IETF Internet-Draft, B. Cain, S. Deering, B. Fenner, I. Kouvelas, A. Thyagarajan
- Protocol Independent Multicast - Sparse Mode (PIM-SM), Protocol Specification (Revised), IETF Internet Draft, B. Fenner, M. Handley, H. Holbrook, I. Kouvelas
- IP Multicast Technology Overview, Cisco white paper www.cisco.com/univercd/cc/td/doc/cisintwk/intsolns/mcst_sol/mcst_ovr.htm
- Interdomain Multicast Solutions Using MSDP, Cisco integration solutions document www.cisco.com/univercd/cc/td/doc/cisintwk/intsolns/mcst_p1/mcstmsdp/index.htm
- How to Configure an RP for PIM Sparse Mode, Cisco configuration guide www.cisco.com/warp/public/cc/pd/iosw/tech/rppim_rg.htm
- "Configuring Multicast Source Discovery Protocol," Cisco IOS IP Configuration Guide, Software Release 12.2 www.cisco.com/univercd/cc/td/doc/product/software/ios122/122cgcr/fipr_c/ipcpt3/1cfmsdp.htm
- "Multicast Source Discovery Protocol Commands," Cisco IOS IP Command Reference, Volume 3 of 3: Multicast, Software Release 12.2 www.cisco.com/univercd/cc/td/doc/product/software/ios122/122cgcr/fiprmc_r/1rfmsdp.htm
- RFC 1112, Host extensions for IP multicasting, S. Deering
- RFC 1918, Address Allocation for Private Internets, Y. Rekhter, B. Moskowitz, D. Karrenberg, G.J. DeGroot, E. Lear
- RFC 2236, Internet Group Management Protocol, Version 2, W. Fenner
- RFC 2858, Multiprotocol Extensions for BGP-4, T. Bates, R. Chandra, D. Katz, Y. Rekhter
- RFC 2362, Protocol Independent Multicast-Sparse Mode (PIM-SM): Protocol Specification, D. Estrin, D. Farinacci, A. Helmy, D. Thaler, S. Deering, M. Handley, V. Jacobson, C. Liu, P. Sharma, L. Wei
- RFC 2365, Administratively Scoped IP Multicast, D. Meyer
- RFC 3180, GLOP Addressing in 233/8, D. Meyer, P. Lothberg
- RFC 3208, PGM Reliable Transport Protocol Specification. T. Speakman, J. Crowcroft, J. Gemmell, D. Farinacci, S. Lin, D. Leshchiner, M. Luby, T. Montgomery, L. Rizzo, A. Tweedly, N. Bhaskar, R. Edmonstone, R. Sumanasekera, L. Vicisano. December 2001. (Status: EXPERIMENTAL)

PART II

Interdomain Multicast with MSDP

Chapter 2 Implementing Interdomain Multicast Using MSDP

Chapter 3 ISP1 Device Characteristics and Configuration Files

Chapter 4 ISP2 Device Characteristics and Configuration Files

Chapter 5 ISP3 and ISP4 Device Characteristics and Configuration Files

This chapter covers the following topics:
- Strategy for Implementing Interdomain Multicast
- Implementing Interdomain Multicast Using MSDP

CHAPTER 2

Implementing Interdomain Multicast Using MSDP

Demand is growing for IP multicast services to extend applications across Internet service provider (ISP) network boundaries to a wider audience. To meet this need, sophisticated protocols such as Protocol Independent Multicast sparse mode (PIM-SM), Multiprotocol Border Gateway Protocol (MBGP), and Multicast Source Discovery Protocol (MSDP) are available in Cisco IOS software that provide solutions for successfully implementing native interdomain multicast service.

This chapter describes how four hypothetical ISPs implement interdomain multicast among them using PIM-SM, MBGP, and MSDP. The solutions presented in this chapter have been tested by customers in the field and verified in a lab environment. The four hypothetical ISPs are representative of typical customer topologies. (The sections, "ISP1 Scenario," "ISP2 Scenario," and "ISP3 and ISP4 Scenario" discuss the specifics of each topology.)

In this chapter, you will learn about various interdomain multicast implementation trade-offs and see a preferred network design that outlines "best practices" for ISP deployment of IP multicast. The actual configuration files that were verified in the lab are included in Chapter 3, "ISP1 Device Characteristics and Configuration Files", Chapter 4, "ISP2 Device Characteristics and Configuration Files, and Chapter 5, "ISP3 Device Characteristics and Configuration Files.

In this solution, implementing interdomain multicast requires the following:

- Establishing an overall interdomain multicast strategy
- Implementing intradomain multicast within each of the individual ISPs
- Implementing interdomain multicast between each of the ISPs
- Connecting customers to the ISP infrastructure

You learn more about each of these requirements in this chapter.

NOTE This chapter covers the basic design and deployment of an interdomain multicast network. Although this chapter discusses PIM-SM, MBGP, and MSDP, it is not intended to be a tutorial of the operations of these protocols. To find resources that discuss more about how these protocols work, refer to the references listed at the end of this chapter.

Strategy for Implementing Interdomain Multicast

The hypothetical interdomain multicast network scenario in this chapter has an ISP backbone that is characteristic of some of the largest ISPs. Figure 2-1 shows the logical connections between four ISP domains in which interdomain multicast will be deployed. Each ISP has established Border Gateway Protocol (BGP) peering and its own autonomous system (AS). As shown in Figure 2-1, ISP1 and ISP2 have implemented route reflectors for their internal BGP peering sessions. The design of each ISP multicast network topology depends on the individual requirements of the ISP.

NOTE The solutions presented in this chapter are based on a hypothetical interdomain ISP environment. All the IP addresses and configuration in this chapter are provided for illustrative purposes only.

Figure 2-1 *Logical Connections of a Typical ISP Interdomain Environment*

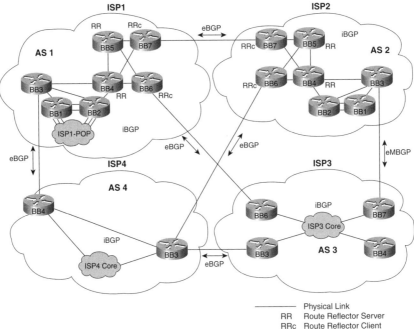

Before implementing interdomain multicast among the 4 ISPs in Figure 2-1, the individual ISPs must establish the following prerequisites:

- An IP address allocation plan
- BGP peering arrangements with the other ISPs
- Customer connections

The ISPs must also consider the benefits and ramifications of implementing interdomain multicast. The benefits of using PIM-SM, MBGP, and MSDP to implement interdomain multicast are as follows:

- Allows each ISP one or more RPs within its own network to reduce its reliance on external RPs. This benefit gives each ISP greater control over its own customer service levels and conserves network capacity.
- Enables an ISP to offer interdomain multicast services to its customers. Content providers can efficiently deliver their products to consumers (for example, applications such as interactive gaming, distance learning, and market data).
- Offers a service provider the ability to maintain its own RPs while also having knowledge of active sources in other domains. A service provider can now set up control measures that previously were not possible. For example, a service provider can filter traffic from certain sources or domains. MSDP allows service providers to control the filtering of incoming and outgoing multicast data streams from a central point. Because the service provider is able to maintain its own RPs and have knowledge of remote sources through MSDP messages, the RPs can exert control over which active source messages it will process/receive. This allows you to filter incoming and outgoing multicast data streams.

The ramifications for using PIM-SM, MBGP, and MSDP to implement interdomain multicast are as follows:

- Multicast forwarding state must be maintained in the router. This situation uses additional memory resources in the router.
- Routers that act as an RP or MSDP peer might experience an additional load on CPU resources.

The strategy for implementing interdomain multicast among the four ISPs has the following three phases:

- Establishing an Overall Intradomain Multicast Strategy
- Establishing an Overall Interdomain Multicast Strategy
- Establishing an Implementation Strategy for Connecting Customers into Infrastructure

The following sections discuss each of these phases.

NOTE The multicast solutions in this chapter were tested with valid IP addresses. Normally, when a configuration file is published, the valid IP addresses are replaced with IP addresses as specified in RFC 1918, "Address Allocation for Private Networks." Because the range of available IP addresses was insufficient to span the range of IP addresses used in this solution, the first octet of the valid IP addresses was replaced with a variable. In the sample configurations provided in the following sections, the first octet of these reserved IP addresses has been replaced with the letter J or the letter K for privacy reasons. The letter J always represents one unique number, and the letter K always represents a unique number that is different from J. The example configurations are intended for illustrative purposes only. The letters J and K must be replaced with valid numbers when these IP addresses are configured in an actual network.

Phase 1: Establishing an Overall Intradomain Multicast Strategy

Before the four ISPs in Figure 2-1 can deploy multicast services between each other, they must each implement multicast within their own networks. As described in Chapter 1, "IP Multicast Technology Overview," PIM-SM is the multicast routing protocol used in these intradomain multicast scenarios. For a brief introduction to PIM and PIM-SM, refer to chapter 1. PIM-SM was originally described in RFC 2362. This RFC is being revised.

NOTE You can find all RFCs online at www.isi.edu/in-notes/rfc*xxx*.txt, where *xxxx* is the number of the RFC. If you do not know the number of the RFC, you can find it by doing a topic search at www.rfc-editor.org/rfcsearch.html.

The following steps describe the general configuration steps each of the four hypothetical ISPs complete to configure intradomain multicast:

Step 1 Configure multicast globally.

To configure multicast globally, use the following two global configuration commands:

```
ip multicast-routing [distributed]
```

The **ip multicast-routing [distributed]** command enables IP multicast forwarding. If disabled, group addressed IP packets of which the router is not a member will be discarded. The default value is for IP multicast routing to be disabled. (The **ip multicast-routing** command was introduced in Cisco IOS Software Release 10.2.)

The **distributed** keyword enables distributed fast switching for the router. The **ip mroute-cache distributed** interface command enables individual interfaces for distributed fast switching. The **distributed** keyword is currently supported on the Cisco 7500 and 12000 router series. (The **distributed** keyword was introduced in Cisco IOS Software Release 11.1(20)CC.)

```
ip multicast multipath
```

The **ip multicast multipath** command enables the router to use different Reverse Path Forwarding (RPF) interfaces for each multicast route that matches the same unicast route prefix when equal cost paths exist for the route prefix. Load sharing is done on a per-(S, G) basis, not on a per-packet basis. (The **ip multicast multipath** command is supported in Cisco IOS Software Releases 12.0, 12.0 S, and 12.0 T.)

Step 2 Configure multicast on the interfaces.

To configure multicast on the interfaces, use the following two interface configuration commands:

```
ip pim sparse-mode
```

The **ip pim sparse-mode** command enables the PIM multicast routing protocol on the interface and configures the interface to operate in sparse mode. A sparse mode interface is used only for multicast forwarding if a join message is received from a downstream router or directly connected members are on the interface. (The **ip pim sparse-mode** command was introduced in Cisco IOS Software Release 10.2.)

```
ip mroute-cache distributed
```

The **ip mroute-cache distributed** command configures IP multicast fast switching. If fast switching is disabled on an incoming interface for a multicast routing table entry, the packet is sent at the process level for all interfaces in the outgoing interface list. If fast switching is disabled on an outgoing interface for a multicast routing table entry, the packet is process level-switched for that interface but may be fast-switched for other interfaces in the outgoing interface list. The default setting is that all interfaces are multicast fast switched. (The **ip mroute-cache** command was introduced in Cisco IOS Software Release 11.0.)

The **distributed** keyword enables the interface to perform distributed fast switching on incoming packets. This command applies to the configuration of the physical interface and not to sub interfaces.

After you configure the **ip mroute-cache distributed** command on the interface, all packets coming in this interface are distributed-switched. You should configure the **ip route-cache distributed** command before you configure the **ip mroute-cache** command on a Cisco 7500 series router (and not on the Cisco 12000 series Gigabit Switch Router). The **distributed** keyword was introduced in Cisco IOS Software Release 11.1(20)CC.

NOTE Cisco Systems recommends that you configure the **ip route-cache distributed** command on all platforms that support it.

Step 3 Select the router to be the RP.

The actual location of the RP should not be a critical decision. Because the RP introduces the source and receiver, it will not necessarily be part of the forwarding path for shortest path trees. Ask yourself if the router powerful enough. Is it in a central location? Be aware that data is not expected to be forwarded by the RP, but only to be an introductory mechanism. Choose any location that is centrally accessible throughout the ISP domain.

Choose an IP address for the RP that can be given out to customers and advertised to other domains. Typically, you assign a unique IP address with a 32-bit mask to a loopback address and use this address for the RP.

Step 4 Configure the RP statically on each router in the network.

To configure the RP, use the **ip pim rp-address** *rp-address access-list* global configuration command. This command configures the PIM RP address for a particular group. First hop routers use the RP address to send register packets on behalf of source multicast hosts. Routers also use the RP address on behalf of multicast hosts that want to become members of a group. These routers send join and prune messages toward the RP. You can configure a single RP for all multicast groups or a subset of the Class D address range, as described by the access list pointer. (The **ip pim rp-address** command was introduced in Cisco IOS Software Release 10.2.)

Phase 2: Establishing an Overall Interdomain Multicast Strategy

To successfully deploy interdomain multicast among the four ISPs, each ISP will use the following protocols:

- Multiprotocol Border Gateway Protocol (MBGP) for interdomain routing
- Multicast Source Discovery Protocol (MSDP) for interdomain source discovery

MBGP and MSDP connect PIM-SM domains. MBGP is a policy-based interdomain routing protocol for choosing the best paths through an IP internetwork. MSDP enables RPs from different domains to exchange information about active sources. For an overview of MBGP and MSDP, refer to Chapter 1.

The following steps describe the general configuration steps each of the four hypothetical ISPs must complete to configure interdomain multicast:

Step 1 Configure MBGP to exchange multicast routing information.

(a) Configure MBGP peering sessions.

The command syntax used to configure MBGP varies depending on which Cisco IOS software release is running on the router.

— For Cisco IOS Software Release 12.0 S, use the following BGP router configuration commands:

`neighbor` *ip-address* `remote-as` *number* [`nlri` {`unicast` | `multicast`}]

This command configures a BGP peer and associated AS number. If only the **multicast** keyword is supplied, only multicast Network Layer Reachability Information (NLRI) is sent to the neighbor. However, if only the **unicast** keyword is supplied, only unicast NLRI is sent to the neighbor. Both keywords may be supplied, which indicates that the neighbor will be sent both types of routes. Unicast NLRI is sent in the conventional encoding and the multicast NLRI is sent in the MP_REACH and MP_UNREACH path attributes. The default is to send unicast NLRI only. This version of BGP negotiates NLRI in the Capabilities Option of the Open message. Therefore, both sides of a BGP connection must be configured consistently with respect to NLRI or the MBGP peering session will not be established.

`neighbor` *peer-group-name* `peer-group` [`nlri` {`unicast` | `multicast`}]

This command configures the peer group to support either unicast NLRI, multicast NLRI, or both. Supplying both the **unicast** and **multicast** keywords indicates that both NLRIs are sent. The default value is unicast only.

`network` *network-number* [`mask` *network-mask*] [`nlri` {`unicast` | `multicast`}]

This command determines if the network in the AS should be injected into the BGP unicast routing information base (RIB) or the MBGP multicast RIB. If both the **unicast** and **multicast** keywords are specified, the network is injected in both RIBs. If the **multicast** keyword only is specified, the network is injected in the multicast RIB only. The default is unicast only.

— For Cisco IOS Software Release 12.0 S, use the following MBGP route map configuration commands:

`match nlri` {`unicast` | `multicast`}

The route-map criteria can be based on the unicast or multicast RIB (or both). If the multicast RIB entry is being processed for a route map with the **match nlri multicast** command, the route-map condition yields TRUE, likewise for the unicast corollary. If both the **unicast** and **multicast** keywords are specified, either RIB entry being processed yields TRUE. The default value is both **unicast** and **multicast**.

You can use this command in conjunction with the **neighbor** *ip-address* **route-map** *map-name* **in** command so that you can use one route-map reference to describe filtering policies for different NLRI types.

`set nlri {unicast | multicast}`

If the route-map match criteria are met, decide if the route should be injected into the unicast or multicast RIB. If you specify both the **unicast** and **multicast** keywords, the route is injected into both RIBs and advertised as a separate NLRI in a BGP Update message. If only the **multicast** keyword is specified, the route is only injected into the multicast RIB. The default value is unicast only in all cases except when the **neighbor** *ip-address* **route-map** *map-name* **out** command references this route map. Use this route map configuration command when referencing a route map by various router configuration commands (that is, **redistribute**, **aggregate-address**, and **neighbor outbound route-map** references).

You can use this command in conjunction with the **neighbor** *ip-address* **default-originate route-map** *map-name* command. If the route map referenced by the **neighbor** command supplies the **set nlri** command, the multicast default route can be generated independently of the unicast default route.

— For Cisco IOS Software Release 12.0 T or 12.1, use the following MBGP address-family configuration commands:

`address-family ipv4 multicast`

This command places the router in address-family configuration mode. The **multicast** keyword specifies that multicast NLRI information is used with neighbors and networks that are explicitly configured under the **address-family ipv4 multicast** command section in the configuration. Routing information for address-family IPv4 is advertised by default when you configure a BGP routing session using the **neighbor remote-as** command, unless you execute the **no bgp default ipv4-activate** command.

`neighbor {ip-address | peer-group-name} activate`

This command enables or disables the exchange of information with a neighboring router. The exchange of addresses with neighbors is enabled by default for the IPv4 address family. For all other address families, you must explicitly activate the neighbor in the appropriate address-family section.

You can find a Cisco Application Note discussing the changes in MBGP commands between Cisco IOS Software Release 12.0 S, 12.0 T, and 12.1 at the following web site:

www.cisco.com/warp/public/cc/pd/iosw/prodlit/mcb12_an.htm

NOTE Cisco Systems strongly recommends that you use the same IP address for BGP and MSDP peering sessions. This is the simplest method for MSDP SA RPF message validation. This address is typically a unique IP address with a 32-bit mask assigned on a loopback interface.

  (b) Verify that MBGP multicast routes are working properly.

  To verify that MBGP multicast routes are working properly, use the following EXEC commands:

  ```
  show ip bgp neighbors
  show ip mbgp
  ```

Step 2 Configure MSDP peering sessions.

  (a) Select an IP address.

  Select an IP address that you will use for MSDP peering sessions. This address is usually a loopback address that is the same as the BGP sessions.

  (b) Configure peering sessions.

  Configure peering sessions from the local RP to the RP in another ISP using the **ip msdp peer** {*peer-name* | *peer-address*} [**connect-source** *type number*] global configuration command. This command configures an MSDP peer. If you also have a BGP peering session with this MSDP peer, use the same IP address for MSDP as you do for BGP. Use the **connect-source** keyword to supply a source IP address for the TCP connection; use the *type* and *number* attributes to identify the specific interface. The IP address of the interface identified is the IP address used to source the IP connection to the remote peer.

Step 3 Configure recommended SA filters.

  The following global configuration commands configure outgoing or incoming filter lists for SA messages sent to an MSDP peer:

  ```
  ip msdp sa-filter out {peer-address | peer-name} [list access-list]
    [route-map map-name]
  ip msdp sa-filter in {peer-address | peer-name} [list access-list]
    [route-map map-name]
  ```

By default, all SA messages received are forwarded to the peer. The *access-list* argument is an extended access list that can describe source/group pairs to pass through the filter. If the **route-map** *map-name* keyword and argument is specified, you can filter based on match criteria in the *map-name* argument. If all match criteria are true, a permit from the route map passes routes through the filter. A deny filters routes. If you use both keywords, all conditions must be true to pass or filter any (S, G) in outgoing SA messages. If neither keyword is specified, all source/group pairs are filtered.

You can find a document describing recommended SA filters at the following web site:

www.cisco.com/warp/public/105/49.html

Step 4 Configure SA caching.

Enable the SA caching feature to cache information on which sources are active in the network. To configure the SA caching, use the **ip msdp cache-sa-state** command. This command indicates to the router that SA state should be cached for faster service.

Step 5 Verify that MSDP peers are working properly.

To verify that MSDP peers are working properly, use the following EXEC commands:

```
show ip msdp peer
show ip msdp sa-cache
```

Step 6 Configure multicast borders appropriately.

To configure the multicast border, use the following two interface configuration commands:

```
ip multicast boundary access-list
ip pim bsr-border
```

The **ip multicast boundary** *access-list* command configures an administratively scoped boundary on the interface for multicast group addresses in the range defined by the simple IP access list *access-list* argument. No multicast data packets may flow across the boundary from either direction, allowing reuse of the same multicast group address in different administrative domains. (The multicast address range from 239.0.0.0 to 239.255.255.255 is designated as the administratively scoped addresses.) For example, to configure a boundary for all administratively scoped addresses, use the following commands:

```
access-list 1 deny 239.0.0.0 0.255.255.255
access-list 1 deny 224.0.1.40
access-list 1 deny 224.0.1.39
access-list 1 permit 224.0.0.0 15.255.255.255
interface ethernet 0
 ip multicast boundary 1
```

The **ip pim bsr-border** command configures the interface to be the PIM domain border. Bootstrap messages cannot pass through this border in either direction. The PIM domain border effectively partitions the network into regions using different RPs that are configured using the bootstrap router feature. No other PIM messages are dropped by this domain border setup. Please note that this command does not set up any multicast boundaries. (The **ip pim border** command was introduced in Cisco IOS Software Release 11.1(20)CC. This command was replaced with the **ip pim bsr-border** command in Cisco IOS Software Release 12.0(7.1).)

Figure 2-2 and Figure 2-3 show the MBGP and MSDP peering sessions established among the four ISPs in which interdomain multicast is being deployed.

Figure 2-2 *MBGP Peering*

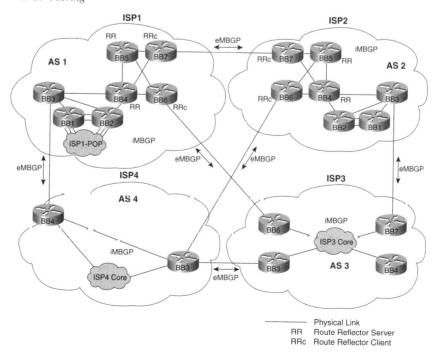

Figure 2-3 *MSDP Peering*

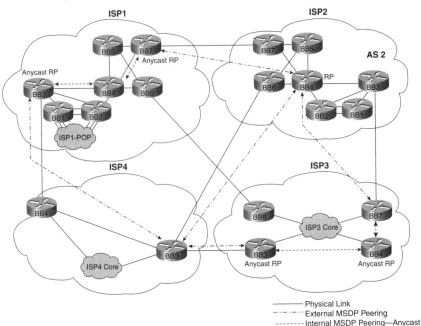

Phase 3: Establishing an Implementation Strategy for Connecting Customers into Infrastructure

Now that all 4 ISPs in Figure 2-1 can share multicast traffic through interdomain routing, the individual ISPs can connect customers into their infrastructure. The following three scenarios describe the types of customers that may want to connect to an ISP to receive multicast traffic:

- **Multicast customer with external RP**—The customer does not run MBGP and does not have its own RP or AS. The customer does not want to have or manage its own multicast domain; it wants only multicast service. The customer will configure its routers to point to the ISP's RP.

- **Multicast customer with internal RP and without MBGP**—The customer does not run MBGP but has its own RP. This customer does not have its own AS but is serious enough about multicast that it has its own RP for its local applications. The customer RP would use MSDP to peer with the ISP's RP. The customer can run Auto-RP in its domain, and the ISP filters Auto-RP on its borders.

- **Multicast customer with internal RP and MBGP**—The customer runs MBGP and has its own RP. This situation is the same peering arrangement as connecting to another ISP. The same border precautions should be taken.

Implementing Interdomain Multicast Using MSDP

This section describes implementing intradomain and interdomain multicast and connecting customers into the infrastructure of an ISP for scenarios described in the following subsections:

- ISP2 Scenario
- ISP1 Scenario
- ISP3 and ISP4 Scenarios

The intradomain multicast deployment in ISP2 is simpler than in ISP1, so ISP2 is discussed first.

NOTE The example configurations provided in the following sections use highlighted text to indicate pertinent configuration commands used for deploying the multicast solutions described in this document.

ISP2 Scenario

This section discusses the following topics:

- **ISP2**—Implementing Intradomain Multicast
- **ISP2**—Implementing Interdomain Multicast
- **ISP2**—Connecting Customers into Infrastructure

ISP2—Implementing Intradomain Multicast

This section addresses the following issues pertaining to intradomain multicast for the ISP2 example:

- Strategy
- Topology
- Benefits and ramifications
- Configuration summary

ISP2 is a new, relatively small ISP that wants to implement the simplest multicast design. ISP2 is not concerned about advertising all of its internal IP addresses to other ISPs. Therefore, ISP2 implemented a single, static RP at the core of its network. The RP is the same router that will peer with other ISPs, and its address is given out to customers.

Figure 2-4 shows the intradomain multicast network diagram for ISP2.

Figure 2-4 *Network Diagram for ISP2—Intradomain Multicast*

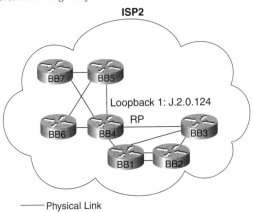

Table 2-1 presents the benefits and ramifications of deploying the ISP2 multicast network.

Table 2-1 *Deploying ISP2 Multicast Network: Benefits and Ramifications*

Benefits	Ramifications
The network topology is a simple multicast implementation.	No redundancy—If the RP router were to fail, all new requests for multicast service would also fail.
The topology creates a deterministic network that is easy to troubleshoot.	No load sharing—All PIM joins must be serviced by a single RP. Under extreme and unlikely circumstances, this situation may have a performance impact on the router acting as the RP.

The following is a summary of the tasks that were performed to configure the devices in ISP2 for intradomain multicast:

Step 1 Configure multicast globally.

The following sample configuration, taken from the configuration file for the ISP2BB4 router, shows how to configure multicast globally on a router. Multicast is configured on all ISP2 routers.

```
ip multicast-routing distributed
```

Step 2 Configure multicast on the interfaces.

The following sample configuration shows how to configure multicast on the interfaces of the ISP2BB4 router. Multicast is configured on the interfaces of all the ISP2 routers.

```
interface POS0/0
 ip pim sparse-mode
 ip mroute-cache distributed

interface POS2/0
 ip pim sparse-mode
 ip mroute-cache distributed

interface POS3/0
 ip pim sparse-mode
 ip mroute-cache distributed

interface GigabitEthernet4/0
 ip mroute-cache distributed

interface GigabitEthernet4/0.430
 ip pim sparse-mode

interface GigabitEthernet4/0.440
 ip pim sparse-mode

interface POS5/0
 ip pim sparse-mode
 ip mroute-cache distributed

interface POS6/0
 ip pim sparse-mode
 ip mroute-cache distributed
```

NOTE You must configure the **ip mroute-cache distributed** command on the main Gigabit Ethernet interface. It is not allowed on sub interfaces.

Step 3 Select the router to be the RP.

The ISP2BB4 router was selected as the RP because of its topologically central location in the ISP2 network. The following sample configuration shows how to configure a unique IP address with a 32-bit mask on the loopback interface of the RP (ISP2BB4):

```
interface Loopback1
 ip address J.2.0.124 255.255.255.255
 ip pim sparse-mode
 ip mroute-cache distributed
 no shutdown
```

Step 4 Configure the RP statically on each router in ISP2.

Configure the RP address on each router in ISP2 with the following command:

```
ip pim rp-address J.2.0.124
```

Step 5 Restrict available multicast groups from using 232/24. (Optional)

Source Specific Multicast (SSM) will use the 232.0.0.0 through 232.255.255.255 address range for specific well-known sources. This address range will not require the use of an RP. The following sample configuration shows how to restrict sources in the 232/8 range from registering with the RP. You need to configure these statements only on the RP.

```
ip pim accept-register list no-ssm-range
```

```
ip access-list extended no-ssm-range deny ip any
    232.0.0.0 0.255.255.255 permit ip any any
```

For the device characteristics and complete configuration files of the devices in ISP2, see Chapter 4, "ISP2 Device Characteristics and Complete Configuration Files."

ISP2—Implementing Interdomain Multicast

This section addresses the following issues related to interdomain multicast for the ISP2 example:

- Topology
- Configuration summary

Figure 2-5 shows the interdomain multicast network diagram for ISP2.

Figure 2-5   *Network Diagram for ISP2—Interdomain Multicast*

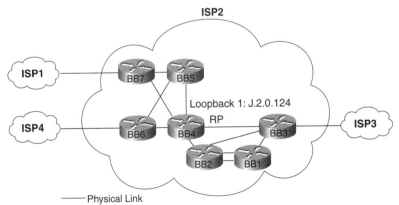

The following is a summary of the tasks to configure the devices in ISP2 for interdomain multicast:

Step 1   Configure MBGP to exchange multicast routing information.

(a) Configure MBGP peering sessions.

The following MBGP peering sessions exist in ISP2:

—ISP2BB7 externally peers with ISP1BB7.

—ISP2BB6 externally peers with ISP1BB3.

—ISP2BB3 externally peers with ISP1BB7.

—All backbone routers in ISP2 internally peer with each other directly or through route reflectors.

The routers in ISP2 are running Cisco IOS Software Release 12.0 S. You must configure the routers for multicast NLRI information. The ISP2INTERNAL peer group is configured on every router in ISP2. The following sample configuration shows how to configure the internal peers:

```
router bgp 2
 neighbor ISP2INTERNAL peer-group nlri unicast multicast
```

The following sample configurations show how to configure the external peers. The configuration is different for each router.

The following configuration is for the ISP2BB7 router:

```
router bgp 2
 neighbor J.2.0.254 remote as 1 nlri unicast multicast
```

The following configuration is for the ISP2BB6 router:

```
router bgp 2
 neighbor ISP2ISP4PEER peer-group nlri unicast multicast
```

The following configuration is for the ISP2BB3 router:

```
router bgp 2
 neighbor ISP2ISP3PEER peer-group nlri unicast multicast
```

(a) Verify that MBGP is configured properly.

The following sample output shows how to verify that the MBGP peers have negotiated for multicast routes:

```
show ip bgp neighbors J.2.0.254

BGP neighbor is J.2.0.254, remote AS 1, external link
 Index 2, Offset 0, Mask 0x4
```

```
BGP version 4, remote router ID J.1.0.207
BGP state = Established, table version = 55643246, up for 4w3d
Last read 00:00:12, last send 00:00:16
Hold time 180, keepalive interval 60 seconds
Neighbor NLRI negotiation:
  Configured for unicast and multicast routes
  Peer negotiated unicast and multicast routes
  Exchanging unicast and multicast routes
Received route refresh capability from peer
Minimum time between advertisement runs is 30 seconds
Received 2126681 messages, 0 notifications, 0 in queue
Sent 2811709 messages, 0 notifications, 0 in queue
Prefix advertised 28942996, suppressed 943, withdrawn 21015964
Route refresh request:received 0, sent 0
Connections established 3; dropped 2
Last reset 4w3d, due to Peer closed the session
Number of unicast/multicast prefixes received 218/0
Connection state is ESTAB, I/O status:1, unread input bytes:0
Local host:J.2.0.253, Local port:179
Foreign host:J.2.0.254, Foreign port:11006

Enqueued packets for retransmit:0, input:0  mis-ordered:0 (0 bytes)

Event Timers (current time is 0x12B681EFC):
Timer          Starts      Wakeups           Next
Retrans        202084      0                 0x0
TimeWait       0           0                 0x0
AckHold        236755      172305            0x0
SendWnd        0           0                 0x0
KeepAlive      0           0                 0x0
GiveUp         0           0                 0x0
PmtuAger       0           0                 0x0
DeadWait       0           0                 0x0

iss:2914616936  snduna:2982467531  sndnxt:2982467531     sndwnd: 15866
irs:2914616299  rcvnxt:2959879526  rcvwnd:      16249 delrcvwnd:   135

SRTT:300 ms, RTTO:607 ms, RTV:3 ms, KRTT:0 ms
minRTT:0 ms, maxRTT:512 ms, ACK hold:200 ms
Flags:passive open, nagle, gen tcbs

Datagrams (max data segment is 536 bytes):
Rcvd:476100 (out of order:0), with data:267701, total data
  bytes:45263226
Sent:488699 (retransmit:0), with data:250296, total data bytes:67850594
```

```
show ip mbgp summary

BGP router identifier J.2.0.207, local AS number 2
MBGP table version is 14925
2 network entries and 1 paths using 222 bytes of memory
90 BGP path attribute entries using 4320 bytes of memory
82 BGP AS-PATH entries using 2336 bytes of memory
BGP activity 1073815/1042808 prefixes, 58323706/58292540 paths

Neighbor        V    AS MsgRcvd MsgSent   TblVer  InQ OutQ Up/Down  State/
PfxRcd
J.2.0.201       4    2   83641 1212820    14925    0    0 8w2d           0
J.2.0.202       4    2   83628 1212935    14925    0    0 8w2d           0
J.2.0.203       4    2 1466577 1212059    14925    0    0 8w1d           1
J.2.0.204       4    2   83645 1213054    14925    0    0 8w2d           0
J.2.0.205       4    2 6290303 1213059    14925    0    0 8w2d           0
J.2.0.206       4    2 1217472 1213014    14925    0    0 8w2d           0
J.2.0.208       4    2   96243 1201558        0    0    0 8w2d           0
 (NoNeg)
J.2.0.254       4    1 2126718 2811770    14925    0    0 4w3d           0
```

Step 2 Configure MSDP peering sessions.

    (a) Select an IP address.

        For MSDP peering sessions, use the same IP address that you used for the BGP peering session. In this case, it is the unique IP address with a 32-bit mask configured on Loopback0.

    (b) Configure peering sessions.

        The ISP2BB4 router peers with the ISP1BB7, ISP4BB3, and ISP3BB7 routers. The following sample configuration shows how to configure these peering sessions:

```
ip msdp peer J.1.0.207 connect-source Loopback0 remote-as 1
ip msdp peer J.4.0.203 connect-source Loopback0 remote-as 4
ip msdp peer J.3.0.207 connect-source Loopback0 remote-as 3
```

Step 3 Configure recommended SA filters.

The following sample configurations show how to configure the SA filters on ISP2's RP (ISP2BB4) for the connections to the ISP1BB7, ISP4BB3, and ISP3BB7 routers.

The following SA filter configuration is for the connection to the ISP1BB7 router:

```
ip msdp sa-filter in J.1.0.207 list 124
ip msdp sa-filter out J.1.0.207 list 124
```

The following SA filter configuration is for the connection to the ISP4BB3 router:

```
ip msdp sa-filter in J.4.0.203 list 124
ip msdp sa-filter out J.4.0.203 list 124
```

The following SA filter configuration is for the connection to the ISP3BB7 router:

```
ip msdp sa-filter in J.3.0.207 list 124
ip msdp sa-filter out J.3.0.207 list 124
```

The following access list is configured on the ISP2BB4 router:

```
access-list 124 deny    ip any host 224.0.2.2
access-list 124 deny    ip any host 224.0.1.3
access-list 124 deny    ip any host 224.0.1.24
access-list 124 deny    ip any host 224.0.1.22
access-list 124 deny    ip any host 224.0.1.2
access-list 124 deny    ip any host 224.0.1.35
access-list 124 deny    ip any host 224.0.1.60
access-list 124 deny    ip any host 224.0.1.39
access-list 124 deny    ip any host 224.0.1.40
access-list 124 deny    ip any 239.0.0.0 0.255.255.255
access-list 124 deny    ip 10.0.0.0 0.255.255.255 any
access-list 124 deny    ip 127.0.0.0 0.255.255.255 any
access-list 124 deny    ip 172.16.0.0 0.15.255.255 any
access-list 124 deny    ip 192.168.0.0 0.0.255.255 any
access-list 124 deny    ip any 232.0.0.0 0.255.255.255
access-list 124 permit  ip any any
```

NOTE The SA filter used in this solution was taken from Cisco System's recommended SA filter list. This list is updated regularly and posted on the following web site:

ftp://ftpeng.cisco.com/ipmulticast.html

Please check the list on a periodic basis for the latest SA filter.

Step 4 Configure SA caching.

The following sample configuration shows how to enable SA caching. Enable this feature on the ISP2BB4 router.

```
ip msdp cache-sa-state
```

Step 5 Verify that MSDP peers are working properly.

The following sample output shows how to verify that the MSDP peers are working properly:

```
show ip msdp peer

MSDP Peer J.1.0.207 (?), AS 1 (configured AS)
Description:
  Connection status:
    State:Up, Resets:2, Connection source:Loopback0 (J.2.0.204)
    Uptime(Downtime):4w3d, Messages sent/received:114677/106473
    Output messages discarded:0
    Connection and counters cleared 7w0d    ago
  SA Filtering:
    Input (S,G) filter:124, route-map:none
    Input RP filter:none, route-map:none
    Output (S,G) filter:124, route-map:none
    Output RP filter:none, route-map:none
  SA-Requests:
    Input filter:none
    Sending SA-Requests to peer:enabled
  Peer ttl threshold:0
  Input queue size:0, Output queue size:0
MSDP Peer J.4.0.203 (?), AS 4 (configured AS)
Description:
  Connection status:
    State:Up, Resets:743, Connection source:Loopback0 (J.2.0.204)
    Uptime(Downtime):1w2d, Messages sent/received:29748/36008
    Output messages discarded:0
    Connection and counters cleared 7w0d    ago
  SA Filtering:
    Input (S,G) filter:124, route-map:none
    Input RP filter:none, route-map:none
    Output (S,G) filter:124, route-map:none
    Output RP filter:none, route-map:none
  SA-Requests:
    Input filter:none
    Sending SA-Requests to peer:enabled
  Peer ttl threshold:0
  Input queue size:0, Output queue size:0
MSDP Peer J.3.0.207 (?), AS 3 (configured AS)
```

```
      Description:
        Connection status:
          State:Up, Resets:8, Connection source:Loopback0 (J.2.0.204)
          Uptime(Downtime):08:12:05, Messages sent/received:1893/493
          Output messages discarded:0
          Connection and counters cleared 7w0d     ago
        SA Filtering:
          Input (S,G) filter:124, route-map:none
          Input RP filter:none, route-map:none
          Output (S,G) filter:124, route-map:none
          Output RP filter:none, route-map:none
        SA-Requests:
          Input filter:none
          Sending SA-Requests to peer:enabled
        Peer ttl threshold:0
        Input queue size:0, Output queue size:0
```

Step 6 Configure multicast borders appropriately.

You must configure multicast borders on every router interface that borders another ISP. For ISP2, you must configure multicast borders on the ISP2BB3, ISP2BB6, and ISP2BB7 routers. The following sample configuration, taken from the configuration file for the ISP2BB7 router, shows how to configure multicast borders:

```
interface POS0/0
 description TO ISP1BB7, POS9/0/0
 ip pim bsr-border
 ip multicast boundary 1
!
access-list 1 deny    224.0.1.39
access-list 1 deny    224.0.1.40
access-list 1 deny    239.0.0.0 0.255.255.255
access-list 1 permit any
```

For the device characteristics and complete configuration files of the devices in ISP2, see Chapter 4, "ISP2 Device Characteristics and Configuration Files."

NOTE In the interdomain multicast scenario, ISP2 does not have customers connected to its network. For an example of how a customer is connected through a point of presence (POP), see the "ISP1—Connecting Customers into Infrastructure" section later in this chapter.

ISP1 Scenario

This section covers the following topics:

- **ISP1**—Implementing Intradomain Multicast
- **ISP1**—Implementing Interdomain Multicast
- **ISP1**—Connecting Customers into Infrastructure

ISP1—Implementing Intradomain Multicast

This section addresses the following issues related to intradomain multicast for the ISP1 example:

- Strategy
- Topology
- Benefits and ramifications
- Configuration summary

ISP1 is a larger, more established ISP that wants the flexibility to decide which of its IP addresses to advertise to other ISPs. ISP1 also wants redundancy and load-sharing capability within its multicast network. ISP1 decided to implement two Anycast RPs at the edge of its network. The two routers provide redundancy for one another by sharing a single logical IP address. Anycast RP enables ISP1 to have more than one physical RP in its domain. The decision to place the RPs at the edge of the network was made to reduce the transit multicast traffic. Therefore, ISP1 implemented two Anycast RPs at the edge of its network.

Anycast RP is a useful application of MSDP. You use this technique to configure a multicast sparse mode network to provide for fault tolerance and load sharing within a single multicast domain. For more information about anycast RP, refer to Chapter 1.

Configure two or more RPs with the same IP address (for example, 10.0.0.1) on loopback interfaces. You should configure the loopback address with a 32-bit mask because it is a host route. Configure all the downstream routers so that they know that 10.0.0.1 is their local RP's IP address. IP routing automatically selects the topologically closest RP for each source and receiver. Because some sources use only one RP and some receivers use a different RP, MSDP is needed to enable the RPs to exchange information about active sources. All the RPs are configured to be MSDP peers of each other. Each RP will know about the active sources in the other RP's area. If any of the RPs were to fail, IP routing would converge and one of the RPs would become the active RP in both areas.

Chapter 2: Implementing Interdomain Multicast Using MSDP

NOTE The Anycast RP example in the previous paragraph used IP addresses from RFC 1918. These IP addresses are normally blocked at interdomain borders and are not accessible to other ISPs. You must use valid IP addresses if you want the RPs to be reachable from other domains.

Figure 2-6 shows the intradomain multicast network diagram for ISP1.

Figure 2-6 *Network Diagram for ISP1—Intradomain Multicast*

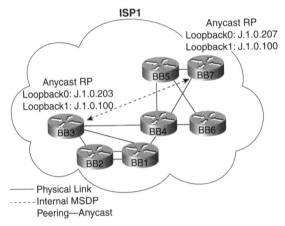

Table 2-2 presents the benefits and ramifications of deploying the ISP1 multicast network.

Table 2-2 *Deploying ISP1 Multicast Network: Benefits and Ramifications*

Benefits	Ramifications
Deploying the ISP1 multicast network offers redundancy capability due to Anycast RPs. If one RP were to fail, the other RP would take over within the convergence time of the unicast routing protocol.	Difficult to implement compared to ISP2 network topology
The deployment offers load-sharing capability due to Anycast RPs. Devices will use the RP they are topologically closest to (based on routing metric) in the network.	Difficult to troubleshoot compared to ISP2 network topology
The Anycast RP mechanism depends only on the fast convergence of unicast routing.	

The following is a summary of the tasks that were performed to configure the devices in ISP1 for intradomain multicast:

Step 1 Configure multicast globally.

The following sample configuration, taken from the configuration file for the ISP1BB4 router, shows how to configure multicast globally on a router. Multicast is configured on all ISP1 routers.

```
ip multicast-routing distributed
```

Step 2 Configure multicast on the interfaces.

The following sample configuration shows how to configure multicast on an interface of the ISP1BB4 router. Multicast is configured on the interfaces of all the ISP1 routers.

```
interface POS1/0/0
 ip pim sparse-mode
 ip mroute-cache distributed
```

Step 3 Select the router to be RP.

To benefit from load sharing and redundancy, ISP1 implemented Anycast RPs in its network. ISP1's Anycast RPs (ISP1BB3 and ISP1BB7) are placed at the edge of the ISP domain. The following sample configuration shows you how to configure a unique IP address with a 32-bit mask on the loopback interfaces of the Anycast RPs. Configure the same unique loopback address on both the ISP1BB3 and ISP1BB7 routers.

```
interface Loopback1
 ip address J.1.0.100 255.255.255.255
 ip pim sparse-mode
```

The following sample configuration shows how to configure an MSDP peering session between the ISP1BB3 and ISP1BB7 routers using the unique IP addresses that were already configured for BGP on the Loopback0 interface:

For the ISP1BB3 router:

```
ip msdp peer J.1.0.207 connect-source Loopback0
ip msdp cache-sa-state
ip msdp originator-id Loopback0
```

For the ISP1BB7 router:

```
ip msdp peer J.1.0.203 connect-source Loopback0
ip msdp cache-sa-state
ip msdp originator-id Loopback0
```

62 Chapter 2: Implementing Interdomain Multicast Using MSDP

NOTE   The configuration shown is applicable for intradomain multicast traffic, but creates a problem if ISP1 is connected to other ISPs. RPF checks will fail if there is a direct MSDP peer relationship between ISP1BB3 and ISP1BB7. The problem and the solution are described in Step 2 of the "ISP1—Implementing Interdomain Multicast" section later in this chapter.

Step 4   Configure the RP statically on each router in ISP1.

The following sample configuration shows how to configure the RP address on each router in ISP1:

```
ip pim rp-address J.1.0.100
```

Step 5   Restrict available multicast groups from using 232/24. (Optional)

SSM will use the 232.0.0.0 through 232.255.255.255 address range for specific well-known sources. This address range does not require the use of an RP. The following sample configuration shows how to restrict sources in the 232/8 range from registering with the RP. These statements need to be configured only on the RP.

```
ip pim accept-register list no-ssm-range

ip access-list extended no-ssm-range deny ip any
    232.0.0.0 0.255.255.255 permit ip any any
```

For the device characteristics and complete configuration files of the devices in ISP1, see Chapter 3, "ISP1 Device Characteristics and Configuration Files."

ISP1—Implementing Interdomain Multicast

This section addresses the following issues related to interdomain multicast for the ISP1 example:

- Topology
- Configuration summary

Figure 2-7 shows the interdomain multicast network diagram for ISP1.

Figure 2-7   *Network Diagram for ISP1—Interdomain Multicast*

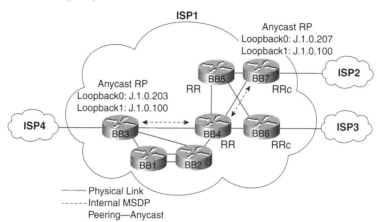

The following is a summary of the tasks that were performed to configure the devices in ISP1 for interdomain multicast:

Step 1   Configure MBGP to exchange multicast routing information.

(a) Configure MBGP peering sessions.

The following MBGP peering sessions exist in ISP1:

—ISP1BB3 externally peers with ISP4BB4.

—ISP1BB6 externally peers with ISP3BB6.

—ISP1BB7 externally peers with ISP2BB7.

—All backbone routers in ISP1 internally peer with each other directly or through route reflectors.

The routers in ISP1 are running Cisco IOS Software Release 12.1 or 12.1 T software. You must configure these routers for multicast NLRI information using the **address-family** address family configuration command. The ISP1INTERNAL peer group is configured on every router in ISP1. The following sample configuration, taken from the configuration file for the ISP1BB3 router, shows how to configure the internal peers. The configuration is slightly different on the ISP1BB6 and ISP1BB7 routers.

```
router bgp 1
 neighbor ISP1INTERNAL peer-group
 neighbor ISP1INTERNAL remote-as 1
 neighbor ISP1INTERNAL update-source Loopback0
 !
 address-family ipv4 multicast
```

```
neighbor ISP1INTERNAL activate
neighbor J.1.0.200 activate
neighbor J.1.0.201 activate
neighbor J.1.0.202 activate
neighbor J.1.0.204 activate
neighbor J.1.0.205 activate
neighbor J.1.0.208 activate
neighbor J.1.0.209 activate
neighbor J.1.0.210 activate
exit-address-family
```

The following sample configurations show how to configure the external peers. The configuration is different for each router.

The following configuration is for the ISP1BB3 router:

```
router bgp 1
 neighbor ISP4ISP1PEER peer-group
 neighbor ISP4ISP1PEER remote-as 4
 neighbor J.4.0.33 peer-group ISP4ISP1PEER
 !
 address-family ipv4 multicast
 neighbor ISP4ISP1PEER activate
 neighbor J.4.0.33 activate
 exit-address-family
```

The following configuration is for the ISP1BB6 router:

```
router bgp 1
 neighbor ISP3ISP1PEER peer-group
 neighbor ISP3ISP1PEER remote-as 3
 neighbor J.3.0.245 peer-group ISP3ISP1PEER
 !
 address-family ipv4 multicast
 neighbor J.3.0.245 activate
 exit-address-family
```

The following configuration is for the ISP1BB7 router:

```
router bgp 1
 neighbor J.2.0.253 remote-as 2
 !
 address-family ipv4 multicast
 neighbor J.2.0.253 activate
 exit-address-family
```

(b) Verify that MBGP is configured properly.

The following sample output shows how to verify that MBGP peers have negotiated for multicast routes:

```
show ip bgp neighbors J.4.0.33

BGP neighbor is J.4.0.33, remote AS 4, external link
 Member of peer-group ISP4ISP1PEER for session parameters
  BGP version 4, remote router ID J.4.0.204
  BGP state = Established, up for 1d01h
  Last read 00:00:19, hold time is 180, keepalive interval is 60 seconds
  Neighbor capabilities:
    Route refresh:advertised and received(new)
    Address family IPv4 Unicast:advertised and received
    Address family IPv4 Multicast:advertised
  Received 1527053 messages, 1 notifications, 0 in queue
  Sent 1525164 messages, 0 notifications, 0 in queue
  Route refresh request:received 0, sent 0
  Default minimum time between advertisement runs is 30 seconds

 For address family:IPv4 Unicast
  BGP table version 7180619, neighbor version 7180618
  Index 2, Offset 0, Mask 0x4
  ISP4ISP1PEER peer-group member
  393 accepted prefixes consume 14148 bytes
  Prefix advertised 3913222, suppressed 15560, withdrawn 569094

 For address family:IPv4 Multicast
  BGP table version 179740, neighbor version 0
  Index 9, Offset 1, Mask 0x2
  0 accepted prefixes consume 0 bytes
  Prefix advertised 0, suppressed 0, withdrawn 0

  Connections established 5; dropped 4
  Last reset 6d02h, due to Peer closed the session
Connection state is ESTAB, I/O status:1, unread input bytes:0
Local host:J.4.0.34, Local port:179
Foreign host:J.4.0.33, Foreign port:11001

Enqueued packets for retransmit:0, input:0  mis-ordered:0 (0 bytes)

Event Timers (current time is 0xC44ED904):
Timer          Starts    Wakeups            Next
Retrans          4226         20             0x0
TimeWait            0          0             0x0
AckHold          2577       2106             0x0
SendWnd             0          0             0x0
KeepAlive           0          0             0x0
```

Chapter 2: Implementing Interdomain Multicast Using MSDP

```
GiveUp              0         0              0x0
PmtuAger            0         0              0x0
DeadWait            0         0              0x0

iss: 788905143   snduna: 789055186   sndnxt: 789055186      sndwnd: 13161
irs: 788903705   rcvnxt: 788982188   rcvwnd:        15115   delrcvwnd: 1269

SRTT:300 ms, RTTO:303 ms, RTV:3 ms, KRTT:0 ms
minRTT:0 ms, maxRTT:304 ms, ACK hold:200 ms
Flags:passive open, nagle, gen tcbs

Datagrams (max data segment is 4430 bytes):
Rcvd:5847 (out of order:0), with data:2577, total data bytes:78482
Sent:6330 (retransmit:20), with data:4205, total data bytes:150042
```

show ip bgp ipv4 multicast summary

```
BGP router identifier J.1.0.203, local AS number 1
BGP table version is 179746, main routing table version 1
3 network entries and 1 paths using 330 bytes of memory
8 BGP path attribute entries using 480 bytes of memory
2 BGP rrinfo entries using 48 bytes of memory
3 BGP AS-PATH entries using 72 bytes of memory
0 BGP route-map cache entries using 0 bytes of memory
0 BGP filter-list cache entries using 0 bytes of memory
BGP activity 399426/517203 prefixes, 3845743/3844578 paths, scan
interval 15 secs

Neighbor       V    AS MsgRcvd MsgSent   TblVer  InQ OutQ Up/Down  State/
PfxRcd
J.1.0.200      4     1   69546 1027381   179746    0    0 5w3d          0
J.1.0.201      4     1   54860 1027256   179746    0    0 2w6d          0
J.1.0.202      4     1   54846 1027272   179746    0    0 2w6d          0
J.1.0.204      4     1 1822972 1027387   179746    0    0 5w3d          0
J.1.0.205      4     1  996842 1027387   179746    0    0 5w3d          1
J.1.0.208      4     1   70235 1027387   179746    0    0 5w3d          0
J.1.0.209      4     1   76084 1027381   179746    0    0 5w3d          0
J.1.0.210      4     1   67412 1027068   179746    0    0 5w2d          0
J.4.0.33       4     4 1527057 1525173        0    0    0 1d01h         0
```

Step 2 Configure MSDP peering sessions.

The configuration of the BGP route reflector servers and route reflector clients adds some complexity to the configuration of ISP1. For example, the MSDP peers must perform an RPF check to verify from which AS the SA messages originated, and the IP addresses must match the IP address of the route reflector server. To ensure that RPF checks always succeeds in the ISP1 network, the route reflector server (ISP1BB4) is configured to have an MSDP peering sessions with the Anycast RPs (ISP1BB3 and ISP1BB7). In addition, the direct peering relationship between ISP1BB3 and ISP1BB7 is removed.

NOTE You have several ways to configure a network to ensure that RPF checks will always succeed. These alternatives will not be discussed in this chapter.

(a) Select an IP address.

For MSDP peering sessions, use the same IP address that you used for the BGP peering session. In this case, it is the unique IP address with a 32-bit mask configured on Loopback0.

(b) Configure peering sessions.

As shown in Figure 2-7, the following new intradomain Anycast peering sessions exist in ISP1:

—ISP1BB3 peers with ISP1BB4

—ISP1BB4 peers with ISP1BB7

The following MSDP peering sessions also exist in ISP1:

—ISP1BB3 peers with ISP4BB3

—ISP1BB7 peers with ISP2BB4

The following sample configurations show how to configure the MSDP peering sessions in ISP1:

The following configuration is for the ISP1BB3 router:

```
ip msdp peer J.4.0.203 connect-source Loopback0 remote-as 4
ip msdp peer J.1.0.204 connect-source Loopback0
ip msdp originator-id Loopback0
```

The following configuration is for the ISP1BB4 router:

```
ip msdp peer J.1.0.203 connect-source Loopback0
ip msdp peer J.1.0.207 connect-source Loopback0
```

The following configuration is for the ISP1BB7 router:

```
ip msdp peer J.2.0.204 connect-source Loopback0 remote-as 2
ip msdp peer J.1.0.204 connect-source Loopback0
ip msdp originator-id Loopback0
```

Step 3 Configure recommended SA filters.

The following sample configurations show how to configure the SA filters on ISP1's RPs (ISP1BB3 and ISP1BB7):

The following configures the SA filters for the ISP1BB3 router (connection to the ISP4BB3 router):

```
ip msdp sa-filter in J.4.0.203 list 124
ip msdp sa-filter out J.4.0.203 list 124
```

The following configures the SA filters for the ISP1BB7 router (connection to the ISP2BB4 router):

```
ip msdp sa-filter in J.2.0.204 list 124
ip msdp sa-filter out J.2.0.204 list 124
```

Configure the following access list on both the ISP1BB3 and ISP1BB7 routers:

```
access-list 124 deny ip any host 224.0.2.2
access-list 124 deny ip any host 224.0.1.3
access-list 124 deny ip any host 224.0.1.24
access-list 124 deny ip any host 224.0.1.22
access-list 124 deny ip any host 224.0.1.2
access-list 124 deny ip any host 224.0.1.35
access-list 124 deny ip any host 224.0.1.60
access-list 124 deny ip any host 224.0.1.39
access-list 124 deny ip any host 224.0.1.40
access-list 124 deny ip any 239.0.0.0 0.255.255.255
access-list 124 deny ip 10.0.0.0 0.255.255.255 any
access-list 124 deny ip 127.0.0.0 0.255.255.255 any
access-list 124 deny ip 172.16.0.0 0.15.255.255 any
access-list 124 deny ip 192.168.0.0 0.0.255.255 any
access-list 124 deny ip any 232.0.0.0 0.255.255.255
```

Step 4 Configure SA caching.

The following sample configuration shows how to enable SA caching. This feature is enabled on all the routers in ISP1 running MSDP (ISP1BB3, ISP1BB4, and ISP1BB7 routers).

```
ip msdp cache-sa-state
```

Step 5 Verify that MSDP peers are working properly.

The following sample output shows how to verify that MSDP peers are working properly:

```
show ip msdp peer J.4.0.203
```

```
              MSDP Peer J.4.0.203 (?), AS 4 (configured AS)
              Description:
                Connection status:
                  State:Up, Resets:4, Connection source:Loopback0 (J.1.0.203)
                  Uptime(Downtime):1d06h, Messages sent/received:4022/5221
                  Output messages discarded:0
                  Connection and counters cleared 5w3d     ago
                SA Filtering:
                  Input (S,G) filter:124, route-map:none
                  Input RP filter:none, route-map:none
                  Output (S,G) filter:124, route-map:none
                  Output RP filter:none, route-map:none
                SA-Requests:
                  Input filter:none
                  Sending SA-Requests to peer:enabled
                Peer ttl threshold:0
                Input queue size:0, Output queue size:0
```

Step 6 Configure multicast borders appropriately.

You must configure multicast borders on every router interface that borders another ISP. For ISP1, configure multicast borders on the ISP1BB3, ISP1BB6, and ISP1BB7 routers. The following sample configuration, taken from the configuration file for the ISP1BB3 router, shows how to configure multicast borders:

```
interface POS9/0/0
 description TO ISP4BB4, POS 12/0/0
 ip pim bsr-border
 ip pim sparse-mode
 ip multicast boundary 10
!
access-list 10 deny     224.0.1.39
access-list 10 deny     224.0.1.40
access-list 10 deny     239.0.0.0 0.255.255.255
access-list 10 permit any
```

For characteristics and complete configuration files of the devices in ISP1, see Chapter 3.

ISP1—Connecting Customers into Infrastructure

This section covers the following scenarios related to connecting customers to ISP1.

- External RP Scenario
- Internal RP Scenario Without MBGP

External RP Scenario

This section addresses the following issues related to using RP in ISP1 for multicast:

- Strategy
- Topology
- Benefits and ramifications
- Configuration summary

In this scenario, the customer uses the RP in ISP1 for multicasting. This customer requires its internal content to be seen by others outside the company.

The network topology for ISP1-POP is the same topology as ISP1 with the addition of a point of presence (POP). In Figure 2-8, ISP1AC2 represents the "external RP customer" scenario.

Figure 2-8 *Network Diagram for ISP1-POP*

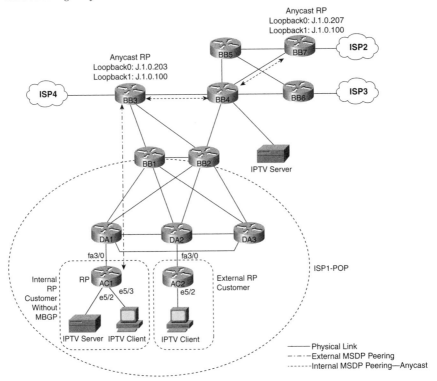

Table 2-3 presents the benefits and ramifications of using RP in ISP1 when deploying a multicast network.

Table 2-3 *Using RP in ISP1 for multicasting: Benefits and Ramifications*

Benefits	Ramifications
Using RP allows controlled access to multicast content on the Internet.	Possibility for a denial-of-service attack by another customer of the ISP
Configuration is simple.	
Using RP requires minimal command configuration.	

The following is a summary of the tasks that were performed to configure the ISP1AC2 router for multicasting using an RP in ISP1:

Step 1 Configure multicast globally.

Use the following configuration:

```
ip multicast-routing
```

Step 2 Configure multicast on the interfaces.

Use the following configuration:

```
interface fa3/0
 ip pim sparse-mode

interface eth5/2
 ip pim sparse-mode
```

Step 3 Configure the RP statically.

Use the following configuration:

```
ip pim rp-address J.1.0.100
```

For characteristics and complete configuration files of the devices in ISP1-POP, see Chapter 3

Internal RP Without MBGP Scenario

This section addresses the following issues related to using RP without MBGP in ISP1 for multicast:

- Strategy
- Topology
- Benefits and ramifications
- Intradomain configuration summary
- Interdomain configuration summary

In this scenario, the customer uses its own internal RP for multicasting without MBGP. This customer wants the flexibility to decide whether its internal multicast content can be seen by others outside of the company. The internal RP allows the customer to filter private multicast traffic.

Refer to figure 2-8 to review the network topology of ISP1-POP. ISP1AC1 represents the "internal RP customer without MBGP" scenario. The customer is in the same AS as the provider.

Table 2-4 presents the benefits and ramifications of deploying the ISP2 multicast network.

Table 2-4 *Using RP Without MBGP in ISP1 for Multicasting: Benefits and Ramifications*

Benefits	Ramifications
Using RP without MBGP allows access to multicast content on the Internet.	More complex to implement than the external RP scenario
The customer can have its own multicast sessions that do not leave the company.	
The customer can limit exposure to multicast denial-of-service attacks.	

The following is a summary of the tasks that were performed to configure the ISP1AC1 router for intradomain multicasting. In this example, the customer has only one router. If the customer has multiple routers, the intradomain multicast tasks should be performed on all of the routers.

Step 1 Configure multicast globally.

Use the following configuration:

```
ip multicast-routing
```

Step 2 Configure multicast on the interfaces.

Use the following configuration:

```
interface FastEthernet3/0
 ip pim sparse-mode

interface Ethernet5/2
 ip pim sparse-mode

interface Ethernet5/3
 ip pim sparse-mode
```

Step 3 Select the router to be the RP.

In this example, the customer has only one router (ISP1AC1). The following sample configuration shows how a unique IP address with a 32-bit mask is configured on the loopback interface of the RP (ISP1AC1).

```
interface Loopback0
  ip address K.250.0.201 255.255.255.255
  ip pim sparse-mode
  ip mroute-cache distributed
  no shut
```

Step 4 Configure the RP statically.

Use the following configuration:

```
ISP1AC1#ip pim rp-address K.250.0.201
```

The following is a summary of the tasks that were performed to configure the ISP1AC1 router for interdomain multicasting. In this example, the customer has only one router. If the customer has multiple routers, the interdomain multicast tasks should be performed on all of the routers.

Step 1 Configure MSDP peering session.

The following sample configuration shows how to configure the peering session between the ISP1AC1 router and the ISP1BB3 router:

The following configuration is for the ISP1AC1 router:

```
ip msdp peer J.1.0.203 connect-source Loopback0
```

The following configuration is for the ISP1BB3 router:

```
ip msdp peer K.250.1.2 connect-source Loopback0
```

Step 2 Configure recommended SA filters.

The following sample configuration shows how to configure the SA filters on the ISP1AC1 router for the connection to the ISP1BB3 router:

```
ip msdp sa-filter in J.1.0.203 list 124
ip msdp sa-filter out J.1.0.203 list 124

access-list 124 deny    ip any host 224.0.2.2
access-list 124 deny    ip any host 224.0.1.3
access-list 124 deny    ip any host 224.0.1.24
access-list 124 deny    ip any host 224.0.1.22
access-list 124 deny    ip any host 224.0.1.2
access-list 124 deny    ip any host 224.0.1.35
access-list 124 deny    ip any host 224.0.1.60
access-list 124 deny    ip any host 224.0.1.39
```

Chapter 2: Implementing Interdomain Multicast Using MSDP

```
access-list 124 deny   ip any host 224.0.1.40
access-list 124 deny   ip any 239.0.0.0 0.255.255.255
access-list 124 deny   ip 10.0.0.0 0.255.255.255 any
access-list 124 deny   ip 127.0.0.0 0.255.255.255 any
access-list 124 deny   ip 172.16.0.0 0.15.255.255 any
access-list 124 deny   ip K.168.0.0 0.0.255.255 any
access-list 124 deny   ip any 232.0.0.0 0.255.255.255
access-list 124 permit ip any any
```

Step 3 Configure SA caching.

The following sample configuration shows how to enable SA caching. This feature is enabled on the ISP1AC1 router.

```
ip msdp cache-sa-state
```

Step 4 Verify that MSDP peers are working properly.

The following sample output shows how to verify that MSDP peers are working properly:

```
show ip msdp peer

MSDP Peer J.1.0.203 (?), AS ?
Description:
  Connection status:
    State:Up, Resets:1, Connection source:Loopback0 (K.250.0.201)
    Uptime(Downtime):2w1d, Messages sent/received:21824/66342
    Output messages discarded:0
    Connection and counters cleared 2w2d    ago
  SA Filtering:
    Input (S,G) filter:124, route-map:none
    Input RP filter:none, route-map:none
    Output (S,G) filter:124, route-map:none
    Output RP filter:none, route-map:none
  SA-Requests:
    Input filter:none
    Sending SA-Requests to peer:disabled
  Peer ttl threshold:0
  Input queue size:0, Output queue size:0
```

Step 5 Configure multicast borders appropriately.

The following sample configuration shows how to configure a multicast border on the ISP1AC1 router. In this sample configuration, access list 1 is used to separate multicast domains by denying the AutoRP groups and the admin address range 239.

```
interface FastEthernet3/0
 ip pim bsr-border
```

```
ip pim sparse-mode
ip multicast boundary 1

access-list 1 deny    224.0.1.39
access-list 1 deny    224.0.1.40
access-list 1 deny    239.0.0.0 0.255.255.255
access-list 1 permit any
```

For characteristics and complete configuration files of the devices in ISP1-POP, see Chapter 3.

ISP3 and ISP4 Scenarios

The detailed network scenarios of ISP3 and ISP4 are not discussed in this chapter. For these two ISPs, the discussion focuses only on the routers that are configured to implement interdomain multicast among the ISP1, ISP2, ISP3, and ISP4 domains.

This section addresses the following issues related to implementing interdomain multicast on ISP3 and ISP4:

- Topology
- Intradomain configuration summary

Figure 2-9 shows the interdomain multicast network diagram for ISP3.

Figure 2-9 *Network Diagram for ISP3—Interdomain Multicast*

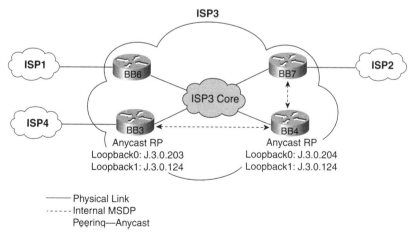

Chapter 2: Implementing Interdomain Multicast Using MSDP

The following is a summary of the tasks that were performed to configure the devices in ISP3 for interdomain multicast:

Step 1 Configure MBGP to exchange multicast routing information.

  (a) Configure MBGP peering sessions.

  The following MBGP peering sessions exist in ISP3:

  —ISP3BB3 externally peers with ISP4BB3.

  —ISP3BB6 externally peers with ISP1BB6.

  —ISP3BB7 externally peers with ISP2BB3.

  —All backbone routers in ISP3 internally peer with each other directly or through route reflectors.

  The routers in ISP3 are running Cisco IOS Software Release 12.1 or 12.1 T software. You must configure these routers for multicast NLRI information using the **address-family** address family configuration command. Configure the ISP3INTERNAL peer group on every router in ISP3. The following sample configuration, taken from the configuration file for the ISP3BB3 router, shows how to configure the internal peers. The configuration is slightly different on the ISP3BB6 and ISP3BB7 routers.

```
router bgp 3
 neighbor ISP3INTERNAL peer-group
 neighbor ISP3INTERNAL remote-as 3
 neighbor ISP3INTERNAL update-source Loopback0
 neighbor J.3.0.201 peer-group ISP3INTERNAL
 neighbor J.3.0.202 peer-group ISP3INTERNAL
 neighbor J.3.0.204 peer-group ISP3INTERNAL
 neighbor J.3.0.205 peer-group ISP3INTERNAL
 neighbor J.3.0.206 peer-group ISP3INTERNAL
 neighbor J.3.0.207 peer-group ISP3INTERNAL
 neighbor J.3.0.240 remote-as 3
 neighbor J.3.0.240 update-source Loopback0
 !
 address-family ipv4 multicast
 neighbor ISP3INTERNAL activate
 neighbor ISP3ISP4PEER activate
 neighbor J.3.0.201 activate
 neighbor J.3.0.202 activate
 neighbor J.3.0.204 activate
 neighbor J.3.0.205 activate
 neighbor J.3.0.206 activate
 neighbor J.3.0.207 activate
```

```
neighbor J.3.0.240 activate
exit-address-family
!
```

The following sample configurations show how to configure the external peers. The configuration is different for each router.

The following configuration is for the ISP3BB3 router:

```
router bgp 3
 neighbor ISP3ISP4PEER peer-group
 neighbor J.3.0.250 remote-as 4
 neighbor J.3.0.250 peer-group ISP3ISP4PEER
 !
 address-family ipv4 multicast
 neighbor ISP3ISP4PEER activate
 neighbor J.3.0.250 activate
 exit-address-family
```

The following configuration is for the ISP3BB6 router:

```
router bgp 3
 neighbor ISP3ISP1PEER peer-group
 neighbor ISP3ISP1PEER remote-as 1
 neighbor J.3.0.246 peer-group ISP3ISP1PEER
 !
 address-family ipv4 multicast
 neighbor ISP3ISP1PEER activate
 neighbor J.3.0.246 activate
 exit-address-family
```

The following configuration is for the ISP3BB7 router:

```
router bgp 3
 neighbor ISP3ISP2PEER peer-group
 neighbor ISP3ISP2PEER remote-as 2
 neighbor J.2.0.245 peer-group ISP3ISP2PEER
 !
 address-family ipv4 multicast
 neighbor ISP3ISP2PEER activate
 neighbor J.2.0.245 activate
 exit-address-family
```

(b) Verify that MBGP is configured properly.

The following sample output shows how to verify that MBGP peers have negotiated for multicast routes:

```
ISP3BB6#show ip bgp neighbors J.3.0.246

BGP neighbor is J.3.0.246, remote AS 1, external link
  Member of peer-group ISP3ISP1PEER for session parameters
```

```
  BGP version 4, remote router ID J.1.0.206
  BGP state = Established, up for 1w0d
  Last read 00:00:49, hold time is 180, keepalive interval is 60
seconds
    Neighbor capabilities:
      Route refresh:advertised and received(new)
      Address family IPv4 Unicast:advertised and received
      Address family IPv4 Multicast:advertised and received
    Received 18404 messages, 0 notifications, 0 in queue
    Sent 18548 messages, 0 notifications, 0 in queue
    Route refresh request:received 0, sent 0
    Default minimum time between advertisement runs is 30 seconds

  For address family:IPv4 Unicast
    BGP table version 726089, neighbor version 726089
    Index 1, Offset 0, Mask 0x2
    ISP3ISP1PEER peer-group member
    50376 accepted prefixes consume 1813536 bytes
    Prefix advertised 388255, suppressed 26, withdrawn 337751

  For address family:IPv4 Multicast
    BGP table version 22917, neighbor version 22917
    Index 8, Offset 1, Mask 0x1
    0 accepted prefixes consume 0 bytes
    Prefix advertised 265, suppressed 0, withdrawn 263

    Connections established 1; dropped 0
    Last reset never
  Connection state is ESTAB, I/O status:1, unread input bytes:0
  Local host:J.3.0.245, Local port:11019
  Foreign host:J.3.0.246, Foreign port:179

  Enqueued packets for retransmit:0, input:0  mis-ordered:0 (0 bytes)

  Event Timers (current time is 0x287B19C4):
  Timer          Starts      Wakeups              Next
  Retrans        14396          46                0x0
  TimeWait           0           0                0x0
  AckHold        14205       11580                0x0
  SendWnd            0           0                0x0
  KeepAlive          0           0                0x0
  GiveUp             0           0                0x0
  PmtuAger           0           0                0x0
  DeadWait           0           0                0x0

  iss:2895360363    snduna:2898650079    sndnxt:2898650079    sndwnd:  14007
  irs:2895361023    rcvnxt:2898664417    rcvwnd:       14970  delrcvwnd: 1414
```

```
            SRTT:300 ms, RTTO:303 ms, RTV:3 ms, KRTT:0 ms
            minRTT:0 ms, maxRTT:484 ms, ACK hold:200 ms
            Flags:higher precedence, nagle

            Datagrams (max data segment is 4430 bytes):
            Rcvd:29082 (out of order:0), with data:14786, total data bytes:3303393
            Sent:27252 (retransmit:46), with data:14751, total data bytes:3289715

            ISP3BB6#show ip bgp ipv4 multicast summary

            BGP router identifier J.3.0.206, local AS number 3
            BGP table version is 22917, main routing table version 1
            6 network entries and 2 paths using 660 bytes of memory
            292 BGP path attribute entries using 17520 bytes of memory
            7 BGP rrinfo entries using 168 bytes of memory
            99 BGP AS-PATH entries using 5832 bytes of memory
            187 BGP extended community entries using 4488 bytes of memory
            0 BGP route-map cache entries using 0 bytes of memory
            0 BGP filter-list cache entries using 0 bytes of memory
            BGP activity 388470/342418 prefixes, 401299/350266 paths, scan interval
            15 secs

            Neighbor      V     AS MsgRcvd MsgSent   TblVer  InQ OutQ Up/Down  State/
            PfxRcd
            J.3.0.201     4     3  11546   12644     22917   0   0   1w0d     0
            J.3.0.202     4     3  11362   12644     22917   0   0   1w0d     0
            J.3.0.203     4     3  11919   12644     22917   0   0   1w0d     1
            J.3.0.204     4     3  11322   11905     22917   0   0   1w0d     0
            J.3.0.205     4     3  11328   11905     22917   0   0   1w0d     1
            J.3.0.207     4     3  11403   11905     22917   0   0   1w0d     0
            J.3.0.241     4     3  12377   12620     0       0   0   2d16h    0
            J.3.0.246     4     1  18405   18549     22917   0   0   1w0d     0
```

Step 2 Configure MSDP peering sessions.

The configuration of the BGP route reflector servers and route reflector clients adds some complexity to the configuration of ISP3. For example, the MSDP peers must perform an RPF check to verify from which AS the SA messages originated, and the IP addresses must match the IP address of the route reflector server. To ensure that RPF checks always succeed in the ISP3 network, configure the router reflector server (ISP3BB4) to have an MSDP peering session with the Anycast RPs (ISP3BB3 and ISP3BB4).

    (a) Select an IP address.

For MSDP peering sessions, use the same IP address that you used for the BGP peering session. In this case, it is the unique IP address with a 32-bit mask configured on Loopback0.

(b) Configure peering sessions.

The following sample configurations show how to configure the MSDP peering sessions in ISP3:

The following configuration is for the ISP3BB3 router:

```
ip msdp peer J.3.0.250 connect-source Loopback0 remote-as 4
ip msdp peer J.3.0.204 connect-source Loopback0 remote-as 3
```

The following configuration is for the ISP3BB4 router:

```
ip msdp peer J.3.0.203 connect-source Loopback0
ip msdp peer J.3.0.207 connect-source Loopback0
```

The following configuration is for the ISP3BB7 router:

```
ip msdp peer J.3.0.204 connect-source Loopback0
ip msdp peer J.2.0.204 connect-source Loopback0 remote-as 2
```

Step 3 Configure recommended SA filters.

The following sample configurations show how to configure the SA filters on ISP3's RPs (ISP3BB3 and ISP3BB4):

The following configures the SA filters for the ISP3BB3 router (connection to the ISP4BB3 router):

```
ip msdp sa-filter in J.3.0.250 list 124
ip msdp sa-filter out J.3.0.250 list 124
```

The following configures the SA filters for the ISP3BB7 router (connection to the ISP2BB3 router):

```
ip msdp sa-filter in J.2.0.204 list 124
ip msdp sa-filter out J.2.0.204 list 124
```

The following access list is configured on both the ISP3BB3 and ISP3BB7 routers:

```
access-list 124 deny   ip any host 224.0.2.2
access-list 124 deny   ip any host 224.0.1.3
access-list 124 deny   ip any host 224.0.1.24
access-list 124 deny   ip any host 224.0.1.22
access-list 124 deny   ip any host 224.0.1.2
access-list 124 deny   ip any host 224.0.1.35
access-list 124 deny   ip any host 224.0.1.60
access-list 124 deny   ip any host 224.0.1.39
```

```
access-list 124 deny    ip any host 224.0.1.40
access-list 124 deny    ip any 239.0.0.0 0.255.255.255
access-list 124 deny    ip 10.0.0.0 0.255.255.255 any
access-list 124 deny    ip 127.0.0.0 0.255.255.255 any
access-list 124 deny    ip 172.16.0.0 0.15.255.255 any
access-list 124 deny    ip K.168.0.0 0.0.255.255 any
access-list 124 permit  ip any any
```

Step 4 Configuring SA caching.

The following sample configuration shows how to enable SA caching. This feature is enabled on all the routers in ISP3 running MSDP (ISP3BB3, ISP3BB4, and ISP3BB7 routers).

```
ip msdp cache-sa-state
```

Step 5 Verify that MSDP peers are working properly.

The following sample output shows how to verify that MSDP peers are working properly:

```
ISP3BB3# show ip msdp peer J.3.0.250

MSDP Peer J.3.0.250 (?), AS 4
Description:
  Connection status:
    State:Up, Resets:1, Connection source:none configured
    Uptime(Downtime):10:05:21, Messages sent/received:605/3321
    Output messages discarded:0
    Connection and counters cleared 2w3d    ago
  SA Filtering:
    Input (S,G) filter:124, route-map:none
    Input RP filter:none, route-map:none
    Output (S,G) filter:124, route-map:none
    Output RP filter:none, route-map:none
  SA-Requests:
    Input filter:none
    Sending SA-Requests to peer:enabled
  Peer ttl threshold:0
  Input queue size:0, Output queue size:0
```

Step 6 Configure multicast borders appropriately.

You must configure multicast borders on every router interface that borders another ISP. For ISP3, configure multicast borders on the ISP3BB3, ISP3BB6, and ISP3BB7 routers.

The following sample configuration, taken from the configuration file for the ISP3BB3 router, shows how to configure multicast borders:

```
interface POS12/0/0
 description Connected to ISP4BB3, POS12/0/0
 ip pim bsr-border
 ip pim sparse-mode
 ip multicast boundary 1
!
access-list 1 deny    224.0.1.39
access-list 1 deny    224.0.1.40
access-list 1 deny    239.0.0.0 0.255.255.255
access-list 1 permit any
```

For characteristics and complete configuration files of the significant devices in ISP3, see Chapter 5, "ISP3 and ISP4 Device Characteristics and Configuration Files."

Figure 2-10 shows the interdomain multicast network diagram for ISP4.

Figure 2-10 *Network Diagram for ISP4—Interdomain Multicast*

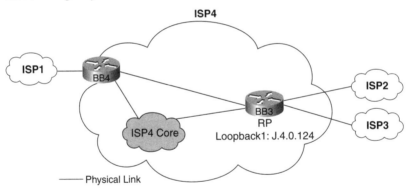

The following is a summary of the tasks that were performed to configure the devices in ISP4 for interdomain multicast:

Step 1 Configure MBGP to exchange multicast routing information.

    (a) Configure MBGP peering sessions.

        The following MBGP peering sessions exist in ISP4:

        —ISP4BB3 externally peers with ISP3BB3.

        —ISP4BB3 externally peers with ISP2BB6.

        —ISP4BB4 externally peers with ISP1BB3.

        —All backbone routers in ISP4 internally peer with each other directly or through router reflectors.

The following sample configurations show how to configure the external peers. The configuration is different for each router.

The following configuration is for the ISP4BB3 router:

```
router bgp 4
 neighbor ISP3ISP4PEER peer-group nlri unicast multicast
 neighbor ISP4ISP2PEER peer-group nlri unicast multicast
 neighbor ISP4INTERNAL peer-group nlri unicast multicast
```

The following configuration is for the ISP4BB4 router:

```
router bgp 4
 neighbor ISP4INTERNAL peer-group nlri unicast multicast
 neighbor ISP4ISP1PEER peer-group nlri unicast multicast
```

(b) Verify that MBGP is configured properly.

The following sample output shows how to verify that the MBGP peers have negotiated for multicast routes:

```
ISP4BB3#show ip bgp neighbors J.3.0.249

BGP neighbor is J.3.0.249, remote AS 3, external link
  Member of peer-group ISP3ISP4PEER for session parameters
  BGP version 4, remote router ID J.3.0.203
  BGP state = Established, up for 00:08:45
  Last read 00:00:46, hold time is 180, keepalive interval is 60 seconds
  Neighbor capabilities:
    Route refresh:advertised and received(new)
    Address family IPv4 Unicast:advertised and received
    Address family IPv4 Multicast:advertised and received
  Received 5414 messages, 0 notifications, 0 in queue
  Sent 4790 messages, 0 notifications, 0 in queue
  Route refresh request:received 0, sent 0
  Default minimum time between advertisement runs is 30 seconds

 For address family:IPv4 Unicast
  BGP table version 243679, neighbor version 243679
  Index 1, Offset 0, Mask 0x2
  ISP3ISP4PEER peer-group member
  102 accepted prefixes consume 3672 bytes
  Prefix advertised 241691, suppressed 2, withdrawn 89926

 For address family:IPv4 Multicast
  BGP table version 7, neighbor version 7
  Index 2, Offset 0, Mask 0x4
  2 accepted prefixes consume 72 bytes
  Prefix advertised 1, suppressed 0, withdrawn 1

  Connections established 4; dropped 3
```

```
    Last reset 00:09:26, due to Address family activated
Connection state is ESTAB, I/O status:1, unread input bytes:0
Local host:J.3.0.250, Local port:179
Foreign host:J.3.0.249, Foreign port:11031

Enqueued packets for retransmit:0, input:0  mis-ordered:0 (0 bytes)

Event Timers (current time is 0x606BEC4):
Timer          Starts      Wakeups            Next
Retrans          44           0               0x0
TimeWait          0           0               0x0
AckHold          33          11               0x0
SendWnd           6           0               0x0
KeepAlive         0           0               0x0
GiveUp            0           0               0x0
PmtuAger          0           0               0x0
DeadWait          0           0               0x0

iss:2625748112  snduna:2625894217  sndnxt:2625894217     sndwnd: 14092
irs:2625727436  rcvnxt:2625873688  rcvwnd:       12635  delrcvwnd:  3749

SRTT:309 ms, RTTO:376 ms, RTV:67 ms, KRTT:0 ms
minRTT:4 ms, maxRTT:552 ms, ACK hold:200 ms
Flags:passive open, nagle, gen tcbs

Datagrams (max data segment is 4430 bytes):
Rcvd:125 (out of order:0), with data:54, total data bytes:146251
Sent:115 (retransmit:6), with data:73, total data bytes:146098

ISP4BB3#show ip mbgp summary

BGP router identifier J.4.0.203, local AS number 4
BGP table version is 7, main routing table version 1
3 network entries and 3 paths using 399 bytes of memory
41 BGP path attribute entries using 2460 bytes of memory
37 BGP AS-PATH entries using 2076 bytes of memory
0 BGP route-map cache entries using 0 bytes of memory
0 BGP filter-list cache entries using 0 bytes of memory
BGP activity 120888/92256 prefixes, 213008/181966 paths, scan interval
15 secs

Neighbor        V    AS MsgRcvd MsgSent  TblVer  InQ OutQ Up/Down  State/
PfxRcd
J.2.0.249       4    2    4049    3878       7    0    0 00:09:19      1
J.3.0.249       4    3    5415    4791       7    0    0 00:09:13      2
J.4.0.201       4    4    1699    1697       0    0    0 00:09:22      0
J.4.0.202       4    4    1691    1697       0    0    0 00:09:17      0
J.4.0.204       4    4    1680    1684       0    0    0 00:09:16      0
```

Step 2 Configure MSDP peering sessions.

  (a) Select an IP address.

  For MSDP peering sessions, use the same IP address that you used for the BGP peering session. In this case, it is the unique IP address with a 32-bit mask configured on Loopback0.

  (b) Configure peering sessions.

  The ISP4BB3 router peers with the ISP1BB3, ISP2BB4, and ISP3BB3 routers. The following sample configuration shows how to configure these peering sessions:

```
ip msdp peer J.3.0.249 connect-source Loopback0 remote-as 3
ip msdp peer J.2.0.204 connect-source Loopback0 remote-as 2
ip msdp peer J.1.0.203 connect-source Loopback0 remote-as 1
```

Step 3 Configure recommended SA filters.

The following sample configurations show how to configure the SA filters on ISP4's RP (ISP4BB3) for the connections to the ISP1BB3, ISP2BB4, and ISP3BB3 routers:

The following configures the SA filters for the connection to the ISP1BB3 router:

```
ip msdp sa-filter in J.1.0.203 list 124
ip msdp sa-filter out J.1.0.203 list 124
```

The following configures the SA filters for the connection to the ISP2BB4 router:

```
ip msdp sa-filter in J.2.0.204 list 124
ip msdp sa-filter out J.2.0.204 list 124
```

The following configures the SA filters for the connection to the ISP3BB3 router:

```
ip msdp sa-filter in J.3.0.249 list 124
ip msdp sa-filter out J.3.0.249 list 124
```

The following access list is configured on the ISP4BB3 router:

```
access-list 124 deny    ip any host 224.0.2.2
access-list 124 deny    ip any host 224.0.1.3
access-list 124 deny    ip any host 224.0.1.24
access-list 124 deny    ip any host 224.0.1.22
access-list 124 deny    ip any host 224.0.1.2
access-list 124 deny    ip any host 224.0.1.35
access-list 124 deny    ip any host 224.0.1.60
access-list 124 deny    ip any host 224.0.1.39
```

```
access-list 124 deny    ip any host 224.0.1.40
access-list 124 deny    ip any 239.0.0.0 0.255.255.255
access-list 124 deny    ip 10.0.0.0 0.255.255.255 any
access-list 124 deny    ip 127.0.0.0 0.255.255.255 any
access-list 124 deny    ip 172.16.0.0 0.15.255.255 any
access-list 124 deny    ip K.168.0.0 0.0.255.255 any
```

Step 4 Configure SA caching.

The following sample configuration shows how to enable SA caching. This feature is enabled on the ISP4BB3 router.

```
ip msdp cache-sa-state
```

Step 5 Verify that MSDP peers are working properly.

The following sample output shows how to verify that the MSDP peers are working properly:

```
ISP4BB3#show ip msdp peer

MSDP Peer J.3.0.249 (?), AS 3
Description:
  Connection status:
    State:Up, Resets:1, Connection source:none configured
    Uptime(Downtime):01:47:57, Messages sent/received:554/111
    Output messages discarded:0
    Connection and counters cleared 1d04h    ago
  SA Filtering:
    Input (S,G) filter:124, route-map:none
    Input RP filter:none, route-map:none
    Output (S,G) filter:124, route-map:none
    Output RP filter:none, route-map:none
  SA-Requests:
    Input filter:none
    Sending SA-Requests to peer:enabled
  Peer ttl threshold:0
  Input queue size:0, Output queue size:0
MSDP Peer J.2.0.204 (?), AS 2 (configured AS)
Description:
  Connection status:
    State:Up, Resets:1, Connection source:Loopback0 (J.4.0.203)
    Uptime(Downtime):00:49:19, Messages sent/received:163/108
    Output messages discarded:0
    Connection and counters cleared 1d04h    ago
  SA Filtering:
    Input (S,G) filter:124, route-map:none
```

```
      Input RP filter:none, route-map:none
      Output (S,G) filter:124, route-map:none
      Output RP filter:none, route-map:none
    SA-Requests:
      Input filter:none
      Sending SA-Requests to peer:enabled
    Peer ttl threshold:0
    Input queue size:0, Output queue size:0
  MSDP Peer J.1.0.203 (?), AS 1 (configured AS)
  Description:
    Connection status:
      State:Up, Resets:1, Connection source:Loopback0 (J.4.0.203)
      Uptime(Downtime):00:49:31, Messages sent/received:155/164
      Output messages discarded:0
      Connection and counters cleared 1d04h    ago
    SA Filtering:
      Input (S,G) filter:124, route-map:none
      Input RP filter:none, route-map:none
      Output (S,G) filter:124, route-map:none
      Output RP filter:none, route-map:none
    SA-Requests:
      Input filter:none
      Sending SA-Requests to peer:enabled
    Peer ttl threshold:0
    Input queue size:0, Output queue size:0
```

Step 6 Configure multicast borders appropriately.

You must configure multicast borders on every router interface that borders another ISP. For ISP4, configure multicast borders on the ISP4BB3 and ISP4BB4 routers. The following sample configuration, taken from the configuration file for the ISP4BB3 router, shows how to configure multicast borders:

```
interface POS5/0/0
  description TO ISP2BB6, POS 0/0
  ip pim bsr-border
  ip pim sparse-mode
  ip multicast boundary 1

interface POS12/0/0
  description To ISP3BB3, POS 12/0/0
  ip pim bsr-border
  ip pim sparse-mode
  ip multicast boundary 1
```

```
access-list 1 deny    224.0.1.39
access-list 1 deny    224.0.1.40
access-list 1 deny    239.0.0.0 0.255.255.255
access-list 1 permit  any
```

For characteristics and complete configuration files of the significant devices in ISP4, see Chapter 5.

Summary

In this chapter, you saw how four hypothetical ISPs implemented interdomain multicast among them using PIM-SM, MBGP, and MSDP. The solutions presented in this chapter were based on actual customer deployments. These solutions were tested in the field and verified in a lab environment. The ISPs are representative of typical customer topologies.

The solution itself was divided into four deployment phases:

- Establishing an overall interdomain multicast strategy
- Implementing intradomain multicast within each of the individual ISPs
- Implementing interdomain multicast between each of the ISPs
- Connecting customers to the ISP infrastructure

The overall interdomain multicast strategy was to deploy intradomain multicast within each of the individual ISPs, to deploy interdomain multicast between each of the ISPs, and, finally, to connect customers to the ISP infrastructure. PIM-SM was the multicast routing protocol used in these intradomain multicast scenarios. MBGP was used for interdomain routing and MSDP was employed for interdomain source discovery. MBGP and MSDP connect PIM-SM domains. Two strategies were presented for connecting customers to the ISP infrastructure: having the customer connect to an external RP in its ISP, and having the customer maintain its own internal RP without MBGP.

Related Documents

- *Changes in MBGP Commands Between 12.0S and 12.0T/12.1*, Cisco Application Note (www.cisco.com/warp/public/cc/pd/iosw/prodlit/mcb12_an.htm)
- *Cisco IOS IP and IP Routing Command Reference*, Release 12.1 (www.cisco.com/univercd/cc/td/doc/product/software/ios121/121cgcr/ip_r/index.htm)
- *Cisco IOS IP and IP Routing Configuration Guide*, Release 12.1 (www.cisco.com/univercd/cc/td/doc/product/software/ios121/121cgcr/ip_c/index.htm)
- Cisco IOS Software IP Multicast Groups External Homepage (ftp://ftpeng.cisco.com/ipmulticast/index.html)
- Cisco IOS Software Multicast Services Web Page (www.cisco.com/go/ipmulticast)

- *IP Multicast Technology Overview*, Cisco white paper
  (www.cisco.com/univercd/cc/td/doc/cisintwk/intsolns/mcst_sol/mcst_ovr.htm)
- *MSDP Feature Broadens Reach of Multicast Services*, Cisco Beyond Basic IP Newsletter V1.22
  (www.cisco.com/warp/public/779/servpro/promotions/bbip/volume_01_issue22.html)
- *Multicast Quick-Start Configuration Guide*, Cisco Tech Note
  (www.cisco.com/warp/customer/105/48.html)
- *Multicast Source Discovery Protocol*, Cisco IOS Software Release 12.0(7)T feature module
  (www.cisco.com/univercd/cc/td/doc/product/software/ios120/120newft/120t/120t7/msdp.htm)
- *Multicast Source Discovery Protocol SA Filter Recommendations*, Cisco Tech Note
  (www.cisco.com/warp/public/105/49.html)
- *Multiprotocol BGP Extensions for IP Multicast*, Cisco IOS Software Release 12.0(7)T feature module
  (www.cisco.com/univercd/cc/td/doc/product/software/ios120/120newft/120t/120t7/mbgp.htm)
- *PIM-SM Protocol Improves Multicast Service Scalability*, Cisco Beyond Basic IP Newsletter V1.11
  (www.cisco.com/warp/public/779/servpro/promotions/bbip/volume_01_issue11.html)
- RFC 1918, *Address Allocation for Private Internets*, Y. Rekhter, B. Moskowitz, D. Karrenberg, G.J. DeGroot, E. Lear
- RFC 2283, *Multiprotocol Extensions for BGP-4*, T. Bates, R. Chandra, D. Katz, Y Rekhter
- RFC 2362, *Protocol Independent Multicast-Sparse Mode (PIM-SM): Protocol Specification* D. Estrin, D. Farinacci, A. Helmy, D. Thaler, S. Deering, M. Handley, V. Jacobson, C. Liu, P. Sharma, L. Wei

This chapter includes the device characteristics and configuration files for the following host names in ISP1 and ISP1-POP, as described in Chapter 2, "Implementing Interdomain Multicast Using MSDP":

- ISP1BB1
- ISP1BB2
- ISP1BB3
- ISP1BB4
- ISP1BB5
- ISP1BB6
- ISP1BB7
- ISP1DA1
- ISP1DA2
- ISP1DA3
- ISP1AC1

CHAPTER 3

ISP1 Device Characteristics and Configuration Files

This chapter provides the characteristics and configuration files for the devices associated with ISP1 and ISP1-POP, as described in Chapter 2, "Implementing Interdomain Multicast Using MSDP." Figure 3-1 and Figure 3-2 show the overall interdomain topology to which ISP1 and ISP1-POP belong. Figure 3-1 shows the MBGP peering sessions and Figure 3-2 shows the MSDP peering sessions established among the four Internet service providers (ISPs) in which interdomain multicast is deployed.

Figure 3-1 *Overall Network Topology with MBGP Peering*

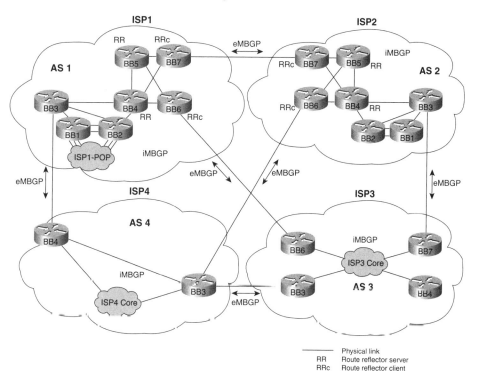

Figure 3-2 *Overall Network Topology with MSDP Peering*

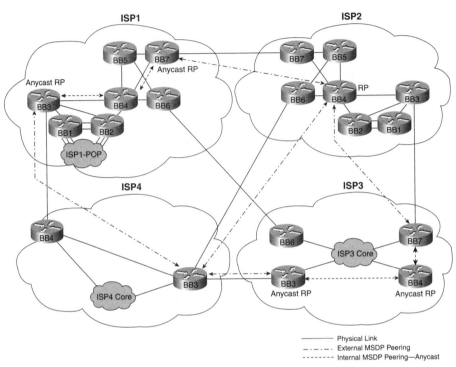

The multicast solutions in this chapter were tested with valid IP addresses. Normally, when a configuration file is published, the valid IP addresses are replaced with IP addresses specified in RFC 1918, "Address Allocation for Private Networks." Because the range of available IP addresses was insufficient to span the range of IP addresses used in this solution, the first octet of the valid IP addresses was replaced with a variable. In the example configurations provided in the following sections, the first octet of these reserved IP addresses has been replaced with the letter J or the letter K for privacy reasons. The letter J always represents one unique number and the letter K always represents a unique number that is different from J.

The example configurations are intended for illustrative purposes only. The letters J and K must be replaced with valid numbers when these IP addresses are configured in an actual network.

NOTE The example configurations provided in the following sections use shaded text to indicate pertinent configuration commands that are used to deploy the IP multicast solutions described in this chapter.

ISP1BB1

ISP1BB1 is a backbone router in ISP1. Figure 3-3 shows the topology of ISP1 and ISP1BB1's location in ISP1.

Figure 3-3 *ISP1BB1*

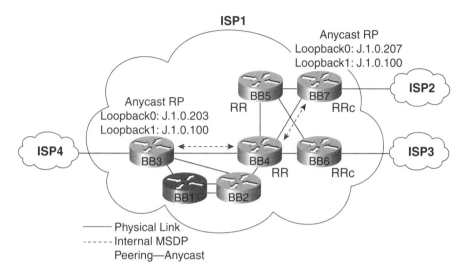

Device Characteristics for ISP1BB1

Table 3-1 lists the hardware and software device characteristics for ISP1BB1.

Table 3-1 *Hardware and Software Device Characteristics for ISP1BB1*

ISP1BB1	Device Characteristics
Host name	ISP1BB1
Chassis type	Cisco 12012 Gigabit Switch Router (GSR)
Physical interfaces	1 Ethernet/IEEE 802.3 12 Packet over SONET (POS)
Hardware components	Cisco 12012/GRP (R5000) processor (revision 0x00) 2 route processor cards 2 clock scheduler cards 3 switch fabric cards 3 four-port OC-2 POS controllers (12 POS)
Software loaded	Cisco IOS Software Release 12.0(10)S
Memory	Cisco 12012/GRP (R5000) processor (revision 0x00): 128 MB

continues

Table 3-1 *Hardware and Software Device Characteristics for ISP1BB1 (Continued)*

ISP1BB1	Device Characteristics
IP addresses	Loopback0: J.1.0.201 255.255.255.255 POS0/0: J.1.0.5 255.255.255.252 POS0/1: J.1.71.2 255.255.255.252 POS0/2: J.1.71.26 255.255.255.252 POS0/3: J.1.71.18 255.255.255.252 POS1/0: J.1.64.1 255.255.255.252 POS1/1: J.1.0.5 255.255.255.252 POS1/2: J.1.0.1 255.255.255.252 POS1/3: J.1.71.9 255.255.255.252

Configuration File for ISP1BB1

ISP1BB1, a core router for ISP1, connects to the ISP1-POP. BGP and MBGP internal peering is configured to all other routers in ISP1 except for Route Reflector clients. For multicast, the router is statically configured to use the anycast RP address of J.1.0.100. Example 3-1 displays the **show running-config** privileged EXEC command output for host ISP1BB1.

Example 3-1 *ISP1BB1 Configuration*

```
ISP1BB1#show running-config
version 12.0
no service pad
service timestamps debug uptime
service timestamps log datetime localtime show-timezone
no service password-encryption
service udp-small-servers
service tcp-small-servers
service download-fl
!
hostname ISP1BB1
!
logging buffered 100000 debugging
no logging console
enable password lab
!
clock timezone PDT -8
clock summer-time PDT recurring
redundancy
 main-cpu
  auto-sync startup-config
!
!
ip subnet-zero
no ip domain-lookup
ip multicast-routing distributed
ip multicast multipath
clns routing
```

Example 3-1 *ISP1BB1 Configuration (Continued)*

```
no tag-switching ip
no tag-switching advertise-tags
!
!
interface Loopback0
 ip address J.1.0.201 255.255.255.255
 ip directed-broadcast
 ip pim sparse-mode
 ip router isis
 ip mroute-cache distributed
!
interface POS0/0
 description to ISP1BB2, POS 0/0
 ip address J.1.0.5 255.255.255.252
 no ip directed-broadcast
 ip pim sparse-mode
 ip router isis
 ip mroute-cache distributed
 crc 32
 clock source internal
 pos ais-shut
 aps revert 1
 aps protect 1 J.1.0.201
!
interface POS0/1
 description TO ISP1DA1, POS 1/0/0
 ip address J.1.71.2 255.255.255.252
 no ip directed-broadcast
 ip pim sparse-mode
 ip router isis
 ip mroute-cache distributed
 tag-switching ip
 crc 16
 clock source internal
!
interface POS0/2
 description TO ISP1DA2, POS 1/0/0
 ip address J.1.71.26 255.255.255.252
 no ip directed-broadcast
 ip pim sparse-mode
 ip router isis
 ip mroute-cache distributed
 tag-switching ip
 crc 16
 clock source internal
!
interface POS0/3
 description TO ISP1DA3, POS 2/0/0
 ip address J.1.71.18 255.255.255.252
 no ip directed-broadcast
 ip pim sparse-mode
 ip router isis
```

continues

Example 3-1 *ISP1BB1 Configuration (Continued)*

```
 ip mroute-cache distributed
 tag-switching ip
 crc 16
 clock source internal
!
interface POS1/0
 description TO ISP1FDR, POS 1/0/0
 ip address J.1.64.1 255.255.255.252
 no ip directed-broadcast
 ip pim sparse-mode
 ip router isis
 ip mroute-cache distributed
 tag-switching ip
 crc 16
 clock source internal
!
interface POS1/1
 description TO ISP1BB2, POS 1/1
 ip address J.1.0.5 255.255.255.252
 no ip directed-broadcast
 ip pim sparse-mode
 ip router isis
 ip mroute-cache distributed
 crc 32
 clock source internal
 pos ais-shut
 aps working 1
!
interface POS1/2
 description to ISP1BB3, POS 1/0/0
 ip address J.1.0.1 255.255.255.252
 no ip directed-broadcast
 ip pim sparse-mode
 ip router isis
 ip mroute-cache distributed
 crc 16
 clock source internal
!
router isis
 net 49.0001.0000.0000.0001.00
 is-type level-1
!
router bgp 1
 no synchronization
 redistribute connected route-map connected-bgp
 neighbor ISP1INTERNAL peer-group nlri unicast multicast
 neighbor ISP1INTERNAL remote-as 1
 neighbor ISP1INTERNAL update-source Loopback0
 neighbor J.1.0.200 peer-group ISP1INTERNAL
 neighbor J.1.0.202 peer-group ISP1INTERNAL
 neighbor J.1.0.203 peer-group ISP1INTERNAL
 neighbor J.1.0.204 peer-group ISP1INTERNAL
```

Example 3-1 *ISP1BB1 Configuration (Continued)*

```
 neighbor J.1.0.205 peer-group ISP1INTERNAL
 neighbor J.1.0.208 peer-group ISP1INTERNAL
 neighbor J.1.0.209 peer-group ISP1INTERNAL
 neighbor J.1.0.210 peer-group ISP1INTERNAL
 no auto-summary
!
no ip classless
ip http server
ip pim rp-address J.1.0.100
!
access-list 112 permit ip J.1.0.0 0.0.255.255 255.255.0.0 0.0.255.255
access-list 112 deny   ip any any
route-map connected-bgp permit 10
 match ip address 112
 set ip next-hop J.1.0.201
 set origin igp
!
snmp-server engineID local 0000000902000010F60873FF
snmp-server community public RO
snmp-server community STSS RW
snmp-server contact sysadmin
snmp-server chassis-id ISP1BB1
!
!
line con 0
 exec-timeout 0 0
 login authentication NOTACACS
 length 40
 transport input none
line aux 0
line vty 0 4
 exec-timeout 0 0
 password lab
!
end
```

ISP1BB2

ISP1BB2 is a backbone router in ISP1. Figure 3-4 shows the topology of ISP1 and ISP1BB2's location in ISP1.

Figure 3-4 *ISP1BB2*

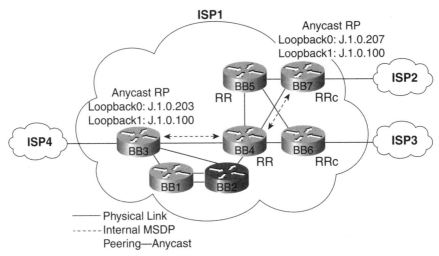

Device Characteristics for ISP1BB2

Table 3-2 lists the hardware and software device characteristics for ISP1BB2.

Table 3-2 *Hardware and Software Device Characteristics for ISP1BB2*

ISP1BB2	Device Characteristics
Host name	ISP1BB2
Chassis type	Cisco 12012 Gigabit Switch Router (GSR)
Physical interfaces	1 Ethernet/IEEE 802.3 16 Packet over SONET (POS)
Hardware components	Cisco 12012/GRP (R5000) processor (revision 0x00) 2 route processor cards 2 clock scheduler cards 3 switch fabric cards 4 four-port OC-2 POS controllers (16 POS)
Software loaded	Cisco IOS Software Release 12.0(10)S
Memory	Cisco 12012/GRP (R5000) processor (revision 0x00): 128 MB

Table 3-2 *Hardware and Software Device Characteristics for ISP1BB2 (Continued)*

ISP1BB2	Device Characteristics
IP addresses	Loopback0: J.1.0.202 255.255.255.255 POS0/0: J.1.0.6 255.255.255.252 POS0/1: J.1.71.6 255.255.255.252 POS0/2: J.1.71.14 255.255.255.252 POS0/3: J.1.71.22 255.255.255.252 POS1/0: J.1.64.9 255.255.255.252 POS1/1: J.1.0.6 255.255.255.252 POS1/2: J.1.0.9 255.255.255.252 POS2/0: J.1.0.13 255.255.255.252

Configuration File for ISP1BB2

ISP1BB2, a core router for ISP1, connects to the ISP1-POP. BGP and MBGP internal peering is configured to all other routers in ISP1 except for Route Reflector clients. For multicast, the router is statically configured to use the anycast RP address of J.1.0.100. Example 3-2 displays the **show running-config** privileged EXEC command output for host ISP1BB2.

Example 3-2 *ISP1BB2 Configuration*

```
ISP1BB2#show running-config
version 12.0
no service pad
service timestamps debug datetime localtime show-timezone
service timestamps log datetime localtime show-timezone
no service password-encryption
service udp-small-servers
service tcp-small-servers
!
hostname ISP1BB2
!
logging buffered 10000 debugging
no logging console
enable password lab
!
clock timezone PDT -8
clock summer-time PDT recurring
redundancy
 main-cpu
  auto-sync startup-config
!
!
ip subnet-zero
no ip domain-lookup
ip multicast-routing distributed
clns routing
no tag-switching ip
no tag-switching advertise-tags
```

continues

Example 3-2 *ISP1BB2 Configuration (Continued)*

```
!
!
interface Loopback0
 ip address J.1.0.202 255.255.255.255
 ip directed-broadcast
 ip pim sparse-mode
 ip router isis
 ip mroute-cache distributed
!
interface POS0/0
 description TO ISP1BB1, POS 0/0
 ip address J.1.0.6 255.255.255.252
 no ip directed-broadcast
 ip pim sparse-mode
 ip router isis
 ip mroute-cache distributed
 crc 32
 clock source internal
 pos ais-shut
 aps revert 1
 aps protect 1 J.1.0.202
!
interface POS0/1
 description TO ISP1DA1, POS 2/0/0
 ip address J.1.71.6 255.255.255.252
 no ip directed-broadcast
 ip pim sparse-mode
 ip router isis
 ip mroute-cache distributed
 load-interval 30
 tag-switching ip
 crc 16
 clock source internal
!
interface POS0/2
 description TO ISP1DA2, POS 2/0/0
 ip address J.1.71.14 255.255.255.252
 no ip directed-broadcast
 ip pim sparse-mode
 ip router isis
 ip mroute-cache distributed
 tag-switching ip
 crc 16
 clock source internal
!
interface POS0/3
 description TO ISP1DA3, POS 3/0/0
 ip address J.1.71.22 255.255.255.252
 no ip directed-broadcast
 ip pim sparse-mode
 ip router isis
 ip mroute-cache distributed
```

Example 3-2 *ISP1BB2 Configuration (Continued)*

```
 tag-switching ip
 crc 16
 clock source internal
!
interface POS1/0
 description TO ISP1FDR, POS 2/0/0
 ip address J.1.64.9 255.255.255.252
 no ip directed-broadcast
 ip pim sparse-mode
 ip router isis
 ip mroute-cache distributed
 tag-switching ip
 crc 16
 clock source internal
!
interface POS1/1
 description TO ISP1BB1, POS 1/1
 ip address J.1.0.6 255.255.255.252
 no ip directed-broadcast
 ip pim sparse-mode
 ip router isis
 ip mroute-cache distributed
 crc 32
 clock source internal
 pos ais-shut
 aps working 1
!
interface POS1/2
 description TO ISP1BB4, POS 1/0/0
 ip address J.1.0.9 255.255.255.252
 no ip directed-broadcast
 ip pim sparse-mode
 ip router isis
 ip mroute-cache distributed
 load-interval 30
 crc 16
 clock source internal
!
interface POS2/0
 description TO ISP1BB3, POS2/0/0
 ip address J.1.0.13 255.255.255.252
 no ip directed-broadcast
 ip pim sparse-mode
 ip router isis
 ip mroute-cache distributed
 crc 16
 clock source internal
!
router isis
 net 49.0001.0000.0000.0002.00
 is-type level-1
!
```

continues

Example 3-2   *ISP1BB2 Configuration (Continued)*

```
router bgp 1
 no synchronization
 redistribute connected route-map connected-bgp
 neighbor ISP1INTERNAL peer-group nlri unicast multicast
 neighbor ISP1INTERNAL remote-as 1
 neighbor ISP1INTERNAL update-source Loopback0
 neighbor J.1.0.200 peer-group ISP1INTERNAL
 neighbor J.1.0.201 peer-group ISP1INTERNAL
 neighbor J.1.0.203 peer-group ISP1INTERNAL
 neighbor J.1.0.204 peer-group ISP1INTERNAL
 neighbor J.1.0.205 peer-group ISP1INTERNAL
 neighbor J.1.0.208 peer-group ISP1INTERNAL
 neighbor J.1.0.209 peer-group ISP1INTERNAL
 neighbor J.1.0.210 peer-group ISP1INTERNAL
 no auto-summary
!
no ip classless
ip http server
ip pim rp-address J.1.0.100
!
access-list 112 permit ip J.1.0.0 0.0.255.255 255.255.0.0 0.0.255.255
access-list 112 deny   ip any any
route-map connected-bgp permit 10
 match ip address 112
 set ip next-hop J.1.0.202
 set origin igp
!
snmp-server engineID local 0000000902000010F6087FFF
snmp-server community public RO
snmp-server community STSS RW
snmp-server contact sysadmin
snmp-server chassis-id ISP1BB2
!
!
line con 0
 exec-timeout 0 0
 login authentication NOTACACS
 transport input none
line aux 0
line vty 0 4
 exec-timeout 0 0
 password lab
!
end
```

ISP1BB3

ISP1BB3 is a backbone router in ISP1. Figure 3-5 shows the topology of ISP1 and ISP1BB3's location in ISP1.

Figure 3-5 *ISP1BB3*

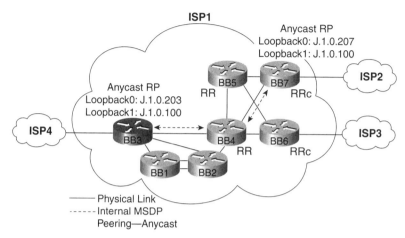

Device Characteristics for ISP1BB3

Table 3-3 lists the hardware and software device characteristics for ISP1BB3.

Table 3-3 *Hardware and Software Device Characteristics for ISP1BB3*

ISP1BB3	Device Characteristics
Host name	ISP1BB3
Chassis type	Cisco 7513 router
Physical interfaces	4 Ethernet/IEEE 802.3 1 FastEthernet/IEEE 802.3 5 Packet over SONET (POS)
Hardware components	Cisco Route/Switch Processor Version 2 (RSP2)(R4700) 6 Versatile Interface Processor Version 2 (VIP2) controllers (1 Fast Ethernet) (4 Ethernet) (5 POS)
Software loaded	Cisco IOS Software Release 12.1(3.3)
Memory	Cisco RSP2 (R4700) processor: 128 MB
IP addresses	Loopback0: J.1.0.203 255.255.255.255 Loopback1: J.1.0.100 255.255.255.255 Ethernet0/0/0: J.1.4.1 255.255.255.0 Ethernet0/0/2: J.1.6.1 255.255.255.248 FastEthernet0/1/0: J.1.7.1 255.255.255.248 POS3/0/0: J.1.0.17 255.255.255.252 POS9/0/0: J.4.0.34 255.255.255.252

Configuration File for ISP1BB3

ISP1BB3, a core router for ISP1, has an external connection to ISP4BB4. BGP and MBGP internal peering is configured to all other routers in ISP1 except for Route Reflector clients. ISP1BB3 has external BGP and MBGP peering to ISP4BB4. For multicast, it is configured as one of the two anycast RPs in ISP1. ISP1BB3 is also configured to have an MSDP internal peering session with ISP1BB4 and an external peering session with ISP4BB3, with SA filters to block unwanted sources and to prevent the unnecessary creation, forwarding, and caching of some well-known domain local sources. Additional filters are set up on the external AS connections to block administratively scoped multicast and RP announce and discovery addresses.

Example 3-3 displays the **show running-config** privileged EXEC command output for host ISP1BB3.

Example 3-3 *ISP1BB3 Configuration*

```
ISP1BB3#show running-config
version 12.1
no service pad
service timestamps debug datetime localtime
service timestamps log datetime localtime
no service password-encryption
service udp-small-servers
service tcp-small-servers
!
hostname ISP1BB3
!
logging buffered 10000 debugging
no logging console
enable password lab
!
!
clock timezone PDT -8
clock summer-time PDT recurring
ip subnet-zero
ip cef distributed
ip domain-name isp1.com
ip name-server J.4.7.10
!
ip multicast-routing distributed
clns routing
no tag-switching ip
no tag-switching advertise-tags
!
!
interface Loopback0
 ip address J.1.0.203 255.255.255.255
 ip directed-broadcast
 ip router isis
 ip pim sparse-mode
!
```

Example 3-3 *ISP1BB3 Configuration (Continued)*

```
interface Loopback1
 ip address J.1.0.100 255.255.255.255
 ip router isis
 ip pim sparse-mode
!
interface Ethernet0/0/0
 description TO RVT100, E3
 ip address J.1.4.1 255.255.255.0
 ip router isis
 ip route-cache distributed
 no ip mroute-cache
!
interface Ethernet0/0/2
 description TO ISP1BB3CL1
 ip address J.1.6.1 255.255.255.248
 ip router isis
 ip pim sparse-mode
 ip route-cache distributed
 ip mroute-cache distributed
 load-interval 30
!
interface POS1/0/0
 description TO ISP1BB1, POS 1/2
 ip address J.1.0.2 255.255.255.252
 ip router isis
 ip pim sparse-mode
 ip route-cache distributed
 ip mroute-cache distributed
 clock source internal
!
interface POS2/0/0
 description TO ISP1BB2, POS 2/0
 ip address J.1.0.14 255.255.255.252
 ip router isis
 ip pim sparse-mode
 ip route-cache distributed
 ip mroute-cache distributed
 clock source internal
!
interface POS3/0/0
 description TO ISP1BB4, POS 2/0/0
 ip address J.1.0.17 255.255.255.252
 ip router isis
 ip pim sparse-mode
 ip route-cache distributed
 ip mroute-cache distributed
 load-interval 30
 clock source internal
!
interface POS9/0/0
 description TO ISP4BB4, POS 12/0/0
 ip address J.4.0.34 255.255.255.252
```

continues

Example 3-3 *ISP1BB3 Configuration (Continued)*

```
 ip router isis
 ip pim bsr-border
 ip pim sparse-mode
 ip multicast boundary 10
 ip route-cache distributed
 ip mroute-cache distributed
 clock source internal
!
router isis
 net 49.0001.0000.0000.0003.00
 is-type level-1
!
router bgp 1
 no synchronization
 bgp log-neighbor-changes
 redistribute connected route-map connected-bgp
 neighbor ISP1INTERNAL peer-group
 neighbor ISP1INTERNAL remote-as 1
 neighbor ISP1INTERNAL update-source Loopback0
 neighbor ISP4ISP1PEER peer-group
 neighbor ISP4ISP1PEER remote-as 4
 neighbor J.1.0.200 peer-group ISP1INTERNAL
 neighbor J.1.0.201 peer-group ISP1INTERNAL
 neighbor J.1.0.202 peer-group ISP1INTERNAL
 neighbor J.1.0.204 peer-group ISP1INTERNAL
 neighbor J.1.0.205 peer-group ISP1INTERNAL
 neighbor J.1.0.208 peer-group ISP1INTERNAL
 neighbor J.1.0.209 peer-group ISP1INTERNAL
 neighbor J.1.0.210 peer-group ISP1INTERNAL
 neighbor J.4.0.33 peer-group ISP4ISP1PEER
 no auto-summary
 !
 address-family ipv4 multicast
 redistribute connected route-map connected-bgp
 neighbor ISP1INTERNAL activate
 neighbor ISP4ISP1PEER activate
 neighbor J.1.0.200 activate
 neighbor J.1.0.201 activate
 neighbor J.1.0.202 activate
 neighbor J.1.0.204 activate
 neighbor J.1.0.205 activate
 neighbor J.1.0.208 activate
 neighbor J.1.0.209 activate
 neighbor J.1.0.210 activate
 neighbor J.4.0.33 activate
 exit-address-family
!
no ip classless
ip http server
ip pim rp-address J.1.0.100
ip msdp peer K.250.1.2 connect-source Loopback0
ip msdp sa-filter in K.250.1.2 list 124
```

Example 3-3 *ISP1BB3 Configuration (Continued)*

```
ip msdp sa-filter out K.250.1.2 list 124
ip msdp peer J.4.0.203 connect-source Loopback0 remote-as 4
ip msdp sa-filter in J.4.0.203 list 124
ip msdp sa-filter out J.4.0.203 list 124
ip msdp peer J.1.0.204 connect-source Loopback0
ip msdp cache-sa-state
ip msdp originator-id Loopback0
!
access-list 10 deny    224.0.1.39
access-list 10 deny    224.0.1.40
access-list 10 deny    239.0.0.0 0.255.255.255
access-list 10 permit any
access-list 112 permit ip J.1.0.0 0.0.255.255 255.255.0.0 0.0.255.255
access-list 112 deny   ip any any
access-list 124 deny   ip any host 224.0.2.2
access-list 124 deny   ip any host 224.0.1.3
access-list 124 deny   ip any host 224.0.1.24
access-list 124 deny   ip any host 224.0.1.22
access-list 124 deny   ip any host 224.0.1.2
access-list 124 deny   ip any host 224.0.1.35
access-list 124 deny   ip any host 224.0.1.60
access-list 124 deny   ip any host 224.0.1.39
access-list 124 deny   ip any host 224.0.1.40
access-list 124 deny   ip any 239.0.0.0 0.255.255.255
access-list 124 deny   ip 10.0.0.0 0.255.255.255 any
access-list 124 deny   ip 127.0.0.0 0.255.255.255 any
access-list 124 deny   ip 172.16.0.0 0.15.255.255 any
access-list 124 deny   ip K.168.0.0 0.0.255.255 any
access-list 124 permit ip any any
route-map connected-bgp permit 10
 match ip address 112
 set origin igp
!
snmp-server engineID local 00000009020000100DDEE000
snmp-server community public RO
snmp-server community STSS RW
snmp-server packetsize 2048
snmp-server contact sysadmin
snmp-server chassis-id ISP1BB3
!
!
line con 0
 exec-timeout 0 0
 login authentication NOTACACS
 length 40
 transport input none
line aux 0
line vty 0 4
 exec-timeout 0 0
 password lab
!
end
```

ISP1BB4

ISP1BB4 is a backbone router in ISP1. Figure 3-6 shows the topology of ISP1 and ISP1BB4's location in ISP1.

Figure 3-6 *ISP1BB4*

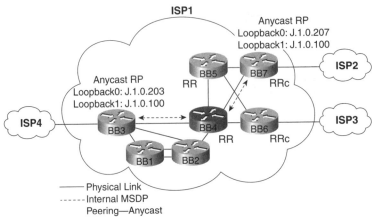

Device Characteristics for ISP1BB4

Table 3-4 lists the device characteristics for ISP1BB4.

Table 3-4 *Hardware and Software Device Characteristics for ISP1BB4*

ISP1BB4	Device Characteristics
Host name	ISP1BB4
Chassis type	Cisco 7513 router
Physical interfaces	4 Ethernet/IEEE 802.3 6 Packet over SONET (POS)
Hardware components	Cisco RSP4 (R5000) processor 7 VIP2 controllers (4 Ethernet) (6 POS)
Software loaded	Cisco IOS Software Release 12.1(3.3)
Memory	Cisco RSP4 (R5000) processor: 256 MB

Table 3-4 *Hardware and Software Device Characteristics for ISP1BB4 (Continued)*

ISP1BB4	Device Characteristics
IP addresses	Loopback0: J.1.0.204 255.255.255.255 Ethernet0/0/0: J.1.8.1 255.255.255.0 Ethernet0/0/2: J.1.10.1 255.255.255.248 Ethernet0/0/3: J.1.10.129 255.255.255.128 POS1/0/0: J.1.0.10 255.255.255.252 POS2/0/0: J.1.0.18 255.255.255.252 POS3/0/0: J.1.0.21 255.255.255.252 POS9/0/0: J.1.0.25 255.255.255.252 POS10/0/0: J.1.0.29 255.255.255.252

Configuration File for ISP1BB4

ISP1BB4 is a core router for ISP1. BGP and MBGP internal peering is configured to all other routers in ISP1 and ISP1BB4 acts as a Route Reflector server to ISP1BB6 and ISP1BB7. For multicast, the router is statically configured to use the anycast RP address of J.1.0.100. ISP1BB4 is also configured to have MSDP internal peering sessions with ISP1BB3 and ISP1BB7 to ensure that RPF checks always succeed for the two anycast RPs in ISP1.

Example 3-4 displays the **show running-config** privileged EXEC command output for host ISP1BB4.

Example 3-4 *ISP1BB4 Configuration*

```
ISP1BB4#show running-config
version 12.1
no service pad
service timestamps debug datetime localtime show-timezone
service timestamps log datetime localtime show-timezone
no service password-encryption
service udp-small-servers
service tcp-small-servers
!
hostname ISP1BB4
!
logging buffered 10000 debugging
enable password lab
!
!
clock timezone PDT -8
clock summer-time PDT recurring
ip subnet-zero
ip cef distributed
ip domain-name isp1.com
ip name-server J.4.7.10
!
ip multicast-routing distributed
clns routing
no tag-switching ip
```

continues

Example 3-4 *ISP1BB4 Configuration (Continued)*

```
 no tag-switching advertise-tags
!
!
interface Loopback0
 ip address J.1.0.204 255.255.255.255
 ip router isis
!
interface Ethernet0/0/0
 description TO RVT100, E4
 ip address J.1.8.1 255.255.255.0
 ip router isis
 ip pim sparse-mode
 ip route-cache distributed
 ip mroute-cache distributed
!
interface Ethernet0/0/2
 description TO ISP1BB4CL1
 ip address J.1.10.1 255.255.255.248
 ip router isis
 ip pim sparse-mode
 ip route-cache distributed
 ip mroute-cache distributed
 tag-switching ip
!
interface Ethernet0/0/3
 description TO ISP1BB4LINUX
 ip address J.1.10.129 255.255.255.128
 ip router isis
 ip pim sparse-mode
 ip route-cache distributed
 ip mroute-cache distributed
!
interface POS1/0/0
 description TO ISP1BB2, POS 1/2
 ip address J.1.0.10 255.255.255.252
 ip router isis
 ip pim sparse-mode
 ip route-cache distributed
 ip mroute-cache distributed
 load-interval 30
 clock source internal
!
interface POS2/0/0
 description TO ISP1BB3, POS 3/0/0
 ip address J.1.0.18 255.255.255.252
 ip router isis
 ip pim sparse-mode
 ip route-cache distributed
 ip mroute-cache distributed
 load-interval 30
 clock source internal
!
```

Example 3-4 *ISP1BB4 Configuration (Continued)*

```
interface POS3/0/0
 description TO ISP1BB5, POS 1/0/0
 ip address J.1.0.21 255.255.255.252
 ip router isis
 ip pim sparse-mode
 ip route-cache distributed
 ip mroute-cache distributed
 load-interval 120
 clock source internal
!
interface POS9/0/0
 description TO ISP1BB6, POS 1/0/0
 ip address J.1.0.25 255.255.255.252
 ip router isis
 ip pim sparse-mode
 ip route-cache distributed
 ip mroute-cache distributed
 load-interval 120
 clock source internal
!
interface POS10/0/0
 description TO ISP1BB7, POS 1/0/0
 ip address J.1.0.29 255.255.255.252
 ip router isis
 ip pim sparse-mode
 ip route-cache distributed
 ip mroute-cache distributed
 clock source internal
!
router isis
 net 49.0001.0000.0000.0004.00
 is-type level-1
!
router bgp 1
 no synchronization
 bgp cluster-id 1111
 bgp log-neighbor-changes
 redistribute connected route-map connected-bgp
 neighbor ISP1INTERNAL peer-group
 neighbor ISP1INTERNAL remote-as 1
 neighbor ISP1INTERNAL update-source Loopback0
 neighbor J.1.0.200 peer-group ISP1INTERNAL
 neighbor J.1.0.201 peer-group ISP1INTERNAL
 neighbor J.1.0.202 peer-group ISP1INTERNAL
 neighbor J.1.0.203 peer-group ISP1INTERNAL
 neighbor J.1.0.205 peer-group ISP1INTERNAL
 neighbor J.1.0.206 remote-as 1
 neighbor J.1.0.206 update-source Loopback0
 neighbor J.1.0.206 route-reflector-client
 neighbor J.1.0.207 remote-as 1
 neighbor J.1.0.207 update-source Loopback0
 neighbor J.1.0.207 route-reflector-client
```

continues

Example 3-4 *ISP1BB4 Configuration (Continued)*

```
 neighbor J.1.0.208 peer-group ISP1INTERNAL
 neighbor J.1.0.209 peer-group ISP1INTERNAL
 neighbor J.1.0.210 peer-group ISP1INTERNAL
 no auto-summary
!
 address-family ipv4 multicast
 redistribute connected route-map connected-bgp
 neighbor ISP1INTERNAL activate
 neighbor J.1.0.200 activate
 neighbor J.1.0.201 activate
 neighbor J.1.0.202 activate
 neighbor J.1.0.203 activate
 neighbor J.1.0.205 activate
 neighbor J.1.0.206 activate
 neighbor J.1.0.207 activate
 neighbor J.1.0.208 activate
 neighbor J.1.0.209 activate
neighbor J.1.0.210 activate
 exit-address-family
!
no ip classless
ip http server
ip pim rp-address J.1.0.100
ip msdp peer J.1.0.203 connect-source Loopback0
ip msdp peer J.1.0.207 connect-source Loopback0
ip msdp cache-sa-state
!
access-list 112 permit ip J.1.0.0 0.0.255.255 255.255.0.0 0.0.255.255
access-list 112 deny   ip any any
route-map connected-bgp permit 10
 match ip address 112
 set origin igp
!
snmp-server engineID local 0000000902000060700F9800
snmp-server community public RO
snmp-server community STSS RW
snmp-server packetsize 2048
snmp-server contact sysadmin
snmp-server chassis-id ISP1BB4
!
!
line con 0
 exec-timeout 0 0
 login authentication NOTACACS
 transport input none
line aux 0
line vty 0 4
 exec-timeout 0 0
 password lab
!
end
```

ISP1BB5

ISP1BB5 is a backbone router in ISP1. Figure 3-7 shows the topology of ISP1 and ISP1BB5's location in ISP1.

Figure 3-7 *ISP1BB5*

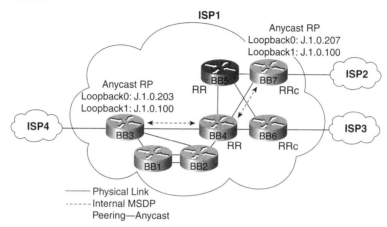

Device Characteristics for ISP1BB5

Table 3-5 lists the hardware and software device characteristics for ISP1BB5.

Table 3-5 *Hardware and Software Device Characteristics for ISP1BB5*

ISP1BB5	Device Characteristics
Host name	ISP1BB5
Chassis type	Cisco 7513 router
Physical interfaces	4 Ethernet/IEEE 802.3 1 FDDI 4 Packet over SONET (POS)
Hardware components	Cisco RSP4 (R5000) processor 5 VIP2 controllers (4 Ethernet) (1 FDDI) (4 POS)
Software loaded	Cisco IOS Software Release 12.1(3.3)
Memory	Cisco RSP4 (R5000) processor: 256 MB

continues

Table 3-5 *Hardware and Software Device Characteristics for ISP1BB5 (Continued)*

ISP1BB5	Device Characteristics
IP addresses	Loopback0: J.1.0.205 255.255.255.255 Ethernet0/0/0: J.1.12.1 255.255.255.0 Ethernet0/0/2: J.1.14.1 255.255.255.248 Ethernet0/0/3: J.1.15.1 255.255.255.128 Fddi0/1/0: J.5.0.1 255.255.255.248 POS1/0/0: J.1.0.22 255.255.255.252 POS2/0/0: J.1.0.33 255.255.255.252 POS9/0/0: J.1.0.37 255.255.255.252

Configuration File for ISP1BB5

ISP1BB5 is a core router for ISP1. BGP and MBGP internal peering is configured to all other routers in ISP1 and acts as a Route Reflector server to ISP1BB6 and ISP1BB7. For multicast, the router is statically configured to use the anycast RP address of J.1.0.100.

Example 3-5 displays the **show running-config** privileged EXEC command output for host ISP1BB5.

Example 3-5 *ISP1BB5 Configuration*

```
ISP1BB5#show running-config
version 12.1
no service pad
service timestamps debug datetime localtime show-timezone
service timestamps log datetime localtime show-timezone
no service password-encryption
service udp-small-servers
service tcp-small-servers
!
hostname ISP1BB5
!
logging buffered 10000 debugging
no logging console
enable password lab
!
!
clock timezone PDT -8
clock summer-time PDT recurring
ip subnet-zero
ip cef distributed
ip domain-name isp1.com
ip name-server J.4.7.10
!
ip multicast-routing distributed
clns routing
no tag-switching ip
no tag-switching advertise-tags
!
```

Example 3-5 *ISP1BB5 Configuration (Continued)*

```
!
interface Loopback0
 ip address J.1.0.205 255.255.255.255
 ip router isis
!
interface Ethernet0/0/0
 description TO RVT100, E5
 ip address J.1.12.1 255.255.255.0
 ip router isis
 ip pim sparse-mode
 ip route-cache distributed
 ip mroute-cache distributed
!
interface Ethernet0/0/2
 description TO ISP1BB5CL1
 ip address J.1.14.1 255.255.255.248
 ip router isis
 ip pim sparse-mode
 ip route-cache distributed
 ip igmp version 1
 ip mroute-cache distributed
!
interface Ethernet0/0/3
 description TO I1EBGP1
 ip address J.1.15.1 255.255.255.128
 ip router isis
 ip pim sparse-mode
 ip route-cache distributed
 ip mroute-cache distributed
!
interface Fddi0/1/0
 description TO NAP
 ip address J.5.0.1 255.255.255.248
 ip router isis
 ip pim sparse-mode
 ip route-cache distributed
 ip mroute-cache distributed
 no keepalive
!
interface POS1/0/0
 description TO ISP1BB4, POS 3/0/0
 ip address J.1.0.22 255.255.255.252
 ip router isis
 ip pim sparse-mode
 ip route-cache distributed
 ip mroute-cache distributed
 load-interval 120
 clock source internal
!
interface POS2/0/0
 description TO ISP1BB6, POS 2/0/0
 ip address J.1.0.33 255.255.255.252
```

continues

Example 3-5 *ISP1BB5 Configuration (Continued)*

```
 ip router isis
 ip pim sparse-mode
 ip route-cache distributed
 ip mroute-cache distributed
 clock source internal
!
interface POS9/0/0
 description TO ISP1BB7, POS 2/0/0
 ip address J.1.0.37 255.255.255.252
 ip router isis
 ip pim sparse-mode
 ip route-cache distributed
 ip mroute-cache distributed
 clock source internal
!
router isis
 net 49.0001.0000.0000.0005.00
 is-type level-1
!
router bgp 1
 no synchronization
 bgp cluster-id 1111
 bgp log-neighbor-changes
 redistribute connected route-map connected-bgp
 redistribute static route-map connected-bgp
 neighbor ISP1INTERNAL peer-group
 neighbor ISP1INTERNAL remote-as 1
 neighbor ISP1INTERNAL update-source Loopback0
 neighbor I1EBGP1 peer-group
 neighbor J.1.0.200 peer-group ISP1INTERNAL
 neighbor J.1.0.201 peer-group ISP1INTERNAL
 neighbor J.1.0.202 peer-group ISP1INTERNAL
 neighbor J.1.0.203 peer-group ISP1INTERNAL
 neighbor J.1.0.204 peer-group ISP1INTERNAL
 neighbor J.1.0.206 route-reflector-client
 neighbor J.1.0.207 remote-as 1
 neighbor J.1.0.207 update-source Loopback0
 neighbor J.1.0.207 route-reflector-client
 neighbor J.1.0.208 peer-group ISP1INTERNAL
 neighbor J.1.0.209 peer-group ISP1INTERNAL
 neighbor J.1.0.210 peer-group ISP1INTERNAL
 neighbor J.1.15.2 remote-as 100
 neighbor J.1.15.2 peer-group I1EBGP1
 neighbor J.1.15.3 remote-as 101
 neighbor J.1.15.3 peer-group I1EBGP1
 neighbor J.1.15.4 remote-as 102
 neighbor J.1.15.4 peer-group I1EBGP1
 neighbor J.1.15.5 remote-as 103
 neighbor J.1.15.5 peer-group I1EBGP1
 neighbor J.1.15.6 remote-as 104
 neighbor J.1.15.6 peer-group I1EBGP1
 neighbor J.1.15.7 remote-as 105
```

Example 3-5 *ISP1BB5 Configuration (Continued)*

```
neighbor J.1.15.7 peer-group I1EBGP1
neighbor J.1.15.8 remote-as 106
neighbor J.1.15.8 peer-group I1EBGP1
neighbor J.1.15.9 remote-as 107
neighbor J.1.15.9 peer-group I1EBGP1
neighbor J.1.15.10 remote-as 108
neighbor J.1.15.11 remote-as 109
neighbor J.1.15.11 peer-group I1EBGP1
neighbor J.1.15.12 remote-as 110
neighbor J.1.15.12 peer-group I1EBGP1
neighbor J.1.15.13 remote-as 111
neighbor J.1.15.13 peer-group I1EBGP1
neighbor J.1.15.14 remote-as 112
neighbor J.1.15.14 peer-group I1EBGP1
neighbor J.1.15.15 remote-as 113
neighbor J.1.15.15 peer-group I1EBGP1
neighbor J.1.15.16 remote-as 114
neighbor J.1.15.16 peer-group I1EBGP1
neighbor J.1.15.17 remote-as 115
neighbor J.1.15.17 peer-group I1EBGP1
neighbor J.1.15.18 remote-as 116
neighbor J.1.15.18 peer-group I1EBGP1
neighbor J.1.15.19 remote-as 117
neighbor J.1.15.19 peer-group I1EBGP1
neighbor J.1.15.20 remote-as 118
neighbor J.1.15.20 peer-group I1EBGP1
neighbor J.1.15.21 remote-as 119
neighbor J.1.15.21 peer-group I1EBGP1
neighbor J.1.15.22 remote-as 120
neighbor J.1.15.22 peer-group I1EBGP1
neighbor J.1.15.23 remote-as 121
neighbor J.1.15.23 peer-group I1EBGP1
neighbor J.1.15.24 remote-as 122
neighbor J.1.15.24 peer-group I1EBGP1
neighbor J.1.15.24 shutdown
neighbor J.1.15.25 remote-as 123
neighbor J.1.15.25 peer-group I1EBGP1
neighbor J.1.15.25 shutdown
neighbor J.1.15.26 remote-as 124
neighbor J.1.15.26 peer-group I1EBGP1
neighbor J.1.15.26 shutdown
neighbor J.1.15.27 remote-as 125
neighbor J.1.15.27 peer-group I1EBGP1
neighbor J.1.15.27 shutdown
neighbor J.1.15.28 remote-as 126
neighbor J.1.15.28 peer-group I1EBGP1
neighbor J.1.15.28 shutdown
neighbor J.1.15.29 remote-as 127
neighbor J.1.15.29 peer-group I1EBGP1
neighbor J.1.15.29 shutdown
neighbor J.1.15.30 remote-as 128
neighbor J.1.15.30 peer-group I1EBGP1
```

continues

Example 3-5 *ISP1BB5 Configuration (Continued)*

```
 neighbor J.1.15.30 shutdown
 neighbor J.1.15.31 remote-as 129
 neighbor J.1.15.31 peer-group I1EBGP1
 neighbor J.1.15.31 shutdown
 neighbor J.1.15.32 remote-as 130
 neighbor J.1.15.32 peer-group I1EBGP1
 neighbor J.1.15.32 shutdown
 neighbor J.1.15.33 remote-as 131
 neighbor J.1.15.33 peer-group I1EBGP1
 neighbor J.1.15.33 shutdown
 neighbor J.1.15.100 remote-as 190
 neighbor J.1.15.100 peer-group I1EBGP1
 neighbor J.1.15.101 remote-as 191
 neighbor J.1.15.101 peer-group I1EBGP1
 neighbor J.1.15.102 remote-as 192
 neighbor J.1.15.102 peer-group I1EBGP1
 no auto-summary
!
 address-family ipv4 multicast
 redistribute connected route-map connected-bgp
 redistribute static route-map connected-bgp
 neighbor ISP1INTERNAL activate
 neighbor J.1.0.200 peer-group ISP1INTERNAL
 neighbor J.1.0.201 peer-group ISP1INTERNAL
 neighbor J.1.0.202 peer-group ISP1INTERNAL
 neighbor J.1.0.203 peer-group ISP1INTERNAL
 neighbor J.1.0.204 peer-group ISP1INTERNAL
 neighbor J.1.0.206 peer-group ISP1INTERNAL
 neighbor J.1.0.208 peer-group ISP1INTERNAL
 neighbor J.1.0.209 peer-group ISP1INTERNAL
 neighbor J.1.0.210 peer-group ISP1INTERNAL
 exit-address-family
!
no ip classless
ip route K.50.0.0 255.255.255.0 J.5.0.5
ip http server
ip pim rp-address J.1.0.100
!
access-list 112 permit ip J.1.0.0 0.0.255.255 255.255.0.0 0.0.255.255
access-list 112 permit ip K.50.0.0 0.0.255.255 255.255.0.0 0.0.255.255
access-list 112 deny   ip any any
route-map connected-bgp permit 10
 match ip address 112
 set origin igp
!
snmp-server engineID local 0000000902000010F6A40000
snmp-server community public RO
snmp-server community STSS RW
snmp-server packetsize 2048
snmp-server contact sysadmin
snmp-server chassis-id ISP1BB5
!
```

Example 3-5 *ISP1BB5 Configuration (Continued)*

```
alias exec cpu show proc cpu | include CPU utilization
!
line con 0
 exec-timeout 0 0
 login authentication NOTACACS
 transport input none
line aux 0
line vty 0 4
 exec-timeout 0 0
 password lab
!
end
```

ISP1BB6

ISP1BB6 is a backbone router in ISP1. Figure 3-8 shows the topology of ISP1 and ISP1BB6's location in ISP1.

Figure 3-8 *ISP1BB6*

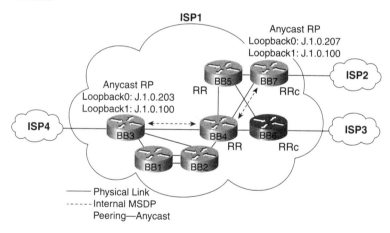

Device Characteristics for ISP1BB6

Table 3-6 lists the hardware and software device characteristics for ISP1BB6.

Table 3-6 *Hardware and Software Device Characteristics for ISP1BB6*

ISP1BB6	Device Characteristics
Host name	ISP1BB6
Chassis type	Cisco 7513 router

continues

Table 3-6 *Hardware and Software Device Characteristics for ISP1BB6 (Continued)*

ISP1BB6	Device Characteristics
Physical interfaces	4 Ethernet/IEEE 802.3 4 Packet over SONET (POS)
Hardware components	Cisco RSP4 (R5000) processor 5 VIP2 controllers (4 Ethernet) (4 POS)
Software loaded	Cisco IOS Software Release 12.1(3.5)T
Memory	Cisco RSP4 (R5000) processor: 128 MB
IP addresses	Loopback0: J.1.0.206 255.255.255.255 Ethernet0/0/0: J.1.16.1 255.255.255.0 Ethernet0/0/2: J.1.18.1 255.255.255.248 POS1/0/0: J.1.0.26 255.255.255.252 POS2/0/0: J.1.0.34 255.255.255.252 POS9/0/0: J.3.0.246 255.255.255.252

Configuration File for ISP1BB6

ISP1BB6 is a core router for ISP1 and has an external connection to ISP3BB6. BGP and MBGP internal peering is only to the Route Reflector servers. BPG and MBGP external peering is with ISP3BB6. For multicast, the router is statically configured to use the anycast RP address of J.1.0.100. Filters are set up on the external AS connections to block administratively scoped multicast and RP announce and discovery addresses.

Example 3-6 displays the **show running-config** privileged EXEC command output for host ISP1BB6.

Example 3-6 *ISP1BB6 Configuration*

```
ISP1BB6#show running-config
version 12.1
service timestamps debug datetime localtime show-timezone
service timestamps log datetime localtime show-timezone
no service password-encryption
service udp-small-servers
service tcp-small-servers
!
hostname ISP1BB6
!
logging buffered 10000 debugging
no logging console
enable password lab
!
!
clock timezone PDT -8
clock summer-time PDT recurring
ip subnet-zero
```

Example 3-6   *ISP1BB6 Configuration (Continued)*

```
ip cef distributed
no ip domain-lookup
ip domain-name cisco.com
!
ip multicast-routing distributed
clns routing
no tag-switching ip
no tag-switching advertise-tags
!
!
interface Loopback0
 ip address J.1.0.206 255.255.255.255
 ip router isis
 ip pim sparse-mode
!
interface Ethernet0/0/0
 description TO RVT100, E6
 ip address J.1.16.1 255.255.255.0
 ip router isis
 ip pim sparse-mode
 ip route-cache distributed
 ip mroute-cache distributed
!
interface Ethernet0/0/2
 description TO ISP1BB6CL1
 ip address J.1.18.1 255.255.255.248
 ip router isis
 ip pim sparse-mode
 ip route-cache distributed
 ip igmp version 1
 ip mroute-cache distributed
!
interface POS1/0/0
 description to ISP1BB4, POS 9/0/0
 ip address J.1.0.26 255.255.255.252
 ip router isis
 ip pim sparse-mode
 ip route-cache distributed
 ip mroute-cache distributed
 load-interval 120
 clock source internal
!
interface POS2/0/0
 description TO ISP1BB5, POS 2/0/0
 ip address J.1.0.34 255.255.255.252
 ip router isis
 ip pim sparse-mode
 ip route-cache distributed
 ip mroute-cache distributed
 load-interval 120
 clock source internal
!
```

continues

Example 3-6 *ISP1BB6 Configuration (Continued)*

```
interface POS9/0/0
 description TO ISP3BB6, POS 12/0/0
 ip address J.3.0.246 255.255.255.252
 ip router isis
 ip pim sparse-mode
 ip multicast boundary 1
 ip route-cache distributed
 ip mroute-cache distributed
 clock source internal
 pos scramble-atm
!
router isis
 net 49.0001.0000.0000.0006.00
 is-type level-1
!
router bgp 1
 no synchronization
 redistribute connected route-map connected-bgp
 neighbor ISP3ISP1PEER peer-group
 neighbor ISP3ISP1PEER remote-as 3
 neighbor ISP3ISP1PEER update-source Loopback0
 neighbor ISP1INTERNAL peer-group
 neighbor J.1.0.204 remote-as 1
 neighbor J.1.0.204 update-source Loopback0
 neighbor J.1.0.205 remote-as 1
 neighbor J.1.0.205 update-source Loopback0
 neighbor J.3.0.245 peer-group ISP3ISP1PEER
 no auto-summary
 !
 address-family ipv4 multicast
 redistribute connected route-map connected-bgp
 neighbor J.1.0.204 activate
 neighbor J.1.0.205 activate
 neighbor J.3.0.245 activate
 exit-address-family
!
no ip classless
ip http server
ip pim rp-address J.1.0.100
!
access-list 1 deny     224.0.1.39
access-list 1 deny     224.0.1.40
access-list 1 deny     239.0.0.0 0.255.255.255
access-list 1 permit any
access-list 50 deny    224.0.1.39
access-list 50 deny    224.0.1.40
access-list 50 deny    239.0.0.0 0.255.255.255
access-list 50 permit 224.0.0.0 15.255.255.255
access-list 112 permit ip J.1.0.0 0.0.255.255 255.255.0.0 0.0.255.255
access-list 112 deny    ip any any
access-list 124 deny    ip any 239.0.0.0 0.255.255.255
access-list 124 permit ip any any
```

Example 3-6 *ISP1BB6 Configuration (Continued)*

```
route-map connected-bgp permit 10
 match ip address 112
 set ip next-hop J.1.0.206
 set origin igp
!
snmp-server engineID local 0000000902000010F6A3B000
snmp-server community STSS RW
snmp-server community public RO
snmp-server packetsize 2048
snmp-server contact sysadmin
snmp-server chassis-id ISP1BB6
!
!
line con 0
 exec-timeout 0 0
 login authentication NOTACACS
 transport input none
line aux 0
line vty 0 4
 exec-timeout 0 0
 password lab
!
end
```

ISP1BB7

ISP1BB7 is a backbone router in ISP1. Figure 3-9 shows the topology of ISP1 and ISP1BB7's location in ISP1.

Figure 3-9 *ISP1BB7*

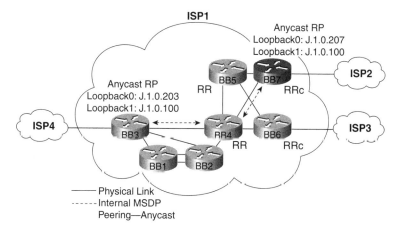

Device Characteristics for ISP1BB7

Table 3-7 lists the hardware and software device characteristics for ISP1BB7.

Table 3-7 *Hardware and Software Device Characteristics for ISP1BB7*

ISP1BB7	Device Characteristics
Host name	ISP1BB7
Chassis type	Cisco 7513 router
Physical interfaces	4 Ethernet/IEEE 802.3 4 Packet over SONET (POS)
Hardware components	Cisco RSP4 (R5000) processor 5 VIP2 controllers (4 Ethernet) (4 POS)
Software loaded	Cisco IOS Software Release 12.1(3.3)
Memory	Cisco RSP4 (R5000) processor: 128 MB
IP addresses	Loopback0: J.1.0.207 255.255.255.255 Loopback1: J.1.0.100 255.255.255.255 Ethernet0/0/0: J.1.20.1 255.255.255.0 Ethernet0/0/2: J.1.22.1 255.255.255.248 POS1/0/0: J.1.0.30 255.255.255.252 POS2/0/0: J.1.0.38 255.255.255.252 POS9/0/0: J.2.0.254 255.255.255.252

Configuration File for ISP1BB7

ISP1BB7, a core router for ISP1, has an external connection to ISP2BB7. BGP and MBGP internal peering is only to the Route Reflector servers. BGP and MBGP external peering is with ISP2BB7. For multicast, ISP1BB7 is configured as one of the two anycast RPs in ISP1. ISP1BB7 is also configured to have an MSDP internal peering session with ISP1BB4 and an external peering session with ISP2BB4, with SA filters to block unwanted sources and to prevent the unnecessary creation, forwarding, and caching of some well-known domain local sources. Additional filters are set up on the external AS connections to block administratively scoped multicast and RP announce and discovery addresses.

Example 3-7 displays the **show running-config** privileged EXEC command output for host ISP1BB7.

Example 3-7 *ISP1BB7 Configuration*

```
ISP1BB7#show running-config
version 12.1
service timestamps debug datetime localtime show-timezone
```

Example 3-7 *ISP1BB7 Configuration (Continued)*

```
service timestamps log datetime localtime show-timezone
no service password-encryption
service udp-small-servers
service tcp-small-servers
!
hostname ISP1BB7
!
logging buffered 10000 debugging
no logging console
enable password lab
!
!
clock timezone PDT -8
clock summer-time PDT recurring
ip subnet-zero
ip cef distributed
no ip domain-lookup
!
ip multicast-routing distributed
clns routing
no tag-switching ip
no tag-switching advertise-tags
!
!
interface Loopback0
 ip address J.1.0.207 255.255.255.255
 ip router isis
 ip pim sparse-mode
!
interface Loopback1
 ip address J.1.0.100 255.255.255.255
 ip router isis
 ip pim sparse-mode
!
interface Ethernet0/0/0
 description to RVT100, E7
 ip address J.1.20.1 255.255.255.0
 ip router isis
 ip pim sparse-mode
 ip route-cache distributed
 ip mroute-cache distributed
!
interface Ethernet0/0/2
 description to ISP1BB7CL1
 ip address J.1.22.1 255.255.255.248
 ip router isis
 ip pim sparse-mode
 ip route-cache distributed
 ip mroute-cache distributed
!
interface Ethernet0/0/3
 description NOT CONNECTED
```

continues

Example 3-7 *ISP1BB7 Configuration (Continued)*

```
 no ip address
 ip route-cache distributed
!
interface POS1/0/0
 description TO ISP1BB4, POS10/0/0
 ip address J.1.0.30 255.255.255.252
 ip router isis
 ip pim sparse-mode
 ip route-cache distributed
 ip mroute-cache distributed
 clock source internal
!
interface POS2/0/0
 description TO ISP1BB5, POS9/0/0
 ip address J.1.0.38 255.255.255.252
 ip router isis
 ip pim sparse-mode
 ip route-cache distributed
 ip mroute-cache distributed
 clock source internal
!
interface POS9/0/0
 description TO ISP2BB7, POS 0/0
 ip address J.2.0.254 255.255.255.252
 ip router isis
 ip pim bsr-border
 ip pim sparse-mode
 ip multicast boundary 1
 ip route-cache distributed
 ip mroute-cache distributed
 clock source internal
!
router isis
 net 49.0001.0000.0000.0007.00
 is-type level-1
!
router bgp 1
 no synchronization
 bgp log-neighbor-changes
 redistribute connected route-map connected-bgp
 neighbor ISP1INTERNAL peer-group
 neighbor J.1.0.204 remote-as 1
 neighbor J.1.0.204 update-source Loopback0
 neighbor J.1.0.205 remote-as 1
 neighbor J.1.0.205 update-source Loopback0
 neighbor J.2.0.253 remote-as 2
 no auto-summary
 !
 address-family ipv4 multicast
 redistribute connected route-map connected-bgp
 neighbor ISP1INTERNAL activate
 neighbor J.1.0.204 activate
```

Example 3-7 *ISP1BB7 Configuration (Continued)*

```
  neighbor J.1.0.205 activate
  neighbor J.2.0.253 activate
  exit-address-family
!
no ip classless
ip http server
ip pim rp-address J.1.0.100
ip msdp peer J.2.0.204 connect-source Loopback0 remote-as 2
ip msdp sa-filter in J.2.0.204 list 124
ip msdp sa-filter out J.2.0.204 list 124
ip msdp peer J.1.0.204 connect-source Loopback0
ip msdp cache-sa-state
ip msdp originator-id Loopback0
!
access-list 1 deny     224.0.1.39
access-list 1 deny     224.0.1.40
access-list 1 deny     239.0.0.0 0.255.255.255
access-list 1 permit any
access-list 112 permit ip J.1.0.0 0.0.255.255 255.255.0.0 0.0.255.255
access-list 112 deny     ip any any
access-list 124 deny     ip any host 224.0.2.2
access-list 124 deny     ip any host 224.0.1.3
access-list 124 deny     ip any host 224.0.1.24
access-list 124 deny     ip any host 224.0.1.22
access-list 124 deny     ip any host 224.0.1.2
access-list 124 deny     ip any host 224.0.1.35
access-list 124 deny     ip any host 224.0.1.60
access-list 124 deny     ip any host 224.0.1.39
access-list 124 deny     ip any host 224.0.1.40
access-list 124 deny     ip any 239.0.0.0 0.255.255.255
access-list 124 deny     ip 10.0.0.0 0.255.255.255 any
access-list 124 deny     ip 127.0.0.0 0.255.255.255 any
access-list 124 deny     ip 172.16.0.0 0.15.255.255 any
access-list 124 deny     ip K.168.0.0 0.0.255.255 any
access-list 124 permit ip any any
route-map connected-bgp permit 10
 match ip address 112
 set origin igp
!
snmp-server engineID local 0000000902000010F6A00800
snmp-server community public RO
snmp-server community STSS RW
snmp-server packetsize 2048
snmp-server contact sysadmin
snmp-server chassis-id ISP1BB7
!
!
line con 0
 exec-timeout 0 0
 login authentication NOTACACS
 transport input none
line aux 0
```

continues

Example 3-7 *ISP1BB7 Configuration (Continued)*

```
line vty 0 4
 exec-timeout 0 0
 password lab
!
end
```

ISP1DA1

ISP1DA1 is a distribution/aggregation (DA) router in ISP1-POP. Figure 3-10 shows the topology of ISP1-POP and ISP1DA1's location in ISP1-POP.

Figure 3-10 *ISP1DA1*

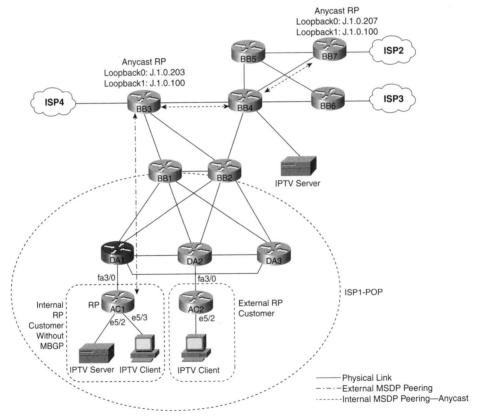

Device Characteristics for ISP1DA1

Table 3-8 lists the hardware and software device characteristics for ISP1DA1.

Table 3-8 *Hardware and Software Device Characteristics for ISP1DA1*

ISP1DA1	Device Characteristics
Host name	ISP1DA1
Chassis type	Cisco 7513 router
Physical interfaces	4 Ethernet/IEEE 802.3 1 Fast Ethernet/IEEE 802.3 1 High-Speed Serial Interface (HSSI) 5 Packet over SONET (POS)
Hardware components	Cisco RSP2 (R4700) processor 1 HSSI Interface Processor (HIP) controller (1 HSSI) 7 VIP2 controllers (1 Fast Ethernet) (4 Ethernet) (1 Channelized T3) (5 POS)
Software loaded	Cisco IOS Software Release 12.1(3)
Memory	Cisco RSP2 (R4700) processor: 128 MB
IP addresses	Loopback0: J.1.0.208 255.255.255.255 Ethernet0/0/0: J.1.73.1 255.255.255.0 Ethernet0/0/2: J.1.74.1 255.255.255.248 FastEthernet0/1/0: K.250.1.1 255.255.255.248 POS1/0/0: J.1.71.1 255.255.255.252 POS2/0/0: J.1.71.5 255.255.255.252 POS9/0/0: J.1.72.5 255.255.255.252 POS10/0/0: J.1.88.5 255.255.255.252

Configuration File for ISP1DA1

ISP1DA1 is a DA router for the POP in ISP1. BGP and MBGP internal peering is configured to all other routers in ISP1 except for Route Reflector clients and access/customer (AC) routers. For multicast, ISP1DA1 uses the anycast RP address of J.1.0.100 as its static RP address.

Example 3-8 displays the **show running-config** privileged EXEC command output for host ISP1DA1.

Example 3-8 *ISP1DA1 Configuration*

```
ISP1DA1#show running-config
version 12.1
service timestamps debug datetime localtime show-timezone
service timestamps log datetime localtime show-timezone
```

continues

Example 3-8 *ISP1DA1 Configuration (Continued)*

```
no service password-encryption
service udp-small-servers
service tcp-small-servers
!
hostname ISP1DA1
!
logging buffered 10000 debugging
no logging console
enable password lab
!
username all
!
!
clock timezone PDT -8
clock summer-time PDT recurring
ip subnet-zero
ip cef distributed
no ip domain-lookup
!
ip multicast-routing distributed
clns routing
no tag-switching ip
no tag-switching advertise-tags
isdn voice-call-failure 0
!
controller T3 4/0/0
!
!
interface Loopback0
 ip address J.1.0.208 255.255.255.255
 ip router isis
!
interface Ethernet0/0/0
 description TO RVT100, E8
 ip address J.1.73.1 255.255.255.0
 ip router isis
 ip pim sparse-mode
 ip route-cache distributed
 ip mroute-cache distributed
!
interface Ethernet0/0/2
 description TO ISP1DA1CL1
 ip address J.1.74.1 255.255.255.248
 ip pim sparse-mode
 ip route-cache distributed
 ip mroute-cache distributed
 load-interval 30
!
interface FastEthernet0/1/0
 description TO ISP1AC1, FA3/0
 ip address K.250.1.1 255.255.255.248
 ip pim sparse-mode
 ip route-cache distributed
 ip mroute-cache distributed
```

Example 3-8 *ISP1DA1 Configuration (Continued)*

```
 full-duplex
!
interface POS1/0/0
 description TO ISP1BB1, POS 0/1
 ip address J.1.71.1 255.255.255.252
 ip router isis
 ip pim sparse-mode
 ip route-cache distributed
 ip mroute-cache distributed
 clock source internal
!
interface POS2/0/0
 description TO ISP1BB2, POS 0/1
 ip address J.1.71.5 255.255.255.252
 ip router isis
 ip pim sparse-mode
 ip route-cache distributed
 ip mroute-cache distributed
 clock source internal
!
interface POS9/0/0
 description TO ISP1DA2, POS 9/0/0
 ip address J.1.72.5 255.255.255.252
 ip router isis
 ip pim sparse-mode
 ip route-cache distributed
 ip mroute-cache distributed
 clock source internal
!
interface POS10/0/0
 description TO ISP1DA3, POS 9/0/0
 ip address J.1.88.5 255.255.255.252
 ip router isis
 ip pim sparse-mode
 ip route-cache distributed
 ip mroute-cache distributed
 clock source internal
!
router isis
 net 49.0001.0000.0000.0011.00
 is-type level-1
!
router bgp 1
 no synchronization
 redistribute connected route-map connected-bgp
 redistribute static
 neighbor ISP1INTERNAL peer-group
 neighbor ISP1INTERNAL remote-as 1
 neighbor ISP1INTERNAL update-source Loopback0
 neighbor J.1.0.200 peer-group ISP1INTERNAL
 neighbor J.1.0.201 peer-group ISP1INTERNAL
 neighbor J.1.0.202 peer-group ISP1INTERNAL
 neighbor J.1.0.203 peer-group ISP1INTERNAL
```

continues

Example 3-8 *ISP1DA1 Configuration (Continued)*

```
 neighbor J.1.0.204 peer-group ISP1INTERNAL
 neighbor J.1.0.205 peer-group ISP1INTERNAL
 neighbor J.1.0.209 peer-group ISP1INTERNAL
 neighbor J.1.0.210 peer-group ISP1INTERNAL
 no auto-summary
 !
 address-family ipv4 multicast
 redistribute connected route-map connected-bgp
 redistribute static
 neighbor ISP1INTERNAL activate
 neighbor J.1.0.200 activate
 neighbor J.1.0.201 activate
 neighbor J.1.0.202 activate
 neighbor J.1.0.203 activate
 neighbor J.1.0.204 activate
 neighbor J.1.0.205 activate
 neighbor J.1.0.209 activate
 neighbor J.1.0.210 activate
 exit-address-family
!
no ip classless
ip route J.1.64.4 255.255.255.255 J.4.71.2
ip route J.1.64.14 255.255.255.255 J.4.71.6
ip route K.250.1.32 255.255.255.224 K.250.1.2
ip http server
ip pim rp-address J.1.0.100
!
access-list 112 permit ip J.1.0.0 0.0.255.255 255.255.0.0 0.0.255.255
access-list 112 permit ip K.250.1.0 0.0.0.255 255.255.0.0 0.0.255.255
route-map connected-bgp permit 10
match ip address 112
set ip next-hop J.1.0.208
set origin igp
!
snmp-server engineID local 00000000902000010F6FAE000
snmp-server community public RO
snmp-server packetsize 2048
snmp-server contact sysadmin
snmp-server chassis-id id ISP1DA1
!
!
line con 0
 exec-timeout 0 0
 length 35
 transport input none
line aux 0
line vty 0 4
 exec-timeout 0 0
 password lab
!
end
```

ISP1DA2

ISP1DA2 is a DA router in ISP1-POP. Figure 3-11 shows the topology of ISP1-POP and ISP1DA2's location in ISP1-POP.

Figure 3-11 *ISP1DA2*

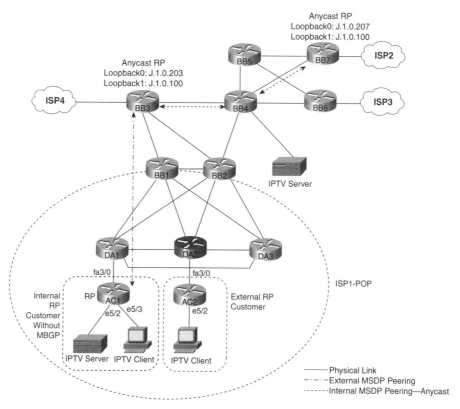

Device Characteristics for ISP1DA2

Table 3-9 lists the hardware and software device characteristics for ISP1DA2.

Table 3-9 *Hardware and Software Device Characteristics for ISP1DA2*

ISP1DA2	Device Characteristics
Host name	ISP1DA2
Chassis type	Cisco 7513 router

continues

Table 3-9 *Hardware and Software Device Characteristics for ISP1DA2 (Continued)*

ISP1DA2	Device Characteristics
Physical interfaces	4 Ethernet/IEEE 802.3 1 Fast Ethernet/IEEE 802.3 5 Packet over SONET (POS)
Hardware components	Cisco RSP2 (R4700) processor 6 VIP2 controllers (1 Fast Ethernet) (4 Ethernet) (5 POS)
Software loaded	Cisco IOS Software Release 12.1(3.5)T
Memory	Cisco RSP2 (R4700) processor: 128 MB
IP addresses	Loopback0: J.1.0.209 255.255.255.255 Ethernet0/0/0: J.1.81.1 255.255.255.0 Ethernet0/0/2: J.1.82.1 255.255.255.248 FastEthernet0/1/0: K.250.1.9 255.255.255.248 POS1/0/0: J.1.71.25 255.255.255.252 POS2/0/0: J.1.71.13 255.255.255.252 POS9/0/0: J.1.72.6 255.255.255.252 POS10/0/0: J.1.80.1 255.255.255.252

Configuration File for ISP1DA2

ISP1DA2 is a DA router for the POP in ISP1. BGP and MBGP internal peering is configured to all other routers in ISP1 except for Route Reflector clients and AC routers. For multicast, ISP1DA2 uses the anycast RP address of J.1.0.100 as its static RP address.

Example 3-9 displays the **show running-config** privileged EXEC command output for host ISP1DA2.

Example 3-9 *ISP1DA2 Configuration*

```
ISP1DA2#show running-config
version 12.1
service timestamps debug uptime
service timestamps log datetime localtime show-timezone
no service password-encryption
service udp-small-servers
service tcp-small-servers
!
hostname ISP1DA2
!
logging buffered 10000 debugging
enable password lab
!
!
clock timezone PDT -8
clock summer-time PDT recurring
ip subnet-zero
ip cef distributed
no ip domain-lookup
```

Example 3-9 *ISP1DA2 Configuration (Continued)*

```
!
ip multicast-routing distributed
clns routing
no tag-switching advertise-tags
no tag-switching ip
!
!
interface Loopback0
 ip address J.1.0.209 255.255.255.255
 ip router isis
!
interface Ethernet0/0/0
 description TO RVT100, E9
 ip address J.1.81.1 255.255.255.0
 ip router isis
 ip pim sparse-mode
 ip route-cache distributed
 ip mroute-cache distributed
!
interface Ethernet0/0/2
 description TO ISP1DA2CL1
 ip address J.1.82.1 255.255.255.248
 ip pim sparse-mode
 ip route-cache distributed
 ip mroute-cache distributed
 load-interval 30
!
interface FastEthernet0/1/0
 description TO ISP1AC2, FA3/0
 ip address K.250.1.9 255.255.255.248
 ip pim sparse-mode
 ip route-cache distributed
 ip mroute-cache distributed
 full-duplex
!
interface POS1/0/0
 description TO ISP1BB1, POS 0/2
 ip address J.1.71.25 255.255.255.252
 ip router isis
 ip pim sparse-mode
 ip route-cache distributed
 ip mroute-cache distributed
 clock source internal
!
interface POS2/0/0
 description TO ISP1BB2, POS 0/2
 ip address J.1.71.13 255.255.255.252
 ip router isis
 ip pim sparse-mode
 ip route-cache distributed
 ip mroute-cache distributed
 clock source internal
!
interface POS9/0/0
```

continues

Example 3-9 *ISP1DA2 Configuration (Continued)*

```
   description TO ISP1DA1, POS 9/0/0
   ip address J.1.72.6 255.255.255.252
   ip router isis
   ip pim sparse-mode
   ip route-cache distributed
   ip mroute-cache distributed
   clock source internal
 !
 interface POS10/0/0
   description TO ISP1DA3, POS 10/0/0
   ip address J.1.80.1 255.255.255.252
   ip router isis
   ip pim sparse-mode
   ip route-cache distributed
   ip mroute-cache distributed
   clock source internal
 !
 router isis
   net 49.0001.0000.0000.0012.00
   is-type level-1
 !
 router bgp 1
   no synchronization
   bgp log-neighbor-changes
   redistribute connected route-map connected-bgp
   neighbor ISP1INTERNAL peer-group
   neighbor ISP1INTERNAL remote-as 1
   neighbor ISP1INTERNAL update-source Loopback0
   neighbor J.1.0.200 peer-group ISP1INTERNAL
   neighbor J.1.0.201 peer-group ISP1INTERNAL
   neighbor J.1.0.202 peer-group ISP1INTERNAL
   neighbor J.1.0.203 peer-group ISP1INTERNAL
   neighbor J.1.0.204 peer-group ISP1INTERNAL
   neighbor J.1.0.205 peer-group ISP1INTERNAL
   neighbor J.1.0.208 peer-group ISP1INTERNAL
   neighbor J.1.0.210 peer-group ISP1INTERNAL
   no auto-summary
 !
   address-family ipv4 multicast
   redistribute connected route-map connected-bgp
   neighbor ISP1INTERNAL activate
   neighbor J.1.0.200 activate
   neighbor J.1.0.201 activate
   neighbor J.1.0.202 activate
   neighbor J.1.0.203 activate
   neighbor J.1.0.204 activate
   neighbor J.1.0.205 activate
   neighbor J.1.0.208 activate
   neighbor J.1.0.210 activate
   exit-address-family
 !
 no ip classless
```

Example 3-9 *ISP1DA2 Configuration (Continued)*

```
ip http server
ip pim rp-address J.1.0.100
!
access-list 112 permit ip J.1.0.0 0.0.255.255 255.255.0.0 0.0.255.255
access-list 112 permit ip K.250.1.0 0.0.0.255 255.255.0.0 0.0.255.255
access-list 112 deny    ip any any
route-map connected-bgp permit 10
 match ip address 112
 set origin igp
!
snmp-server engineID local 0000000902000010F6A02000
snmp-server community public RO
snmp-server community STSS RW
snmp-server packetsize 2048
snmp-server contact sysadmin
snmp-server chassis-id ISP1DA2
!
!
line con 0
 exec-timeout 0 0
 length 40
 transport input none
line aux 0
line vty 0 4
 exec-timeout 0 0
 password lab
!
end
```

ISP1DA3

ISP1DA3 is a DA router in ISP1-POP. Figure 3-12 shows the topology of ISP1-POP and ISP1DA3's location in ISP1-POP.

Figure 3-12 *ISP1DA3*

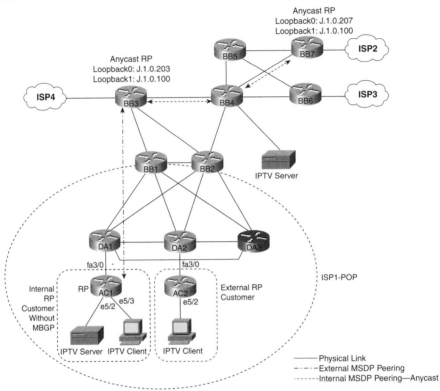

Device Characteristics for ISP1DA3

Table 3-10 lists the hardware and software device characteristics for ISP1DA3.

Table 3-10 *Hardware and Software Device Characteristics for ISP1DA3*

ISP1DA3	Device Characteristics
Host name	ISP1DA3
Chassis type	Cisco 7513 router
Physical interfaces	4 Ethernet/IEEE 802.3 5 Packet over SONET (POS)

Table 3-10 *Hardware and Software Device Characteristics for ISP1DA3 (Continued)*

ISP1DA3	Device Characteristics
Hardware components	Cisco RSP2 (R4700) processor 1 Ethernet Interface Processor (EIP) controller (4 Ethernet) 5 VIP2 controllers (5 POS)
Software loaded	Cisco IOS Software Release 12.1(3)
Memory	Cisco RSP2 (R4700) processor: 128 MB
IP addresses	Loopback0: J.1.0.210 255.255.255.255 Ethernet0/0: J.1.89.1 255.255.255.0 Ethernet0/2: J.1.90.1 255.255.255.248 POS1/0/0: J.1.71.17 255.255.255.252 POS2/0/0: J.1.71.21 255.255.255.252 POS9/0/0: J.1.88.6 255.255.255.252 POS10/0/0: J.1.80.2 255.255.255.252

Configuration File for ISP1DA3

ISP1DA3 is a DA router for the POP in ISP1. BGP and MBGP internal peering is configured to all other routers in ISP1 except for Route Reflector clients and AC routers. For multicast, ISP1DA3 uses the anycast RP address of J.1.0.100 as its static RP address.

Example 3-10 displays the **show running-config** privileged EXEC command output for host ISP1DA3.

Example 3-10 *ISP1DA3 Configuration*

```
ISP1DA3#show running-config
version 12.1
service timestamps debug uptime
service timestamps log datetime localtime show-timezone
no service password-encryption
service udp-small-servers
service tcp-small-servers
!
hostname ISP1DA3
!
logging buffered 10000 debugging
no logging console
enable password lab
!
!
clock timezone PDT -8
clock summer-time PDT recurring
ip subnet-zero
ip cef distributed
no ip domain-lookup
!
```

continues

Example 3-10 *ISP1DA3 Configuration (Continued)*

```
ip multicast-routing distributed
clns routing
no tag-switching ip
no tag-switching advertise-tags
!
!
interface Loopback0
 ip address J.1.0.210 255.255.255.255
 ip router isis
!
interface Ethernet0/0
 description To RVT100 EX
 ip address J.1.89.1 255.255.255.0
 ip router isis
 ip pim sparse-mode
!
interface Ethernet0/2
 description TO ISP1DA3CL1
 ip address J.1.90.1 255.255.255.0
 ip router isis
 ip pim sparse-mode
 ip route-cache distributed
 ip mroute-cache distributed
!
interface Ethernet0/3
 description NOT CONNECTED
 no ip address
 ip pim sparse-mode
 load-interval 30
!
interface POS1/0/0
 description TO ISP1BB1, POS 0/3
 ip address J.1.71.17 255.255.255.252
 ip router isis
 ip pim sparse-mode
 ip route-cache distributed
 ip mroute-cache distributed
 clock source internal
!
interface POS2/0/0
 description TO ISP1BB2, POS 0/3
 ip address J.1.71.21 255.255.255.252
 ip router isis
 ip pim sparse-mode
 ip route-cache distributed
 ip mroute-cache distributed
 clock source internal
!
interface POS9/0/0
 description TO ISP1DA1, POS 10/0/0
 ip address J.1.88.6 255.255.255.252
 ip router isis
 ip pim sparse-mode
 ip route-cache distributed
```

Example 3-10 *ISP1DA3 Configuration (Continued)*

```
  ip mroute-cache distributed
  clock source internal
 !
 interface POS10/0/0
  description TO ISP1DA2, POS 10/0/0
  ip address J.1.80.2 255.255.255.252
  ip router isis
  ip pim sparse-mode
  ip route-cache distributed
  ip mroute-cache distributed
  clock source internal
 !
 router isis
  net 49.0001.0000.0000.0013.00
  is-type level-1
 !
 router bgp 1
  no synchronization
  redistribute connected route-map connected-bgp
  neighbor ISP1INTERNAL peer-group
  neighbor ISP1INTERNAL remote-as 1
  neighbor ISP1INTERNAL update-source Loopback0
  neighbor J.1.0.200 peer-group ISP1INTERNAL
  neighbor J.1.0.201 peer-group ISP1INTERNAL
  neighbor J.1.0.202 peer-group ISP1INTERNAL
  neighbor J.1.0.203 peer-group ISP1INTERNAL
  neighbor J.1.0.204 peer-group ISP1INTERNAL
  neighbor J.1.0.205 peer-group ISP1INTERNAL
  neighbor J.1.0.208 peer-group ISP1INTERNAL
  neighbor J.1.0.209 peer-group ISP1INTERNAL
  no auto-summary
 !
  address-family ipv4 multicast
  redistribute connected route-map connected-bgp
  neighbor ISP1INTERNAL activate
  neighbor J.1.0.200 activate
  neighbor J.1.0.201 activate
  neighbor J.1.0.202 activate
  neighbor J.1.0.203 activate
  neighbor J.1.0.204 activate
  neighbor J.1.0.205 activate
  neighbor J.1.0.208 activate
  neighbor J.1.0.209 activate
  exit-address-family
 !
 no ip classless
 ip http server
 ip pim rp-address J.1.0.100
 !
 access-list 112 permit ip J.1.0.0 0.0.255.255 255.255.0.0 0.0.255.255
 access-list 112 deny    ip any any
 route-map connected-bgp permit 10
 match ip address 112
 set ip next-hop J.1.0.210
```

continues

Example 3-10 *ISP1DA3 Configuration (Continued)*

```
set origin igp
!
snmp-server engineID local 0000000902000009ED110800
snmp-server community public RO
snmp-server community STSS RW
snmp-server packetsize 2048
snmp-server contact sysadmin
snmp-server system-shutdown
snmp-server enable traps snmp
snmp-server enable traps channel
snmp-server enable traps isdn call-information
snmp-server enable traps isdn layer2
snmp-server enable traps config
snmp-server enable traps entity
snmp-server enable traps envmon
snmp-server enable traps bgp
snmp-server enable traps frame-relay
!
!
line con 0
 exec-timeout 0 0
 transport input none
line aux 0
line vty 0 4
 exec-timeout 0 0
 password lab
!
end
```

ISP1AC1

ISP1AC1 is an AC router in ISP1-POP. Figure 3-13 shows the topology of ISP1-POP and ISP1AC1's location in ISP1-POP.

Figure 3-13 *ISP1AC1*

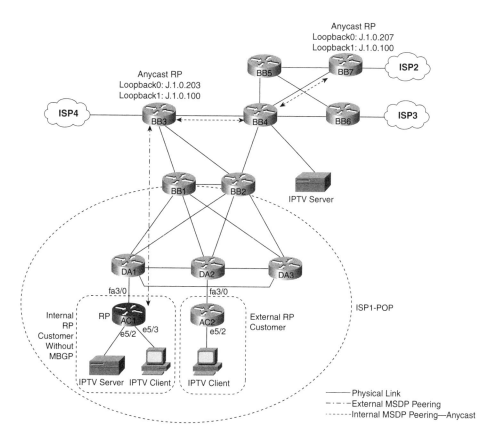

Device Characteristics for ISP1AC1

Table 3-11 lists the hardware and software device characteristics for ISP1AC1.

Table 3-11   *Hardware and Software Device Characteristics for ISP1AC1*

ISP1AC1	Device Characteristics
Host name	ISP1AC1
Chassis type	Cisco 7206VXR
Physical interfaces	8 Ethernet/IEEE 802.3 3 Fast Ethernet/IEEE 802.3

continues

Table 3-11 *Hardware and Software Device Characteristics for ISP1AC1 (Continued)*

ISP1AC1	Device Characteristics
Hardware components	Cisco 7206VXR (NPE300) processor
Software loaded	Cisco IOS Software Release 12.1(4.4)PI
Memory	Cisco 7206VXR (NPE300) processor (revision D): 40 MB
IP addresses	Loopback0: K.250.0.201 255.255.255.255 FastEthernet3/0: K.250.1.2 255.255.255.248 Ethernet5/2: K.250.1.33 255.255.255.248 Ethernet5/3: K.250.1.41 255.255.255.248

Configuration File for ISP1AC1

ISP1AC1 is an AC router for the POP in ISP1. Routing is achieved through a default route. For multicast, ISP1AC1 acts as an RP for any customers connecting to it. ISP1AC1 also learns about other sources by having an internal MSDP peering session with ISP1BB3 with SA filters to block unwanted sources and to prevent the unnecessary creation, forwarding, and caching of some well-known domain local sources.

Example 3-11 displays the **show running-config** privileged EXEC command output for host ISP1AC1.

Example 3-11 *ISP1AC1 Configuration*

```
ISP1AC1#show running-config
version 12.1
no service single-slot-reload-enable
service timestamps debug datetime localtime show-timezone
service timestamps log datetime localtime show-timezone
no service password-encryption
service udp-small-servers
service tcp-small-servers
!
hostname ISP1AC1
!
logging buffered 1000000 debugging
logging rate-limit console 10 except errors
no logging console
aaa new-model
aaa authentication login default group tacacs+ enable
aaa authentication login NOTACACS enable
aaa accounting commands 15 default start-stop group tacacs+
aaa accounting system default start-stop group tacacs+
enable password lab
!
clock timezone PST -8
clock summer-time PST recurring
ip subnet-zero
ip cef
```

Example 3-11 *ISP1AC1 Configuration (Continued)*

```
!
!
no ip finger
no ip domain-lookup
!
ip multicast-routing
call rsvp-sync
!
!
interface Loopback0
 ip address K.250.0.201 255.255.255.255
 ip pim sparse-mode
!
interface FastEthernet3/0
 description To ISP1DA1, FA0/1/0
 ip address K.250.1.2 255.255.255.248
 ip pim bsr-border
 ip pim sparse-mode
 ip multicast boundary 1
 duplex full
!
interface Ethernet5/2
 description TO ISP1AC1IPTV
 ip address K.250.1.33 255.255.255.248
 ip pim sparse-mode
 duplex half
!
interface Ethernet5/3
 description TO ISP1AC1CL1
 ip address K.250.1.41 255.255.255.248
 ip pim sparse-mode
 duplex half
!
ip classless
ip route 0.0.0.0 0.0.0.0 K.250.1.1
no ip http server
ip pim rp-address K.250.0.201
ip msdp peer J.1.0.203 connect-source FastEthernet3/0
ip msdp sa-filter in J.1.0.203 list 124
ip msdp sa-filter out J.1.0.203 list 124
ip msdp cache-sa-state
ip msdp redistribute list 124
!
access-list 1 deny     224.0.1.39
access-list 1 deny     224.0.1.40
access-list 1 deny     239.0.0.0 0.255.255.255
access-list 1 permit any
access-list 124 deny   ip any host 224.0.2.2
access-list 124 deny   ip any host 224.0.1.3
access-list 124 deny   ip any host 224.0.1.24
access-list 124 deny   ip any host 224.0.1.22
access-list 124 deny   ip any host 224.0.1.2
access-list 124 deny   ip any host 224.0.1.35
access-list 124 deny   ip any host 224.0.1.60
```

continues

Example 3-11 *ISP1AC1 Configuration (Continued)*

```
access-list 124 deny    ip any host 224.0.1.39
access-list 124 deny    ip any host 224.0.1.40
access-list 124 deny    ip any 239.0.0.0 0.255.255.255
access-list 124 deny    ip 10.0.0.0 0.255.255.255 any
access-list 124 deny    ip 127.0.0.0 0.255.255.255 any
access-list 124 deny    ip 172.16.0.0 0.15.255.255 any
access-list 124 deny    ip K.168.0.0 0.0.255.255 any
access-list 124 deny    ip any 232.0.0.0 0.255.255.255
access-list 124 permit ip any any
snmp-server engineID local 00000009020000024ADFB800
snmp-server community public RO
snmp-server community STSS RW
snmp-server packetsize 2048
snmp-server contact sysadmin
snmp-server chassis-id ISP1AC1
!
tacacs-server key cisco12345
!
alias exec int_desc show int | include Description
alias exec cpu show proc cpu | include CPU
alias exec mem show mem free | include Processor
!
line con 0
 exec-timeout 0 0
 login authentication NOTACACS
 transport input none
line aux 0
 exec-timeout 0 0
line vty 0 4
 exec-timeout 0 0
 password lab
line vty 5 15
!
exception protocol ftp
exception region-size 36864
exception flash all disk0:
ntp clock-period 17180280
ntp update-calendar
end
```

ISP1AC2

ISP1AC2 is an AC router in ISP1-POP. Figure 3-14 shows the topology of ISP1-POP and ISP1AC2's location in ISP1-POP.

Figure 3-14 *Figure 3-14ISP1AC2*

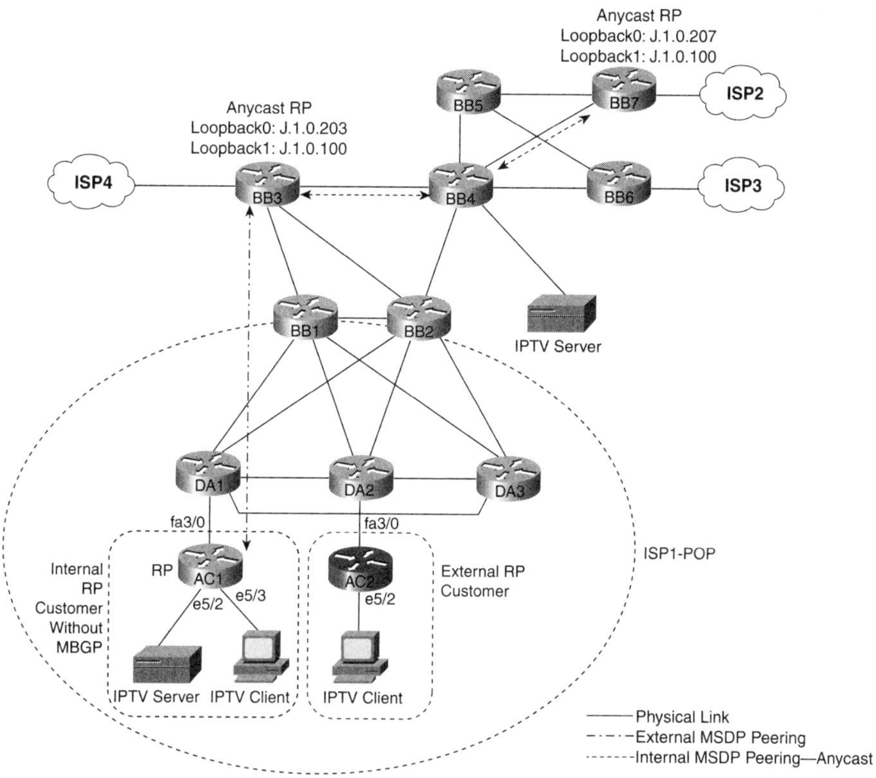

Device Characteristics for ISP1AC2

Table 3-12 lists the hardware and software device characteristics for ISP1AC2.

Table 3-12 *Hardware and Software Device Characteristics for ISP1AC2*

ISP1AC2	Device Characteristics
Host name	ISP1AC2
Chassis type	Cisco 7206 router
Physical interfaces	8 Ethernet/IEEE 802.3 1 Fast Ethernet/IEEE 802.3
Hardware components	Cisco 7206 (NPE200) processor (revision B)

continues

Table 3-12 *Hardware and Software Device Characteristics for ISP1AC2 (Continued)*

ISP1AC2	Device Characteristics
Software loaded	Cisco IOS Software Release 12.1(3.4)T
Memory	Cisco 7206 (NPE200) processor (revision B): 112 MB
IP addresses	FastEthernet3/0: K.250.1.10 255.255.255.248 Ethernet5/2: K.250.1.49 255.255.255.248

Configuration File for ISP1AC2

ISP1AC2 is an AC router for the POP in ISP1. Routing is achieved through a default route. For multicast, ISP1AC2 uses the anycast RP address of J.1.0.100 as its static RP address.

Example 3-12 displays the **show running-config** privileged EXEC command output for host ISP1AC2.

Example 3-12 *ISP1AC2 Configuration*

```
ISP1AC2#show running-config
version 12.1
no service pad
service timestamps debug datetime localtime show-timezone
service timestamps log datetime localtime show-timezone
no service password-encryption
service udp-small-servers
service tcp-small-servers
!
hostname ISP1AC2
!
logging buffered 1000000 debugging
enable password lab
!
!
clock timezone PST -8
clock summer-time PST recurring
ip subnet-zero
ip cef
no ip domain-lookup
!
ip multicast-routing
!
!
interface FastEthernet3/0
 description TO ISP1DA2, FA0/1/0
 ip address K.250.1.10 255.255.255.248
 ip pim sparse-mode
 full-duplex
!
interface Ethernet5/2
 description TO ISP1AC2CL1
```

Example 3-12 *ISP1AC2 Configuration (Continued)*

```
  ip address K.250.1.49 255.255.255.248
  ip pim sparse-mode
!
ip classless
ip route 0.0.0.0 0.0.0.0 K.250.1.9
no ip http server
ip pim rp-address J.1.0.100
!
snmp-server community public RO
snmp-server community STSS RW
snmp-server packetsize 2048
snmp-server chassis-id ISP1AC2
!
alias exec int_desc show int | include Description
alias exec cpu show proc cpu | include CPU
alias exec mem show mem free | include Processor
!
line con 0
 exec-timeout 0 0
 login authentication NOTACACS
 transport input none
line aux 0
 exec-timeout 0 0
line vty 0 4
 exec-timeout 0 0
 password lab
!
end
```

This chapter includes the device characteristics and configuration files for the following host names in ISP2, as described in Chapter 2, "Implementing Interdomain Multicast Using MSDP":

- ISP2BB1
- ISP2BB2
- ISP2BB3
- ISP2BB4
- ISP2BB5
- ISP2BB6
- ISP2BB7

CHAPTER 4

ISP2 Device Characteristics and Configuration Files

This chapter provides the characteristics and configuration files for the devices associated with ISP2, as described in Chapter 2. Figure 4-1 and Figure 4-2 show the overall interdomain topology to which ISP2 belongs. Figure 4-1 shows the MBGP peering sessions and Figure 4-2 shows the MSDP peering sessions established among the four ISPs in which interdomain multicast is deployed.

Figure 4-1 *Overall Network Topology with MBGP Peering*

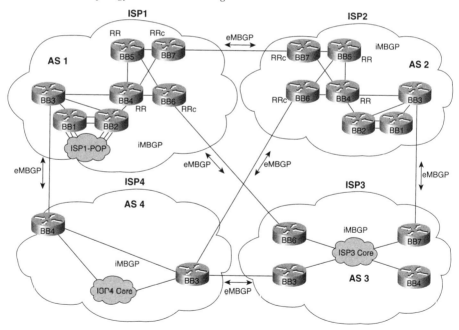

Figure 4-2 *Overall Network Topology with MSDP Peering*

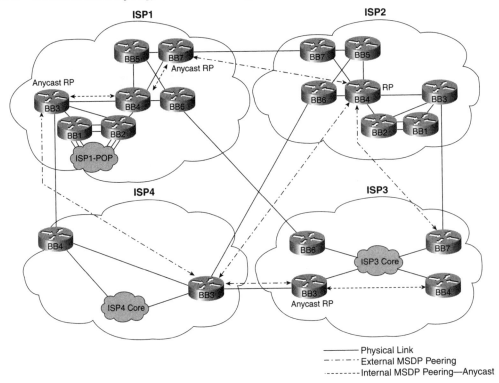

The multicast solutions in this chapter were tested with valid IP addresses. Normally, when a configuration file is published, the valid IP addresses are replaced with IP addresses, as specified in RFC 1918, "Address Allocation for Private Networks." Because the range of available IP addresses was insufficient to span the range of IP addresses used in this solution, the first octet of the valid IP addresses was replaced with a variable. In the example configurations provided in the following sections, the first octet of reserved IP addresses has been replaced with the letter J or the letter K for privacy reasons. The letter J always represents one unique number and the letter K always represents a unique number that is different from J.

The example configurations are intended for illustrative purposes only. The letters J and K must be replaced with valid numbers when these IP addresses are configured in an actual network.

NOTE The example configurations provided in the following sections use highlighted text to indicate pertinent configuration commands used for deploying the IP multicast solutions described in this chapter.

ISP2BB1

ISP2BB1 is a backbone router in ISP2. Figure 4-3 shows the topology of ISP2 and ISP2BB1's location in ISP2.

Figure 4-3 *ISP2BB1*

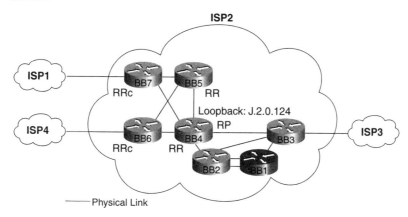

Device Characteristics for ISP2BB1

Table 4-1 lists the hardware and software device characteristics for ISP2BB1.

Table 4-1 *Hardware and Software Device Characteristics for ISP2BB1*

ISP2BB1	Device Characteristics
Host name	ISP2BB1
Chassis type	Cisco 12008 Gigabit Switch Router (GSR)
Physical interfaces	1 Ethernet/IEEE 802.3 1 Gigabit Ethernet/IEEE 802.3 4 ATM 3 Packet over SONET (POS)
Hardware components	Cisco 12008/GRP (R5000) processor (revision 0x01) 2 route processor cards 2 clock scheduler cards 3 switch fabric cards 1 quad-port OC 3c ATM controller (4 ATM) 2 OC-12 POS controllers (2 POS) 1 single-port Gigabit Ethernet/IEEE 802.3z controller (1 Gigabit Ethernet)
Software loaded	Cisco IOS Software Release 12.0(10)S

continues

Table 4-1 *Hardware and Software Device Characteristics for ISP2BB1 (Continued)*

ISP2BB1	Device Characteristics
Memory	Cisco 12008/GRP (R5000) processor (revision 0×01): 128 MB
IP addresses	Loopback0: J.2.0.201 255.255.255.255 ATM0/0.201 point-to-point: J.2.64.1 255.255.255.252 ATM0/0.203 point-to-point: J.2.64.9 255.255.255.252 ATM0/0.205 point-to-point: J.2.64.17 255.255.255.252 ATM0/0.207 point-to-point: J.2.64.25 255.255.255.252 ATM0/1.202 point-to-point: J.2.64.5 255.255.255.252 ATM0/1.204 point-to-point: J.2.64.13 255.255.255.252 ATM0/1.206 point-to-point: J.2.64.21 255.255.255.252 ATM0/1.208 point-to-point: J.2.64.29 255.255.255.252 POS1/0: J.2.0.1 255.255.255.252 POS2/0: J.2.0.1 255.255.255.252 POS3/0: J.2.0.13 255.255.255.252 GigabitEthernet6/0.130: J.2.3.1 255.255.255.248 GigabitEthernet6/0.140: J.2.4.1 255.255.255.0

Configuration File for ISP2BB1

ISP2BB1 is a core router for ISP2. BGP and MBGP internal peering is configured to all other routers in ISP2 except for Route Reflector clients. For multicast, the router is statically configured to use ISP2BB4 as its rendezvous point (RP).

Example 4-1 displays the **show running-config** privileged EXEC command output for host ISP2BB1.

Example 4-1 *ISP2BB1 Configuration*

```
ISP2BB1#show running-config
version 12.0
no service pad
service timestamps debug datetime localtime show-timezone
service timestamps log datetime localtime show-timezone
no service password-encryption
service udp-small-servers
service tcp-small-servers
!
hostname ISP2BB1
!
enable password lab
!
clock timezone PDT -8
clock summer-time PDT recurring
redundancy
main-cpu
  auto-sync startup-config
!
!
ip subnet-zero
```

Example 4-1 *ISP2BB1 Configuration (Continued)*

```
no ip bootp server
no ip domain-lookup
ip multicast-routing distributed
clns routing
!
!
interface Loopback0
 description Needed for BGP and ISIS
 ip address J.2.0.201 255.255.255.255
 no ip directed-broadcast
 ip pim sparse-mode
 ip router isis
 ip mroute-cache distributed
!
interface ATM0/0
 description To ISP2DASW1, 0/0/0
 no ip address
 no ip directed-broadcast
 no ip mroute-cache
 atm sonet stm-1
 atm pvc 16 0 16 ilmi
 no atm enable-ilmi-trap
 no atm ilmi-keepalive
!
interface ATM0/0.201 point-to-point
 description To ISP2DA1 ATM0/0/0.201
 ip address J.2.64.1 255.255.255.252
 no ip directed-broadcast
 ip pim sparse-mode
 ip router isis
 atm pvc 201 0 201 aal5snap
 no atm enable-ilmi-trap
 isis metric 15 level-1
 isis hello-multiplier 12 level-1
 isis hello-interval 5 level-1
 isis retransmit-throttle-interval 250
 isis retransmit-interval 140
 isis lsp-interval 50
!
interface ATM0/0.203 point-to-point
 description To ISP2DA2
 ip address J.2.64.9 255.255.255.252
 no ip directed-broadcast
 ip pim sparse-mode
 ip router isis
 atm pvc 203 0 203 aal5snap
 no atm enable-ilmi-trap
 isis metric 5 level-1
 isis hello-multiplier 12 level-1
 isis hello-interval 5 level-1
 isis retransmit-throttle-interval 250
 isis retransmit-interval 140
```

continues

Example 4-1   *ISP2BB1 Configuration (Continued)*

```
 isis lsp-interval 50
!
interface ATM0/0.205 point-to-point
 description To ISP2DA3
 ip address J.2.64.17 255.255.255.252
 no ip directed-broadcast
 ip pim sparse-mode
 ip router isis
 atm pvc 205 0 205 aal5snap
 no atm enable-ilmi-trap
 isis metric 5 level-1
 isis hello-multiplier 12 level-1
 isis hello-interval 5 level-1
 isis retransmit-throttle-interval 250
 isis retransmit-interval 140
 isis lsp-interval 50
!
interface ATM0/0.207 point-to-point
 description To ISP2DA4
 ip address J.2.64.25 255.255.255.252
 no ip directed-broadcast
 ip pim sparse-mode
 ip router isis
 atm pvc 207 0 207 aal5snap
 no atm enable-ilmi-trap
 isis metric 5 level-1
 isis hello-multiplier 12 level-1
 isis hello-interval 5 level-1
 isis retransmit-throttle-interval 250
 isis retransmit-interval 140
 isis lsp-interval 50
!
interface ATM0/1
 description To ISP2DASW2, 0/0/0
 no ip address
 no ip directed-broadcast
 no ip mroute-cache
 atm sonet stm-1
 atm pvc 16 0 16 ilmi
 no atm enable-ilmi-trap
 no atm ilmi-keepalive
!
interface ATM0/1.202 point-to-point
 description To ISP2DA1 ATM12/0/0.202
 ip address J.2.64.5 255.255.255.252
 no ip directed-broadcast
 ip pim sparse-mode
 ip router isis
 atm pvc 202 0 202 aal5snap
 no atm enable-ilmi-trap
 isis metric 15 level-1
 isis hello-multiplier 12 level-1
 isis hello-interval 5 level-1
```

Example 4-1 *ISP2BB1 Configuration (Continued)*

```
  isis retransmit-throttle-interval 250
  isis retransmit-interval 140
  isis lsp-interval 50
 !
 interface ATM0/1.204 point-to-point
  description To ISP2DA2
  ip address J.2.64.13 255.255.255.252
  no ip directed-broadcast
  ip pim sparse-mode
  ip router isis
  atm pvc 204 0 204 aal5snap
  no atm enable-ilmi-trap
  isis metric 5 level-1
  isis hello-multiplier 12 level-1
  isis hello-interval 5 level-1
  isis retransmit-throttle-interval 250
  isis retransmit-interval 140
  isis lsp-interval 50
 !
 interface ATM0/1.206 point-to-point
  description To ISP2DA3
  ip address J.2.64.21 255.255.255.252
  no ip directed-broadcast
  ip pim sparse-mode
  ip router isis
  atm pvc 206 0 206 aal5snap
  no atm enable-ilmi-trap
  isis metric 5 level-1
  isis hello-multiplier 12 level-1
  isis hello-interval 5 level-1
  isis retransmit-throttle-interval 250
  isis retransmit-interval 140
  isis lsp-interval 50
 !
 interface ATM0/1.208 point-to-point
  description To ISP2DA4
  ip address J.2.64.29 255.255.255.252
  no ip directed-broadcast
  ip pim sparse-mode
  ip router isis
  atm pvc 208 0 208 aal5snap
  no atm enable-ilmi-trap
  isis metric 5 level-1
  isis hello-multiplier 12 level-1
  isis hello-interval 5 level-1
  isis retransmit-throttle-interval 250
  isis retransmit-interval 140
  isis lsp-interval 50
 !
 interface POS1/0
  description TO ISP2BB2, POS 2/0
  ip address J.2.0.1 255.255.255.252
```

continues

Example 4-1 *ISP2BB1 Configuration (Continued)*

```
  no ip directed-broadcast
  ip pim sparse-mode
  ip router isis
  ip mroute-cache distributed
  crc 32
  clock source internal
  pos ais-shut
  aps revert 1
  aps protect 1 J.2.0.201
 !
 interface POS2/0
  description TO ISP2BB2, POS 1/0
  ip address J.2.0.1 255.255.255.252
  no ip directed-broadcast
  ip pim sparse-mode
  ip router isis
  ip mroute-cache distributed
  load-interval 30
  crc 32
  clock source internal
  pos ais-shut
  aps working 1
 !
 interface POS3/0
  description TO ISP2BB3, POS 1/0
  ip address J.2.0.13 255.255.255.252
  no ip directed-broadcast
  ip pim sparse-mode
  ip router isis
  ip mroute-cache distributed
  crc 32
  clock source internal
 !
 interface GigabitEthernet6/0
  no ip address
  no ip directed-broadcast
  load-interval 30
 !
 interface GigabitEthernet6/0.130
  description Client/Server
  encapsulation dot1Q 130
  ip address J.2.3.1 255.255.255.248
  no ip directed-broadcast
  ip pim sparse-mode
  ip router isis
 !
 interface GigabitEthernet6/0.140
  description OPEN
  encapsulation dot1Q 140
  ip address J.2.4.1 255.255.255.0
  no ip directed-broadcast
  ip pim sparse-mode
  ip router isis
```

Example 4-1 *ISP2BB1 Configuration (Continued)*

```
!
router isis
 redistribute static ip metric 0 metric-type internal level-1
 net 49.0002.0000.0000.0001.00
 is-type level-1
!
router bgp 2
 no synchronization
 redistribute connected route-map connected-bgp
 neighbor ISP2INTERNAL peer-group nlri unicast multicast
 neighbor ISP2INTERNAL remote-as 2
 neighbor ISP2INTERNAL update-source Loopback0
 neighbor J.2.0.202 peer-group ISP2INTERNAL
 neighbor J.2.0.203 peer-group ISP2INTERNAL
 neighbor J.2.0.204 peer-group ISP2INTERNAL
 neighbor J.2.0.205 peer-group ISP2INTERNAL
 neighbor J.2.0.206 peer-group ISP2INTERNAL
 neighbor J.2.0.207 peer-group ISP2INTERNAL
 neighbor J.2.0.208 peer-group ISP2INTERNAL
 no auto-summary
!
no ip classless
ip route 191.3.0.0 255.255.0.0 J.2.0.208
ip route 191.4.0.0 255.255.0.0 J.2.0.208
ip http server
ip pim rp-address J.2.0.124
!
logging trap emergencies
access-list 112 permit ip J.2.0.0 0.0.255.255 255.255.0.0 0.0.255.255
access-list 112 deny   ip any any
arp J.2.2.10 0010.8001.e228 ARPA
route-map connected-bgp permit 10
 match ip address 112
 set ip next-hop J.2.0.201
 set origin igp
!
snmp-server engineID local 00000009020000101F4530C0
snmp-server community public RO
snmp-server community STSS RW
snmp-server contact sysadmin
snmp-server chassis-id ISP2BB1
!
!
line con 0
 exec-timeout 0 0
 login authentication NOTACACS
 transport input none
line aux 0
line vty 0 4
 exec-timeout 0 0
 password lab
 length 0
!
end
```

ISP2BB2

ISP2BB2 is a backbone router in ISP2. Figure 4-4 shows the topology of ISP2 and ISP2BB2's location in ISP2.

Figure 4-4 *ISP2BB2*

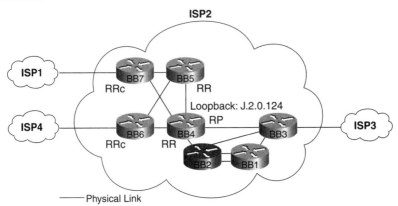

Device Characteristics for ISP2BB2

Table 4-2 lists the hardware and software device characteristics for ISP2BB2.

Table 4-2 *Hardware and Software Device Characteristics for ISP2BB2*

ISP2BB2	Device Characteristics
Host name	ISP2BB2
Chassis type	Cisco 12008 Gigabit Switch Router (GSR)
Physical interfaces	1 Ethernet/IEEE 802.3 1 Gigabit Ethernet/IEEE 802.3 4 ATM 3 Packet over SONET (POS)
Hardware components	Cisco 12008/GRP (R5000) processor (revision 0×01) 2 route processor cards 2 clock scheduler cards 3 switch fabric cards 1 quad-port OC-3c ATM controller (4 ATM) 2 OC-12 POS controllers (2 POS) 2 OC-48 POS E.D. controllers (2 POS) 1 single-port Gigabit Ethernet/IEEE 802.3z controller (1 Gigabit Ethernet)
Software loaded	Cisco IOS Software Release 12.0(10)S

Table 4-2 *Hardware and Software Device Characteristics for ISP2BB2 (Continued)*

ISP2BB2	Device Characteristics
Memory	Cisco 12008/GRP (R5000) processor (revision 0×01): 128 MB
IP addresses	Loopback0: J.2.0.202 255.255.255.255 ATM0/0.211 point-to-point: J.2.64.41 255.255.255.252 ATM0/0.213 point-to-point: J.2.64.49 255.255.255.252 ATM0/0.215 point-to-point: J.2.64.57 255.255.255.252 ATM0/0.217 point-to-point: J.2.64.65 255.255.255.252 ATM0/1.212 point-to-point: J.2.64.45 255.255.255.252 ATM0/1.214 point-to-point: J.2.64.53 255.255.255.252 ATM0/1.216 point-to-point: J.2.64.61 255.255.255.252 ATM0/1.218 point-to-point: J.2.64.69 255.255.255.252 POS1/0: J.2.0.2 255.255.255.252 POS2/0: J.2.0.2 255.255.255.252 POS3/0: J.2.0.21 255.255.255.252 POS4/0: J.2.0.25 255.255.255.252 GigabitEthernet6/0.230: J.2.7.1 255.255.255.248 GigabitEthernet6/0.240: J.2.8.1 255.255.255.0

Configuration File for ISP2BB2

ISP2BB2 is a core router for ISP2. BGP and MBGP internal peering is configured to all other routers in ISP2 except for Route Reflector clients. For multicast, the router is statically configured to use ISP2BB4 as its RP.

Example 4-2 displays the **show running-config** privileged EXEC command output for host ISP2BB2.

Example 4-2 *ISP2BB2 Configuration*

```
ISP2BB2#show running-config
version 12.0
no service pad
service timestamps debug datetime localtime show-timezone
service timestamps log datetime localtime show-timezone
no service password-encryption
service udp-small-servers
service tcp-small-servers
!
hostname ISP2BB2
!
enable password lab
!
clock timezone PDT -8
clock summer-time PDT recurring
redundancy
main-cpu
auto-sync startup-config
!
```

continues

Example 4-2 *ISP2BB2 Configuration (Continued)*

```
!
ip subnet-zero
no ip bootp server
no ip domain-lookup
ip multicast-routing distributed
ip multicast multipath
clns routing
!
!
interface Loopback0
 description Needed for BGP and ISIS
 ip address J.2.0.202 255.255.255.255
 no ip directed-broadcast
 ip pim sparse-mode
 ip router isis
 ip mroute-cache distributed
!
interface ATM0/0
 description To ISP2DASW1, 0/0/1
 no ip address
 no ip directed-broadcast
 no ip mroute-cache
 atm sonet stm-1
 atm pvc 16 0 16 ilmi
 no atm enable-ilmi-trap
 no atm ilmi-keepalive
!
interface ATM0/0.211 point-to-point
 description To ISP2DA1 2/0
 ip address J.2.64.41 255.255.255.252
 no ip directed-broadcast
 ip pim sparse-mode
 ip router isis
 atm pvc 211 0 211 aal5snap
 no atm enable-ilmi-trap
 isis metric 15 level-1
 isis hello-multiplier 12 level-1
 isis hello-interval 5 level-1
 isis retransmit-throttle-interval 250
 isis retransmit-interval 140
 isis lsp-interval 50
!
interface ATM0/0.213 point-to-point
 description To ISP2DA2 1/0
 ip address J.2.64.49 255.255.255.252
 no ip directed-broadcast
 ip pim sparse-mode
 ip router isis
 no atm enable-ilmi-trap
 isis metric 5 level-1
 isis hello-multiplier 12 level-1
 isis hello-interval 5 level-1
```

Example 4-2 *ISP2BB2 Configuration (Continued)*

```
   isis retransmit-throttle-interval 250
   isis retransmit-interval 140
   isis lsp-interval 50
 !
 interface ATM0/0.215 point-to-point
  description To ISP2DA3 0
  ip address J.2.64.57 255.255.255.252
  no ip directed-broadcast
  ip pim sparse-mode
  ip router isis
  atm pvc 215 0 215 aal5snap
  no atm enable-ilmi-trap
  isis metric 5 level-1
  isis hello-multiplier 12 level-1
  isis hello-interval 5 level-1
  isis retransmit-throttle-interval 250
  isis retransmit-interval 140
  isis lsp-interval 50
 !
 interface ATM0/0.217 point-to-point
  description To ISP2DA4 1/0
  ip address J.2.64.65 255.255.255.252
  no ip directed-broadcast
  ip pim sparse-mode
  ip router isis
  atm pvc 217 0 217 aal5snap
  no atm enable-ilmi-trap
  isis metric 5 level-1
  isis hello-multiplier 12 level-1
  isis hello-interval 5 level-1
  isis retransmit-throttle-interval 250
  isis retransmit-interval 140
  isis lsp-interval 50
 !
 interface ATM0/1
  description To ISP2DASW2, 0/0/1
  no ip address
  no ip directed-broadcast
  no ip mroute-cache
  atm sonet stm-1
  atm pvc 16 0 16 ilmi
  no atm enable-ilmi-trap
  no atm ilmi-keepalive
 !
 interface ATM0/1.212 point-to-point
  description To ISP2DA1 3/0
  ip address J.2.64.45 255.255.255.252
  no ip directed-broadcast
  ip pim sparse-mode
  ip router isis
  atm pvc 212 0 212 aal5snap
  no atm enable-ilmi-trap
```

continues

Example 4-2 *ISP2BB2 Configuration (Continued)*

```
 isis metric 15 level-1
 isis hello-multiplier 12 level-1
 isis hello-interval 5 level-1
 isis retransmit-throttle-interval 250
 isis retransmit-interval 140
 isis lsp-interval 50
!
interface ATM0/1.214 point-to-point
 description To ISP2DA2 2/0
 ip address J.2.64.53 255.255.255.252
 no ip directed-broadcast
 ip pim sparse-mode
 ip router isis
 atm pvc 214 0 214 aal5snap
 no atm enable-ilmi-trap
 isis metric 5 level-1
 isis hello-multiplier 12 level-1
 isis hello-interval 5 level-1
 isis retransmit-throttle-interval 250
 isis retransmit-interval 140
 isis lsp-interval 50
!
interface ATM0/1.216 point-to-point
 description To ISP2DA3
 ip address J.2.64.61 255.255.255.252
 no ip directed-broadcast
 ip pim sparse-mode
 ip router isis
 atm pvc 216 0 216 aal5snap
 no atm enable-ilmi-trap
 isis metric 5 level-1
 isis hello-multiplier 12 level-1
 isis hello-interval 5 level-1
 isis retransmit-throttle-interval 250
 isis retransmit-interval 140
 isis lsp-interval 50
!
interface ATM0/1.218 point-to-point
 description To ISP2DA4 2/0
 ip address J.2.64.69 255.255.255.252
 no ip directed-broadcast
 ip pim sparse-mode
 ip router isis
 atm pvc 218 0 218 aal5snap
 no atm enable-ilmi-trap
 isis metric 5 level-1
 isis hello-multiplier 12 level-1
 isis hello-interval 5 level-1
 isis retransmit-throttle-interval 250
 isis retransmit-interval 140
 isis lsp-interval 50
!
```

Example 4-2 *ISP2BB2 Configuration (Continued)*

```
interface POS1/0
 description TO ISP2BB1, POS 2/0
 ip address J.2.0.2 255.255.255.252
 no ip directed-broadcast
 ip pim sparse-mode
 ip router isis
 ip mroute-cache distributed
 load-interval 30
 crc 32
 clock source internal
 pos ais-shut
 aps working 1
!
interface POS2/0
 description TO ISP2BB1, POS 1/0
 ip address J.2.0.2 255.255.255.252
 no ip directed-broadcast
 ip pim sparse-mode
 ip router isis
 ip mroute-cache distributed
 load-interval 30
 crc 32
 clock source internal
 pos ais-shut
 aps revert 1
 aps protect 1 J.2.0.202
!
interface POS3/0
 description TO ISP2BB3, POS 2/0
 ip address J.2.0.21 255.255.255.252
 no ip directed-broadcast
 ip pim sparse-mode
 ip router isis
 ip mroute-cache distributed
 crc 32
 clock source internal
!
interface POS4/0
 description TO ISP2BB4, POS 2/0
 ip address J.2.0.25 255.255.255.252
 no ip directed-broadcast
 ip pim sparse-mode
 ip router isis
 ip mroute-cache distributed
 crc 32
 clock source internal
!
interface GigabitEthernet6/0
 no ip address
 no ip directed-broadcast
 load-interval 30
!
```

continues

Example 4-2 *ISP2BB2 Configuration (Continued)*

```
interface GigabitEthernet6/0.230
 description Client/Server
 encapsulation dot1Q 230
 ip address J.2.7.1 255.255.255.248
 no ip directed-broadcast
 ip pim sparse-mode
 ip router isis
!
interface GigabitEthernet6/0.240
 description OPEN
 encapsulation dot1Q 240
 ip address J.2.8.1 255.255.255.0
 no ip directed-broadcast
 ip pim sparse-mode
 ip router isis
!
router isis
 redistribute static ip metric 0 metric-type internal level-1
 net 49.0002.0000.0000.0002.00
 is-type level-1
!
router bgp 2
 no synchronization
 redistribute connected route-map connected-bgp
 neighbor ISP2INTERNAL peer-group nlri unicast multicast
 neighbor ISP2INTERNAL remote-as 2
 neighbor ISP2INTERNAL update-source Loopback0
 neighbor J.2.0.201 peer-group ISP2INTERNAL
 neighbor J.2.0.203 peer-group ISP2INTERNAL
 neighbor J.2.0.204 peer-group ISP2INTERNAL
 neighbor J.2.0.205 peer-group ISP2INTERNAL
 neighbor J.2.0.206 peer-group ISP2INTERNAL
 neighbor J.2.0.207 peer-group ISP2INTERNAL
 neighbor J.2.0.208 peer-group ISP2INTERNAL
 no auto-summary
!
no ip classless
ip route 191.3.0.0 255.255.0.0 J.2.0.208
ip route 191.4.0.0 255.255.0.0 J.2.0.208
ip pim rp-address J.2.0.124
!
logging trap emergencies
access-list 112 permit ip J.2.0.0 0.0.255.255 255.255.0.0 0.0.255.255
access-list 112 deny   ip any any
arp J.2.6.2 0010.8001.e240 ARPA
arp J.2.6.10 0010.8001.e248 ARPA
route-map connected-bgp permit 10
 match ip address 112
 set ip next-hop J.2.0.202
 set origin igp
!
snmp-server engineID local 00000009020000101F4544C0
```

Example 4-2 *ISP2BB2 Configuration (Continued)*

```
snmp-server community public RO
snmp-server community STSS RW
snmp-server contact sysadmin
snmp-server chassis-id ISP2BB2
!
!
line con 0
 exec-timeout 0 0
 login authentication NOTACACS
 transport input none
line aux 0
line vty 0 4
 exec-timeout 0 0
 password lab
 length 0
!
end
```

ISP2BB3

ISP2BB3 is a backbone router in ISP2. Figure 4-5 shows the topology of ISP2 and ISP2BB3's location in ISP2.

Figure 4-5 *ISP2BB3*

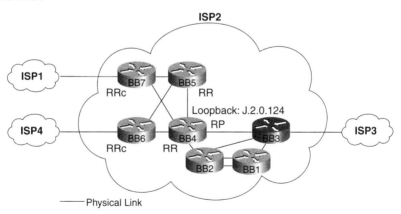

Device Characteristics for ISP2BB3

Table 4-3 lists the hardware and software device characteristics for ISP2BB3.

Table 4-3 *Hardware and Software Device Characteristics for ISP2BB3*

ISP2BB3	Device Characteristics
Host name	ISP2BB3
Chassis type	Cisco 12008 Gigabit Switch Router (GSR)
Physical interfaces	1 Ethernet/IEEE 802.3 1 Gigabit Ethernet/IEEE 802.3 7 Packet over SONET (POS)
Hardware components	Cisco 12008/GRP (R5000) processor (revision 0x01) 1 route processor card 1 clock scheduler card 3 switch fabric cards 1 four-port OC-3 POS controller (4 POS) 3 OC-48 POS E.D. controllers (3 POS) 1 single-port Gigabit Ethernet/IEEE 802.3z controller (1 Gigabit Ethernet)
Software loaded	Cisco IOS Software Release 12.0(10)S
Memory	Cisco 12008/GRP (R5000) processor (revision 0x01): 128 MB
IP addresses	Loopback0: J.2.0.203 255.255.255.255 POS0/0: J.2.0.245 255.255.255.252 POS0/1: J.2.182.1 255.255.255.240 POS0/2: J.2.192.1 255.255.255.240 POS1/0: J.2.0.14 255.255.255.252 POS2/0: J.2.0.22 255.255.255.252 POS4/0: J.2.0.33 255.255.255.252 GigabitEthernet6/0.310: J.2.9.1 255.255.255.0 GigabitEthernet6/0.330: J.2.11.1 255.255.255.248 GigabitEthernet6/0.340: J.2.12.1 255.255.255.0

Configuration File for ISP2BB3

ISP2BB3 is a core router for ISP2 and has an external connection to ISP3BB7. BGP and MBGP internal peering is configured to all other routers in ISP2 except for Route Reflector clients. ISP2BB3 also has an external BGP and MBGP peering to ISP3BB7. For multicast, the router is statically configured to use ISP2BB4 as its RP. Filters are set up on external AS connections to block administratively-scoped multicast and RP announce and discovery addresses.

Example 4-3 displays the **show running-config** privileged EXEC command output for host ISP2BB3.

Example 4-3 *ISP2BB3 Configuration*

```
ISP2BB3#show running-config
version 12.0
no service pad
service timestamps debug datetime localtime show-timezone
service timestamps log datetime localtime show-timezone
no service password-encryption
service udp-small-servers
service tcp-small-servers
!
hostname ISP2BB3
!
enable password lab
!
clock timezone PDT -8
clock summer-time PDT recurring
!
!
ip subnet-zero
no ip domain-lookup
ip multicast-routing distributed
clns routing
!
!
interface Loopback0
 ip address J.2.0.203 255.255.255.255
 no ip directed-broadcast
 ip pim sparse-mode
 ip router isis
 ip mroute-cache distributed
!
interface POS0/0
 description TO ISP3BB7, POS12/0/0
 ip address J.2.0.245 255.255.255.252
 no ip directed-broadcast
 ip pim bsr-border
 ip pim sparse-mode
 ip multicast boundary 1
 ip router isis
 ip mroute-cache distributed
 crc 16
 clock source internal
!
interface POS0/1
 ip address J.2.182.17 255.255.255.240 secondary
 ip address J.2.182.33 255.255.255.240 secondary
 ip address J.2.182.49 255.255.255.240 secondary
 ip address J.2.182.65 255.255.255.240 secondary
 ip address J.2.182.81 255.255.255.240 secondary
 ip address J.2.182.97 255.255.255.240 secondary
```

continues

Example 4-3 *ISP2BB3 Configuration (Continued)*

```
  ip address J.2.182.113 255.255.255.240 secondary
  ip address J.2.182.129 255.255.255.240 secondary
  ip address J.2.182.145 255.255.255.240 secondary
  ip address J.2.182.161 255.255.255.240 secondary
  ip address J.2.182.177 255.255.255.240 secondary
  ip address J.2.182.195 255.255.255.240 secondary
  ip address J.2.182.209 255.255.255.240 secondary
  ip address J.2.182.225 255.255.255.240 secondary
  ip address J.2.182.241 255.255.255.240 secondary
  ip address J.2.183.1 255.255.255.240 secondary
  ip address J.2.183.17 255.255.255.240 secondary
  ip address J.2.183.33 255.255.255.240 secondary
  ip address J.2.183.49 255.255.255.240 secondary
  ip address J.2.183.65 255.255.255.240 secondary
  ip address J.2.183.81 255.255.255.240 secondary
  ip address J.2.183.97 255.255.255.240 secondary
  ip address J.2.183.113 255.255.255.240 secondary
  ip address J.2.183.129 255.255.255.240 secondary
  ip address J.2.183.145 255.255.255.240 secondary
  ip address J.2.183.161 255.255.255.240 secondary
  ip address J.2.183.177 255.255.255.240 secondary
  ip address J.2.183.193 255.255.255.240 secondary
  ip address J.2.183.209 255.255.255.240 secondary
  ip address J.2.183.225 255.255.255.240 secondary
  ip address J.2.183.241 255.255.255.240 secondary
  ip address J.2.184.1 255.255.255.240 secondary
  ip address J.2.184.17 255.255.255.240 secondary
  ip address J.2.184.33 255.255.255.240 secondary
  ip address J.2.184.49 255.255.255.240 secondary
  ip address J.2.184.65 255.255.255.240 secondary
  ip address J.2.184.81 255.255.255.240 secondary
  ip address J.2.184.97 255.255.255.240 secondary
  ip address J.2.184.113 255.255.255.240 secondary
  ip address J.2.184.129 255.255.255.240 secondary
  ip address J.2.184.145 255.255.255.240 secondary
  ip address J.2.184.161 255.255.255.240 secondary
  ip address J.2.184.177 255.255.255.240 secondary
  ip address J.2.182.1 255.255.255.240
  no ip directed-broadcast
  ip router isis
  no ip mroute-cache
  no keepalive
  crc 16
  clock source internal
!
interface POS0/2
  ip address J.2.192.17 255.255.255.240 secondary
  ip address J.2.192.33 255.255.255.240 secondary
  ip address J.2.192.49 255.255.255.240 secondary
  ip address J.2.192.65 255.255.255.240 secondary
  ip address J.2.192.81 255.255.255.240 secondary
  ip address J.2.192.97 255.255.255.240 secondary
```

Example 4-3 *ISP2BB3 Configuration (Continued)*

```
  ip address J.2.192.113 255.255.255.240 secondary
  ip address J.2.192.129 255.255.255.240 secondary
  ip address J.2.192.145 255.255.255.240 secondary
  ip address J.2.192.161 255.255.255.240 secondary
  ip address J.2.192.177 255.255.255.240 secondary
  ip address J.2.192.195 255.255.255.240 secondary
  ip address J.2.192.209 255.255.255.240 secondary
  ip address J.2.192.225 255.255.255.240 secondary
  ip address J.2.192.241 255.255.255.240 secondary
  ip address J.2.193.1 255.255.255.240 secondary
  ip address J.2.193.17 255.255.255.240 secondary
  ip address J.2.193.33 255.255.255.240 secondary
  ip address J.2.193.49 255.255.255.240 secondary
  ip address J.2.193.65 255.255.255.240 secondary
  ip address J.2.193.81 255.255.255.240 secondary
  ip address J.2.193.97 255.255.255.240 secondary
  ip address J.2.193.113 255.255.255.240 secondary
  ip address J.2.193.129 255.255.255.240 secondary
  ip address J.2.193.145 255.255.255.240 secondary
  ip address J.2.193.161 255.255.255.240 secondary
  ip address J.2.193.177 255.255.255.240 secondary
  ip address J.2.193.193 255.255.255.240 secondary
  ip address J.2.193.209 255.255.255.240 secondary
  ip address J.2.193.225 255.255.255.240 secondary
  ip address J.2.193.241 255.255.255.240 secondary
  ip address J.2.194.1 255.255.255.240 secondary
  ip address J.2.194.17 255.255.255.240 secondary
  ip address J.2.194.33 255.255.255.240 secondary
  ip address J.2.194.49 255.255.255.240 secondary
  ip address J.2.194.65 255.255.255.240 secondary
  ip address J.2.194.81 255.255.255.240 secondary
  ip address J.2.194.97 255.255.255.240 secondary
  ip address J.2.194.113 255.255.255.240 secondary
  ip address J.2.194.129 255.255.255.240 secondary
   ip address J.2.194.145 255.255.255.240 secondary
  ip address J.2.194.161 255.255.255.240 secondary
  ip address J.2.194.177 255.255.255.240 secondary
  ip address J.2.192.1 255.255.255.240
  no ip directed-broadcast
  ip router isis
  no ip mroute-cache
  no keepalive
  crc 16
  clock source internal
 !
 interface POS1/0
  description TO ISP2BB1/0, POS 3/0
  ip address J.2.0.14 255.255.255.252
  no ip directed-broadcast
  ip pim sparse-mode
  ip router isis
  ip mroute-cache distributed
```

continues

Example 4-3 *ISP2BB3 Configuration (Continued)*

```
 load-interval 30
 crc 32
 clock source internal
!
interface POS2/0
 description TO ISP2BB2, POS3/0
 ip address J.2.0.22 255.255.255.252
 no ip directed-broadcast
 ip pim sparse-mode
 ip router isis
 ip mroute-cache distributed
 crc 32
 clock source internal
!
interface POS4/0
 description TO ISP2BB4, POS3/0
 ip address J.2.0.33 255.255.255.252
 no ip directed-broadcast
 ip pim sparse-mode
 ip router isis
 ip mroute-cache distributed
 crc 32
 clock source internal
!
interface GigabitEthernet6/0
 no ip address
 no ip directed-broadcast
!
interface GigabitEthernet6/0.310
 description RVT200
 encapsulation dot1Q 310
 ip address J.2.9.1 255.255.255.0
 no ip directed-broadcast
 ip router isis
!
interface GigabitEthernet6/0.330
 description To Client/Server
 encapsulation dot1Q 330
 ip address J.2.11.1 255.255.255.248
 no ip directed-broadcast
 ip pim sparse-mode
 ip router isis
 ip mrm test-sender
!
interface GigabitEthernet6/0.340
 description OPEN
 encapsulation dot1Q 340
 ip address J.2.12.1 255.255.255.0
 no ip directed-broadcast
 ip pim sparse-mode
 ip router isis
!
```

Example 4-3 *ISP2BB3 Configuration (Continued)*

```
router isis
 net 49.0002.0000.0000.0003.00
 is-type level-1
!
router bgp 2
 no synchronization
 redistribute connected route-map connected-bgp
 neighbor ISP2INTERNAL peer-group nlri unicast multicast
 neighbor ISP2INTERNAL remote-as 2
 neighbor ISP2INTERNAL update-source Loopback0
 neighbor ISP2ISP3PEER peer-group nlri unicast multicast
 neighbor ISP2ISP3PEER remote-as 3
 neighbor J.2.0.201 peer-group ISP2INTERNAL
 neighbor J.2.0.202 peer-group ISP2INTERNAL
 neighbor J.2.0.204 peer-group ISP2INTERNAL
 neighbor J.2.0.205 peer-group ISP2INTERNAL
 neighbor J.2.0.206 peer-group ISP2INTERNAL
 neighbor J.2.0.207 peer-group ISP2INTERNAL
 neighbor J.2.0.208 peer-group ISP2INTERNAL
 neighbor J.2.0.246 peer-group ISP2ISP3PEER
 no auto-summary
!
no ip classless
ip http server
ip http authentication local
ip pim rp-address J.2.0.124
!
ip mrm manager test1
 manager GigabitEthernet6/0.330 group 224.10.10.10
 senders 1
 senders 10
 receivers 20 sender-list 10
!
logging trap emergencies
access-list 1 deny    224.0.1.39
access-list 1 deny    224.0.1.40
access-list 1 deny    239.0.0.0 0.255.255.255
access-list 1 permit any
access-list 10 permit J.2.11.1
access-list 20 permit J.2.11.9
access-list 112 permit ip J.2.0.0 0.0.255.255 255.255.0.0 0.0.255.255
access-list 112 deny   ip any any
access-list 124 deny   ip any 229.0.0.0 0.255.255.255
access-list 124 deny   ip any 239.0.0.0 0.255.255.255
access-list 124 permit ip any any
arp J.2.10.10 0010.8001.e268 ARPA
arp J.2.10.2 0010.8001.e260 ARPA
route-map connected-bgp permit 10
 match ip address 112
 set ip next-hop J.2.0.203
 set origin igp
!
```

continues

Example 4-3 *ISP2BB3 Configuration (Continued)*

```
snmp-server engineID local 00000009020000101F453CC0
snmp-server community public RO
snmp-server community STSS RW
snmp-server contact sysadmin
snmp-server chassis-id ISP2BB3
!
!
line con 0
 exec-timeout 0 0
 login authentication NOTACACS
 transport input none
line aux 0
line vty 0 4
 exec-timeout 0 0
 password lab
!
end
```

ISP2BB4

ISP2BB4 is a backbone router in ISP2. Figure 4-6 shows the topology of ISP2 and ISP2BB4's location in ISP2.

Figure 4-6 *ISP2BB4*

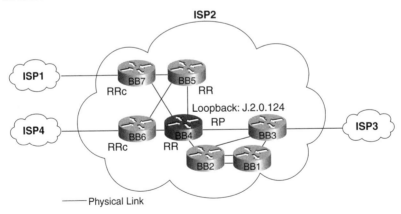

Device Characteristics for ISP2BB4

Table 4-4 lists the hardware and software device characteristics for ISP2BB4.

Table 4-4 *Hardware and Software Device Characteristics for ISP2BB4*

ISP2BB4	Device Characteristics
Host name	ISP2BB4
Chassis type	Cisco 12008 Gigabit Switch Router (GSR)
Physical interfaces	1 Ethernet/IEEE 802.3 1 Gigabit Ethernet/IEEE 802.3 6 Packet over SONET (POS)
Hardware components	Cisco 12008/GRP (R5000) processor (revision 0×01) 1 route processor card 1 clock scheduler card 3 switch fabric cards 4 OC-12 POS controllers (4 POS) 2 OC-48 POS E.D. controllers (2 POS) 1 single-port Gigabit Ethernet/IEEE 802.3z controller (1 Gigabit Ethernet)
Software loaded	Cisco IOS Software Release 12.0(10)S
Memory	Cisco 12008/GRP (R5000) processor (revision 0×01): 128 MB
IP addresses	Loopback0: J.2.0.204 255.255.255.255 Loopback1: J.2.0.124 255.255.255.255 POS0/0: J.2.0.49 255.255.255.252 POS2/0: J.2.0.26 255.255.255.252 POS3/0: J.2.0.34 255.255.255.252 GigabitEthernet4/0.421: J.2.14.9 255.255.255.248 GigabitEthernet4/0.440: J.2.14.1 255.255.255.0 POS5/0: J.2.0.41 255.255.255.252 POS6/0: J.2.0.45 255.255.255.252

Configuration File for ISP2BB4

ISP2BB4 is a core router for ISP2. BGP and MBGP internal peering is configured to all other routers in ISP2 and ISP2BB4 acts as a Route Reflector server to ISP2BB6 and ISP2BB7. For multicast, the router is configured to act as the RP for all of ISP2. Additionally, ISP2BB4 is configured to have MSDP external peering sessions with ISP1BB7, ISP3BB7, and ISP4BB3, with SA filters to block unwanted sources and prevent the unnecessary creation, forwarding, and caching of some well-known domain local sources.

Example 4-4 displays the **show running-config** privileged EXEC command output for host ISP2BB4.

Example 4-4 *ISP2BB4 Configuration*

```
ISP2BB4#show running-config
version 12.0
no service pad
service timestamps debug datetime localtime show-timezone
service timestamps log datetime localtime show-timezone
no service password-encryption
service udp-small-servers
service tcp-small-servers
!
hostname ISP2BB4
!
enable password lab
!
clock timezone PDT -8
clock summer-time PDT recurring
!
!
ip subnet-zero
no ip domain-lookup
ip multicast-routing distributed
clns routing
!
!
interface Loopback0
 ip address J.2.0.204 255.255.255.255
 no ip directed-broadcast
 ip pim sparse-mode
 ip router isis
 ip mroute-cache distributed
!
interface Loopback1
 ip address J.2.0.124 255.255.255.255
 no ip directed-broadcast
 ip pim sparse-mode
 ip router isis
 ip mroute-cache distributed
!
interface POS0/0
 description TO ISP2BB7, POS 4/0
 ip address J.2.0.49 255.255.255.252
 no ip directed-broadcast
 ip pim sparse-mode
 ip router isis
 ip mroute-cache distributed
 crc 32
 clock source internal
!
interface POS2/0
 description TO ISP2BB2, POS 4/0
```

Example 4-4 *ISP2BB4 Configuration (Continued)*

```
  ip address J.2.0.26 255.255.255.252
  no ip directed-broadcast
  ip pim sparse-mode
  ip router isis
  ip mroute-cache distributed
  crc 32
  clock source internal
 !
 interface POS3/0
  description TO ISP2BB3, POS 4/0
  ip address J.2.0.34 255.255.255.252
  no ip directed-broadcast
  ip pim sparse-mode
  ip router isis
  ip mroute-cache distributed
  crc 32
  clock source internal
 !
 interface GigabitEthernet4/0
  no ip address
  no ip directed-broadcast
 !
 interface GigabitEthernet4/0.430
  description To Client/Server
  encapsulation dot1Q 430
  ip address J.2.15.1 255.255.255.248
  no ip directed-broadcast
  ip pim sparse-mode
  ip router isis
 !
 interface GigabitEthernet4/0.440
  description OPEN
  encapsulation dot1Q 440
  ip address J.2.16.1 255.255.255.0
  no ip directed-broadcast
  ip pim sparse-mode
  ip router isis
 !
 interface POS5/0
  description TO ISP2BB5, POS 4/0
  ip address J.2.0.41 255.255.255.252
  no ip directed-broadcast
  ip pim sparse-mode
  ip router isis
  ip mroute-cache distributed
  crc 32
  clock source internal
 !
 interface POS6/0
  description TO ISP2BB6, POS 4/0
  ip address J.2.0.45 255.255.255.252
  no ip directed-broadcast
```

continues

Example 4-4 *ISP2BB4 Configuration (Continued)*

```
 ip pim sparse-mode
 ip router isis
 ip mroute-cache distributed
 crc 32
 clock source internal
!
router isis
 net 49.0002.0000.0000.0004.00
 is-type level-1
!
router bgp 2
 no synchronization
 redistribute connected route-map connected-bgp
 neighbor ISP2INTERNAL peer-group nlri unicast multicast
 neighbor ISP2INTERNAL remote-as 2
 neighbor ISP2INTERNAL update-source Loopback0
 neighbor J.2.0.201 peer-group ISP2INTERNAL
 neighbor J.2.0.202 peer-group ISP2INTERNAL
 neighbor J.2.0.203 peer-group ISP2INTERNAL
 neighbor J.2.0.205 peer-group ISP2INTERNAL
 neighbor J.2.0.206 peer-group ISP2INTERNAL
 neighbor J.2.0.207 peer-group ISP2INTERNAL
 neighbor J.2.0.208 peer-group ISP2INTERNAL
 no auto-summary
!
no ip classless
ip pim rp-address J.2.0.124
ip msdp peer J.1.0.207 connect-source Loopback0 remote-as 1
ip msdp sa-filter in J.1.0.207 list 124
ip msdp sa-filter out J.1.0.207 list 124
ip msdp peer J.4.0.203 connect-source Loopback0 remote-as 4
ip msdp sa-filter in J.4.0.203 list 124
ip msdp sa-filter out J.4.0.203 list 124
ip msdp peer J.3.0.207 connect-source Loopback0 remote-as 3
ip msdp sa-filter in J.3.0.207 list 124
ip msdp sa-filter out J.3.0.207 list 124
ip msdp cache-sa-state
!
logging trap emergencies
access-list 112 permit ip J.2.0.0 0.0.255.255 255.255.0.0 0.0.255.255
access-list 112 deny   ip any any
access-list 124 deny   ip any host 224.0.2.2
access-list 124 deny   ip any host 224.0.1.3
access-list 124 deny   ip any host 224.0.1.24
access-list 124 deny   ip any host 224.0.1.22
access-list 124 deny   ip any host 224.0.1.2
access-list 124 deny   ip any host 224.0.1.35
access-list 124 deny   ip any host 224.0.1.60
access-list 124 deny   ip any host 224.0.1.39
access-list 124 deny   ip any host 224.0.1.40
access-list 124 deny   ip any 239.0.0.0 0.255.255.255
access-list 124 deny   ip 10.0.0.0 0.255.255.255 any
```

Example 4-4 *ISP2BB4 Configuration (Continued)*

```
access-list 124 deny    ip 127.0.0.0 0.255.255.255 any
access-list 124 deny    ip 172.16.0.0 0.15.255.255 any
access-list 124 deny    ip K.168.0.0 0.0.255.255 any
access-list 124 permit ip any any
arp J.2.14.10 0010.8001.e288 ARPA
arp J.2.14.2 0010.8001.e280 ARPA
route-map connected-bgp permit 10
 match ip address 112
 set ip next-hop J.2.0.204
 set origin igp
!
snmp-server engineID local 00000009020000101F454080
snmp-server community public RO
snmp-server community STSS RW
snmp-server contact sysadmin
snmp-server chassis-id ISP2BB4
!
!
line con 0
 exec-timeout 0 0
 login authentication NOTACACS
 transport input none
line aux 0
line vty 0 4
 exec-timeout 0 0
 password lab
!
end
```

ISP2BB5 for Solutions Using MSDP

ISP2BB5 is a backbone router in ISP2. Figure 4-7 shows the topology of ISP2 and ISP2BB5's location in ISP2.

Figure 4-7 *ISP2BB5*

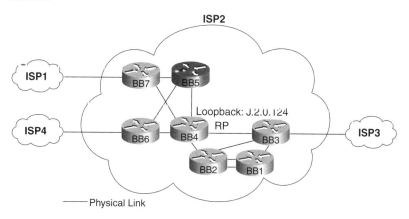

Device Characteristics for ISP2BB5

Table 4-5 lists the hardware and software device characteristics for ISP2BB5.

Table 4-5 *Hardware and Software Device Characteristics for ISP2BB5*

ISP2BB5	Device Characteristics
Host name	ISP2BB5
Chassis type	Cisco 12008 Gigabit Switch Router (GSR)
Physical interfaces	1 Ethernet/IEEE 802.3 1 Gigabit Ethernet/IEEE 802.3 6 Packet over SONET (POS)
Hardware components	Cisco 12008/GRP (R5000) processor (revision 0x01) 1 route processor card 1 clock scheduler card 3 switch fabric cards 6 OC-12 POS controllers (6 POS) 1 single-port Gigabit Ethernet/IEEE 802.3z controller (1 Gigabit Ethernet)
Software loaded	Cisco IOS Software Release 12.0(10)S
Memory	Cisco 12008/GRP (R5000) processor (revision 0x01): 128 MB
IP addresses	Loopback0: J.2.0.205 255.255.255.255 POS0/0: J.2.0.57 255.255.255.252 POS4/0: J.2.0.42 255.255.255.252 GigabitEthernet5/0.530: J.2.19.1 255.255.255.248 GigabitEthernet5/0.540: J.2.20.1 255.255.255.0 POS6/0: J.2.0.53 255.255.255.252

Configuration File for ISP2BB5

ISP2BB5 is a core router for ISP2. BGP and MBGP internal peering is configured to all other routers in ISP2 and acts as a Route Reflector server to ISP2BB6 and ISP2BB7. For multicast, the router is statically configured to use ISP2BB4 as its RP.

Example 4-5 displays the **show running-config** privileged EXEC command output for host ISP2BB5.

Example 4-5 *ISP2BB5 Configuration*

```
ISP2BB5#show running-config
version 12.0
no service pad
service timestamps debug datetime localtime show-timezone
service timestamps log datetime localtime show-timezone
```

Example 4-5 *ISP2BB5 Configuration (Continued)*

```
no service password-encryption
service udp-small-servers
service tcp-small-servers
!
hostname ISP2BB5
!
no logging console
enable password lab
!
clock timezone PDT -8
clock summer-time PDT recurring
!
!
ip subnet-zero
no ip domain-lookup
ip multicast-routing distributed
clns routing
!
!
interface Loopback0
 ip address J.2.0.205 255.255.255.255
 no ip directed-broadcast
 ip pim sparse-mode
 ip router isis
 ip mroute-cache distributed
!
interface POS0/0
 description TO ISP2BB7, POS 5/0
 ip address J.2.0.57 255.255.255.252
 no ip directed-broadcast
 ip pim sparse-mode
 ip router isis
 ip mroute-cache distributed
 crc 32
 clock source internal
!
interface POS4/0
 description TO ISP2BB4, POS 5/0
 ip address J.2.0.42 255.255.255.252
 no ip directed-broadcast
 ip pim sparse-mode
 ip router isis
 ip mroute-cache distributed
 crc 32
 clock source internal
!
interface GigabitEthernet5/0
 no ip address
 no ip directed-broadcast
!
interface GigabitEthernet5/0.530
 description To Client/Server
```

continues

Example 4-5 *ISP2BB5 Configuration (Continued)*

```
   encapsulation dot1Q 530
   ip address J.2.19.1 255.255.255.248
   no ip directed-broadcast
   ip pim sparse-mode
   ip router isis
  !
  interface GigabitEthernet5/0.540
   description TO BGPTool
   encapsulation dot1Q 540
   ip address J.2.20.1 255.255.255.0
   no ip directed-broadcast
   ip pim sparse-mode
   ip router isis
  !
  interface POS6/0
   description TO ISP2BB6, POS 5/0
   ip address J.2.0.53 255.255.255.252
   no ip directed-broadcast
   ip pim sparse-mode
   ip router isis
   ip mroute-cache distributed
   crc 32
   clock source internal
  !
  router isis
   net 49.0002.0000.0000.0005.00
   is-type level-1
  !
  router bgp 2
   no synchronization
   redistribute connected route-map connected-bgp
   neighbor ISP2INTERNAL peer-group nlri unicast multicast
   neighbor ISP2INTERNAL remote-as 2
   neighbor ISP2INTERNAL update-source Loopback0
   neighbor I2EBGP1 peer-group
   neighbor J.2.0.201 peer-group ISP2INTERNAL
   neighbor J.2.0.202 peer-group ISP2INTERNAL
   neighbor J.2.0.203 peer-group ISP2INTERNAL
   neighbor J.2.0.204 peer-group ISP2INTERNAL
   neighbor J.2.0.206 peer-group ISP2INTERNAL
   neighbor J.2.0.207 peer-group ISP2INTERNAL
   neighbor J.2.0.208 peer-group ISP2INTERNAL
   neighbor J.2.20.2 remote-as 200
   neighbor J.2.20.2 peer-group I2EBGP1
   neighbor J.2.20.3 remote-as 201
   neighbor J.2.20.3 peer-group I2EBGP1
   neighbor J.2.20.4 remote-as 202
   neighbor J.2.20.4 peer-group I2EBGP1
   neighbor J.2.20.5 remote-as 203
   neighbor J.2.20.5 peer-group I2EBGP1
   neighbor J.2.20.6 remote-as 204
   neighbor J.2.20.6 peer-group I2EBGP1
```

Example 4-5 *ISP2BB5 Configuration (Continued)*

```
neighbor J.2.20.7 remote-as 205
neighbor J.2.20.7 peer-group I2EBGP1
neighbor J.2.20.8 remote-as 206
neighbor J.2.20.8 peer-group I2EBGP1
neighbor J.2.20.9 remote-as 207
neighbor J.2.20.9 peer-group I2EBGP1
neighbor J.2.20.10 remote-as 208
neighbor J.2.20.10 peer-group I2EBGP1
neighbor J.2.20.11 remote-as 209
neighbor J.2.20.11 peer-group I2EBGP1
neighbor J.2.20.12 remote-as 210
neighbor J.2.20.12 peer-group I2EBGP1
neighbor J.2.20.13 remote-as 211
neighbor J.2.20.13 peer-group I2EBGP1
neighbor J.2.20.14 remote-as 212
neighbor J.2.20.14 peer-group I2EBGP1
neighbor J.2.20.15 remote-as 213
neighbor J.2.20.15 peer-group I2EBGP1
neighbor J.2.20.16 remote-as 214
neighbor J.2.20.16 peer-group I2EBGP1
neighbor J.2.20.17 remote-as 215
neighbor J.2.20.17 peer-group I2EBGP1
neighbor J.2.20.18 remote-as 216
neighbor J.2.20.18 peer-group I2EBGP1
neighbor J.2.20.19 remote-as 217
neighbor J.2.20.19 peer-group I2EBGP1
neighbor J.2.20.20 remote-as 218
neighbor J.2.20.20 peer-group I2EBGP1
neighbor J.2.20.21 remote-as 219
neighbor J.2.20.21 peer-group I2EBGP1
neighbor J.2.20.22 remote-as 220
neighbor J.2.20.22 peer-group I2EBGP1
neighbor J.2.20.23 remote-as 221
neighbor J.2.20.23 peer-group I2EBGP1
neighbor J.2.20.24 remote-as 222
neighbor J.2.20.24 peer-group I2EBGP1
neighbor J.2.20.25 remote-as 223
neighbor J.2.20.25 peer-group I2EBGP1
neighbor J.2.20.26 remote-as 224
neighbor J.2.20.26 peer-group I2EBGP1
neighbor J.2.20.27 remote-as 225
neighbor J.2.20.27 peer-group I2EBGP1
neighbor J.2.20.28 remote-as 226
neighbor J.2.20.28 peer-group I2EBGP1
neighbor J.2.20.29 remote-as 227
neighbor J.2.20.29 peer-group I2EBGP1
neighbor J.2.20.30 remote-as 228
neighbor J.2.20.30 peer-group I2EBGP1
neighbor J.2.20.31 remote-as 229
neighbor J.2.20.31 peer-group I2EBGP1
neighbor J.2.20.32 remote-as 230
neighbor J.2.20.32 peer-group I2EBGP1
```

continues

Example 4-5 *ISP2BB5 Configuration (Continued)*

```
 neighbor J.2.20.33 remote-as 231
 neighbor J.2.20.33 peer-group I2EBGP1
 neighbor J.2.20.100 remote-as 290
 neighbor J.2.20.100 peer-group I2EBGP1
 neighbor J.2.20.101 remote-as 291
 neighbor J.2.20.101 peer-group I2EBGP1
 no auto-summary
!
no ip classless
ip pim rp-address J.2.0.124
!
logging trap emergencies
access-list 112 permit ip J.2.0.0 0.0.255.255 255.255.0.0 0.0.255.255
access-list 112 deny   ip any any
arp J.2.18.2 0010.8001.e2a0 ARPA
arp J.2.18.10 0010.8001.e2a8 ARPA
route-map connected-bgp permit 10
 match ip address 112
 set ip next-hop J.2.0.205
 set origin igp
!
snmp-server engineID local 00000009020000101F4534A0
snmp-server community public RO
snmp-server community STSS RW
snmp-server contact sysadmin
snmp-server chassis-id ISP2BB5
!
!
line con 0
 exec-timeout 0 0
 login authentication NOTACACS
 transport input none
line aux 0
line vty 0 4
 exec-timeout 0 0
 password lab
!
end
```

ISP2BB6

ISP2BB6 is a backbone router in ISP2. Figure 4-8 shows the topology of ISP2 and ISP2BB6's location in ISP2.

Figure 4-8 *ISP2BB6*

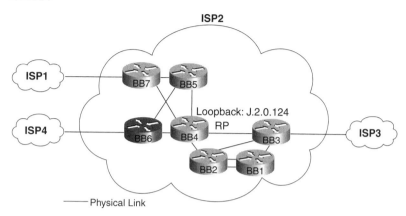

Device Characteristics for ISP2BB6

Table 4-6 lists the hardware and software device characteristics for ISP2BB6.

Table 4-6 *Hardware and Software Device Characteristics for ISP2BB6*

ISP2BB6	Device Characteristics
Host name	ISP2BB6
Chassis type	Cisco 12008 Gigabit Switch Router (GSR)
Physical interfaces	1 Ethernet/IEEE 802.3 1 Gigabit Ethernet/IEEE 802.3 7 Packet over SONET (POS)
Hardware components	Cisco 12008/GRP (R5000) processor (revision 0x01) 1 route processor card 1 clock scheduler card 3 switch fabric cards 1 four-port OC-3 POS controller (4 POS) 3 OC-12 POS controllers (3 POS) 1 single-port Gigabit Ethernet/IEEE 802.3z controller (1 Gigabit Ethernet)
Software loaded	Cisco IOS Software Release 12.0(10)S
Memory	Cisco 12008/GRP (R5000) processor (revision 0x01): 128 MB
IP addresses	Loopback0: J.2.0.206 255.255.255.255 POS0/0: J.2.0.249 255.255.255.252 POS4/0: J.2.0.46 255.255.255.252 POS5/0: J.2.0.54 255.255.255.252 GigabitEthernet6/0.630: J.2.23.1 255.255.255.248 GigabitEthernet6/0.640: J.2.24.1 255.255.255.0

Configuration File for ISP2BB6

ISP2BB6 is a core router for ISP2 and has an external connection to ISP4BB3. BGP and MBGP internal peering is only to the Route Reflector servers. BPG and MBGP external peering is with ISP4BB3. For multicast, the router is statically configured to use ISP2BB4 as its RP. Additionally, filters are set up on the external AS connections to block administratively-scoped multicast and RP announce and discovery addresses.

Example 4-6 displays the **show running-config** privileged EXEC command output for host ISP2BB6.

Example 4-6 *ISP2BB6 Configuration*

```
ISP2BB6#show running-config
version 12.0
no service pad
service timestamps debug datetime localtime show-timezone
service timestamps log datetime localtime show-timezone
no service password-encryption
service udp-small-servers
service tcp-small-servers
!
hostname ISP2BB6
!
no logging console
enable password lab
!
clock timezone PDT -8
clock summer-time PDT recurring
!
!
ip subnet-zero
no ip domain-lookup
ip multicast-routing distributed
clns routing
!
!
interface Loopback0
 ip address J.2.0.206 255.255.255.255
 no ip directed-broadcast
 ip pim sparse-mode
 ip router isis
 ip mroute-cache distributed
!
interface POS0/0
 description TO ISP4BB3, POS5/0/0
 ip address J.2.0.249 255.255.255.252
 no ip directed-broadcast
 ip pim bsr-border
 ip pim sparse-mode
 ip multicast boundary 1
 ip router isis
 ip mroute-cache distributed
 crc 16
 clock source internal
!
```

Example 4-6 *ISP2BB6 Configuration (Continued)*

```
interface POS4/0
 description TO ISP2BB4, POS 6/0
 ip address J.2.0.46 255.255.255.252
 no ip directed-broadcast
 ip pim sparse-mode
 ip router isis
 ip mroute-cache distributed
 crc 32
 clock source internal
!
interface POS5/0
 description TO ISP2BB5, POS6/0
 ip address J.2.0.54 255.255.255.252
 no ip directed-broadcast
 ip pim sparse-mode
 ip router isis
 ip mroute-cache distributed
 crc 32
 clock source internal
!
interface GigabitEthernet6/0
 no ip address
 no ip directed-broadcast
!
interface GigabitEthernet6/0.630
 description Client/Server
 encapsulation dot1Q 630
 ip address J.2.23.1 255.255.255.248
 no ip directed-broadcast
 ip pim sparse-mode
 ip router isis
!
interface GigabitEthernet6/0.640
 description OPEN
 encapsulation dot1Q 640
 ip address J.2.24.1 255.255.255.0
 no ip directed-broadcast
 ip pim sparse-mode
 ip router isis
!
router isis
 net 49.0002.0000.0000.0006.00
 is-type level-1
!
router bgp 2
 no synchronization
 redistribute connected route-map connected-bgp
 neighbor ISP2INTERNAL peer-group nlri unicast multicast
 neighbor ISP2INTERNAL remote-as 2
 neighbor ISP2INTERNAL update-source Loopback0
 neighbor ISP2ISP4PEER peer-group nlri unicast multicast
 neighbor ISP2ISP4PEER remote-as 4
 neighbor J.2.0.201 peer-group ISP2INTERNAL
```

continues

Example 4-6 *ISP2BB6 Configuration (Continued)*

```
    neighbor J.2.0.202 peer-group ISP2INTERNAL
    neighbor J.2.0.203 peer-group ISP2INTERNAL
    neighbor J.2.0.204 peer-group ISP2INTERNAL
    neighbor J.2.0.205 peer-group ISP2INTERNAL
    neighbor J.2.0.207 peer-group ISP2INTERNAL
    neighbor J.2.0.208 peer-group ISP2INTERNAL
    neighbor J.2.0.250 peer-group ISP2ISP4PEER
    no auto-summary
!
no ip classless
ip http server
ip http authentication local
ip pim rp-address J.2.0.124
!
logging trap emergencies
access-list 1 deny     224.0.1.39
access-list 1 deny     224.0.1.40
access-list 1 deny     239.0.0.0 0.255.255.255
access-list 1 permit any
access-list 112 permit ip J.2.0.0 0.0.255.255 255.255.0.0 0.0.255.255
access-list 112 deny   ip any any
access-list 124 deny   ip any 229.0.0.0 0.255.255.255
access-list 124 deny   ip any 239.0.0.0 0.255.255.255
access-list 124 permit ip any any
arp J.2.22.2 0010.8001.e300 ARPA
arp J.2.22.10 0010.8001.e308 ARPA
route-map connected-bgp permit 10
 match ip address 112
 set ip next-hop J.2.0.206
 set origin igp
!
snmp-server engineID local 00000009020000101F4548C0
snmp-server community public RO
snmp-server community STSS RW
snmp-server contact sysadmin
snmp-server chassis-id ISP2BB6
!
!
line con 0
 exec-timeout 0 0
 login authentication NOTACACS
 transport input none
line aux 0
line vty 0 4
 exec-timeout 0 0
 password lab
!
end
```

ISP2BB7 for Solutions Using MSDP

ISP2BB7 is a backbone router in ISP2. Figure 4-9 shows the topology of ISP2 and ISP2BB7's location in ISP2.

Figure 4-9 *ISP2BB7*

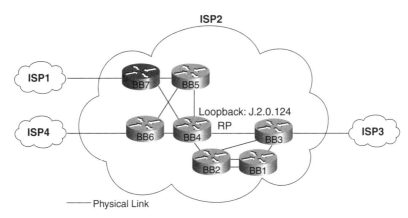

Device Characteristics for ISP2BB7

Table 4-7 lists the hardware and software device characteristics for ISP2BB7.

Table 4-7 *Hardware and Software Device Characteristics for ISP2BB7*

ISP2BB7	Device Characteristics
Host name	ISP2BB7
Chassis type	Cisco 12008 Gigabit Switch Router (GSR)
Physical interfaces	1 Ethernet/IEEE 802.3 1 Gigabit Ethernet/IEEE 802.3 7 Packet over SONET (POS)
Hardware components	Cisco 12008/GRP (R5000) processor (revision 0×01) 1 route processor card 1 clock scheduler card 3 switch fabric cards 1 four-port OC-3 POS controller (4 POS) 3 OC-12 POS controllers (3 POS) 1 single-port Gigabit Ethernet/IEEE 802.3z controller (1 Gigabit Ethernet)
Software loaded	Cisco IOS Software Release 12.0(10)S

continues

Table 4-7 *Hardware and Software Device Characteristics for ISP2BB7 (Continued)*

ISP2BB7	Device Characteristics
Memory	Cisco 12008/GRP (R5000) processor (revision 0×01): 128 MB
IP addresses	Loopback0: J.2.0.207 255.255.255.255 POS0/0: J.2.0.253 255.255.255.252 POS4/0: J.2.0.50 255.255.255.252 POS5/0: J.2.0.58 255.255.255.252 GigabitEthernet6/0.732: J.2.27.17 255.255.255.248 GigabitEthernet6/0.740: J.2.28.1 255.255.255.0

Configuration File for ISP2BB7

ISP1BB7 is a core router for ISP2 and has an external connection to ISP1BB7. BGP and MBGP internal peering is only to the Route Reflector servers. BGP and MBGP external peering is with ISP1BB7. For multicast, the router is statically configured to use ISP2BB4 as its RP. Filters are set up on the external AS connections to block administratively-scoped multicast and RP announce and discovery addresses. Example 4-7 displays the **show running-config** privileged EXEC command output for host ISP2BB7.

Example 4-7 *ISP2BB7 Configuration*

```
ISP2BB7#show running-config
version 12.0
no service pad
service timestamps debug datetime localtime show-timezone
service timestamps log datetime localtime show-timezone
no service password-encryption
service udp-small-servers
service tcp-small-servers
!
hostname ISP2BB7
!
no logging console
enable password lab
!
clock timezone PDT -8
clock summer-time PDT recurring
!
!
ip subnet-zero
no ip domain-lookup
ip multicast-routing distributed
clns routing
!
!
interface Loopback0
 ip address J.2.0.207 255.255.255.255
 no ip directed-broadcast
 ip pim sparse-mode
 ip router isis
```

Example 4-7 *ISP2BB7 Configuration (Continued)*

```
 ip mroute-cache distributed
!
interface POS0/0
 description TO ISP1BB7, POS9/0/0
 ip address J.2.0.253 255.255.255.252
 no ip directed-broadcast
 ip pim bsr-border
 ip pim sparse-mode
 ip multicast boundary 1
 ip router isis
 ip mroute-cache distributed
 crc 16
 clock source internal
!
interface POS4/0
 description TO ISP2BB4, POS 0/0
 ip address J.2.0.50 255.255.255.252
 no ip directed-broadcast
 ip pim sparse-mode
 ip router isis
 ip mroute-cache distributed
 crc 32
 clock source internal
!
interface POS5/0
 description TO ISP2BB5, POS 0/0
 ip address J.2.0.58 255.255.255.252
 no ip directed-broadcast
 ip pim sparse-mode
 ip router isis
 ip mroute-cache distributed
 crc 32
 clock source internal
!
interface GigabitEthernet6/0
 no ip address
 no ip directed-broadcast
 load-interval 30
!
interface GigabitEthernet6/0.730
 description Client/Server
 encapsulation dot1Q 730
 ip address J.2.27.1 255.255.255.248
 no ip directed-broadcast
 ip pim sparse-mode
 ip router isis
!
interface GigabitEthernet6/0.740
 description OPEN
 encapsulation dot1Q 740
 ip address J.2.28.1 255.255.255.0
 no ip directed-broadcast
```

continues

Example 4-7 *ISP2BB7 Configuration (Continued)*

```
 ip pim sparse-mode
 ip router isis
!
router isis
 net 49.0002.0000.0000.0007.00
 is-type level-1
!
router bgp 2
 no synchronization
 redistribute connected route-map connected-bgp
 neighbor ISP2INTERNAL peer-group nlri unicast multicast
 neighbor ISP2INTERNAL remote-as 2
 neighbor ISP2INTERNAL update-source Loopback0
 neighbor J.2.0.201 peer-group ISP2INTERNAL
 neighbor J.2.0.202 peer-group ISP2INTERNAL
 neighbor J.2.0.203 peer-group ISP2INTERNAL
 neighbor J.2.0.204 peer-group ISP2INTERNAL
 neighbor J.2.0.205 peer-group ISP2INTERNAL
 neighbor J.2.0.206 peer-group ISP2INTERNAL
 neighbor J.2.0.208 peer-group ISP2INTERNAL
 neighbor J.2.0.254 remote-as 1 nlri unicast multicast
!
no ip classless
ip pim rp-address J.2.0.124
!
logging trap emergencies
access-list 1 deny    224.0.1.39
access-list 1 deny    224.0.1.40
access-list 1 deny    239.0.0.0 0.255.255.255
access-list 1 permit any
access-list 112 permit ip J.2.0.0 0.0.255.255 255.255.0.0 0.0.255.255
access-list 112 deny   ip any any
access-list 124 deny   ip any 229.0.0.0 0.255.255.255
access-list 124 deny   ip any 239.0.0.0 0.255.255.255
access-list 124 permit ip any any
arp J.2.26.10 0010.8001.e328 ARPA
arp J.2.26.2 0010.8001.e320 ARPA
route-map connected-bgp permit 10
 match ip address 112
 set ip next-hop J.2.0.207
 set origin igp
!
snmp-server engineID local 00000009020000101F4538C0
snmp-server community public RO
snmp-server community STSS RW
snmp-server contact sysadmin
snmp-server chassis-id ISP2BB7
!
!
line con 0
 exec-timeout 0 0
```

Example 4-7 *ISP2BB7 Configuration (Continued)*

```
 login authentication NOTACACS
 transport input none
line aux 0
line vty 0 4
 exec-timeout 0 0
 password lab
!
end
```

This chapter includes the device characteristics and configuration files for the following host names in ISP3 and ISP4, as described in Chapter 2, "Implementing Interdomain Multicast Using MSDP":

- ISP3BB3
- ISP3BB4
- ISP3BB6
- ISP3BB7
- ISP4BB3
- ISP4BB4

CHAPTER 5

ISP3 and ISP4 Device Characteristics and Configuration Files

This chapter provides the device characteristics and configuration files for the devices associated with ISP3 and ISP4 as described in Chapter 2. Figure 5-1 and Figure 5-2 show the overall interdomain topology to which ISP3 and ISP4 belong. Figure 5-1 shows the MBGP peering sessions and Figure 5-2 shows the MSDP peering sessions established among the four ISPs in which interdomain multicast is being deployed.

Figure 5-1 *Overall Network Topology with MBGP Peering*

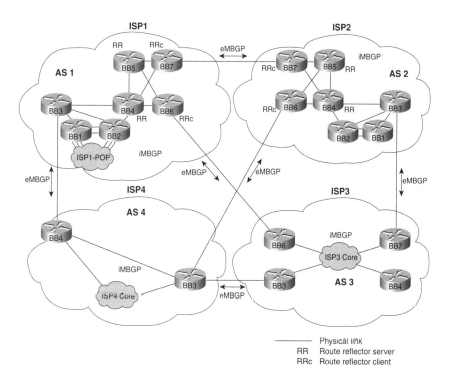

Figure 5-2 *Overall Network Topology with MSDP Peering*

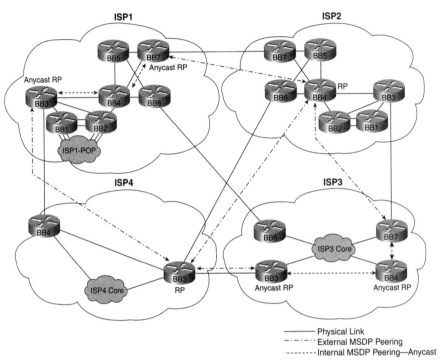

The multicast solutions in this document were tested with valid IP addresses. Normally, when a configuration file is published, the valid IP addresses are replaced with IP addresses, as specified in RFC 1918, "Address Allocation for Private Networks." Because the range of available IP addresses was insufficient to span the range of IP addresses used in this solution, the first octet of the valid IP addresses was replaced with a variable. In the example configurations provided in the following sections, the first octet of reserved IP addresses has been replaced with the letter J or the letter K for privacy reasons. The letter J always represents one unique number, and the letter K always represents a unique number that is different from J.

The example configurations are intended for illustrative purposes only. The letters J and K must be replaced with valid numbers when these IP addresses are configured in an actual network.

NOTE The example configurations provided in the following sections use highlighted text to indicate pertinent configuration commands used for deploying the IP multicast solutions described in this chapter.

ISP3BB3

ISP3BB3 is a backbone router in ISP3. Figure 5-3 shows the topology of ISP3 and ISP3BB3's location in ISP3.

Figure 5-3 *ISP3BB3*

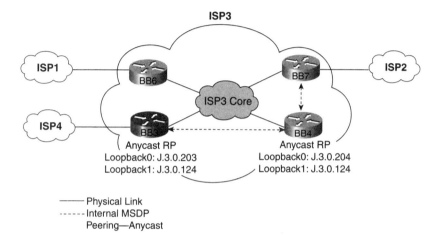

Device Characteristics for ISP3BB3

Table 5-1 lists the hardware and software device characteristics for ISP3BB3.

Table 5-1 *Hardware and Software Device Characteristics for ISP3BB3*

ISP3BB3	Device Characteristics
Host name	ISP3BB3
Chassis type	Cisco 7513 router
Physical interfaces	4 Ethernet/IEEE 802.3 1 Fast Ethernet/IEEE 802.3 1 FDDI 1 ATM 3 Packet over SONET (POS)
Hardware components	Cisco Route/Switch Processor Version 2 (RSP2) (R4700) 3 Versatile Interface Processor Version 2 (VIP2) controllers (4 Ethernet) (2 POS) 3 VIP2 R5K controllers (1 Fast Ethernet) (1 FDDI) (1 ATM) (1 POS)
Software loaded	Cisco IOS Release 12.0(11.5)S

continues

Table 5-1 *Hardware and Software Device Characteristics for ISP3BB3 (Continued)*

ISP3BB3	Device Characteristics
Memory	Cisco RSP2 (R4700) processor: 128 MB
IP addresses	Loopback0: J.3.0.203 255.255.255.255 Loopback1: J.3.0.124 255.255.255.255 Ethernet0/0/2: J.3.6.1 255.255.255.248 ATM1/0/0.113 point-to-point: J.3.0.6 255.255.255.252 ATM1/0/0.123 point-to-point: J.3.0.26 255.255.255.252 ATM1/0/0.134 point-to-point: J.3.0.45 255.255.255.252 ATM1/0/0.135 point-to-point: J.3.0.49 255.255.255.252 ATM1/0/0.136 point-to-point: J.3.0.53 255.255.255.252 ATM1/0/0.137 point-to-point: J.3.0.57 255.255.255.252 FastEthernet9/1/0: J.3.6.9 255.255.255.248 POS12/0/0: J.3.0.249 255.255.255.252

Configuration File for ISP3BB3

ISP3BB3 is a core router for ISP3 and has an external connection to ISP4BB3. BGP and MBGP internal peering is configured to all other routers in ISP3 except for Route Reflector clients. It also has an external BGP and MBGP peering to ISP4BB3. For multicast, ISP3BB3 is configured as one of the two anycast RPs in ISP3. ISP3BB3 is configured to have an MSDP internal peering session with ISP3BB4 and an external peering session with ISP4BB3, with Source Active (SA) filters to block unwanted sources and prevent the unnecessary creation, forwarding, and caching of some well-known domain local sources. Additional filters are set up on the external autonomous system (AS) connections to block administratively-scoped multicast and RP announce and discovery addresses.

Example 5-1 displays the **show running-config** privileged EXEC command output for host ISP3BB3.

Example 5-1 *ISP3BB3 Configuration*

```
ISP3BB3#show running-config
version 12.0
service timestamps debug datetime localtime show-timezone
service timestamps log datetime localtime show-timezone
no service password-encryption
service udp-small-servers
service tcp-small-servers
!
hostname ISP3BB3
!
logging buffered 1000000 debugging
no logging console
enable password lab
!
username cwuser privilege 15 password 0 cwuser
clock timezone PST -8
```

Example 5-1 *ISP3BB3 Configuration (Continued)*

```
clock summer-time PST recurring
ip subnet-zero
ip cef distributed
no ip domain-lookup
ip multicast-routing distributed
!
!
clns routing
!
!
interface Loopback0
 ip address J.3.0.203 255.255.255.255
 no ip directed-broadcast
!
interface Loopback1
 ip address J.3.0.124 255.255.255.255
 no ip directed-broadcast
 ip pim sparse-mode
!
interface Ethernet0/0/2
 description to ISP3BB3CL1
 ip address J.3.6.1 255.255.255.248
 no ip directed-broadcast
 ip route-cache distributed
 no cdp enable
!
interface ATM1/0/0
 description TO ISP3BPX2, 2.1
 no ip address
 no ip directed-broadcast
 ip route-cache distributed
 atm sonet stm-1
 atm pvc 16 0 16 ilmi
 no atm enable-ilmi-trap
 no atm ilmi-keepalive
!
interface ATM1/0/0.113 point-to-point
 description To ISP3BB1
 ip address J.3.0.6 255.255.255.252
 no ip redirects
 no ip directed-broadcast
 no ip proxy-arp
 ip pim sparse-mode
 atm pvc 113 0 113 aal5snap
 no atm enable-ilmi-trap
 tag-switching ip
!
interface ATM1/0/0.123 point-to-point
 description To ISP3BB2
 ip address J.3.0.26 255.255.255.252
 no ip redirects
 no ip directed-broadcast
```

continues

Example 5-1 *ISP3BB3 Configuration (Continued)*

```
 no ip proxy-arp
 ip pim sparse-mode
 atm pvc 123 0 123 aal5snap
 no atm enable-ilmi-trap
 tag-switching ip
!
interface ATM1/0/0.134 point-to-point
 description To ISP3BB4
 ip address J.3.0.45 255.255.255.252
 no ip redirects
 no ip directed-broadcast
 no ip proxy-arp
 ip pim sparse-mode
 atm pvc 134 0 134 aal5snap
 no atm enable-ilmi-trap
 tag-switching ip
!
interface ATM1/0/0.135 point-to-point
 description To ISP3BB5
 ip address J.3.0.49 255.255.255.252
 no ip redirects
 no ip directed-broadcast
 no ip proxy-arp
 ip pim sparse-mode
 atm pvc 135 0 135 aal5snap
 no atm enable-ilmi-trap
 tag-switching ip
!
interface ATM1/0/0.136 point-to-point
 description To ISP3BB6
 ip address J.3.0.53 255.255.255.252
 no ip redirects
 no ip directed-broadcast
 no ip proxy-arp
 ip pim sparse-mode
 atm pvc 136 0 136 aal5snap
 no atm enable-ilmi-trap
 tag-switching ip
!
interface ATM1/0/0.137 point-to-point
 description To ISP3BB7
 ip address J.3.0.57 255.255.255.252
 no ip redirects
 no ip directed-broadcast
 no ip proxy-arp
 ip pim sparse-mode
 atm pvc 137 0 137 aal5snap
 no atm enable-ilmi-trap
 tag-switching ip
!
interface POS12/0/0
 description To ISP4BB3, POS12/0/0
```

Example 5-1 *ISP3BB3 Configuration (Continued)*

```
  ip address J.3.0.249 255.255.255.252
  no ip directed-broadcast
  ip pim bsr-border
  ip pim sparse-mode
  ip multicast boundary 1
  ip route-cache distributed
  clock source internal
  pos scramble-atm
  pos flag c2 22
  no cdp enable
 !
 router ospf 3
 log-adjacency-changes
 network J.3.0.0 0.0.0.255 area 0
 network J.3.4.0 0.0.3.255 area 3
 maximum-paths 6
 !
 router bgp 3
 no synchronization
 redistribute connected route-map connected-bgp
 redistribute ospf 3
 neighbor ISP3INTERNAL peer-group nlri unicast multicast
 neighbor ISP3INTERNAL remote-as 3
 neighbor ISP3INTERNAL update-source Loopback0
 neighbor ISP3ISP4PEER peer-group nlri unicast multicast
 neighbor J.3.0.201 peer-group ISP3INTERNAL
 neighbor J.3.0.202 peer-group ISP3INTERNAL
 neighbor J.3.0.204 peer-group ISP3INTERNAL
 neighbor J.3.0.205 peer-group ISP3INTERNAL
 neighbor J.3.0.208 peer-group ISP3INTERNAL
 neighbor J.3.0.208 shutdown
 neighbor J.3.0.209 peer-group ISP3INTERNAL
 neighbor J.3.0.209 shutdown
 neighbor J.3.0.240 peer-group ISP3INTERNAL
 neighbor J.3.0.241 peer-group ISP3INTERNAL
 neighbor J.3.0.250 remote-as 4
 neighbor J.3.0.250 peer-group ISP3ISP4PEER
 no auto-summary
 !
 ip classless
 ip http server
 ip pim rp-address J.3.0.124
 ip pim accept-rp J.3.0.124
 ip pim send-rp-announce Loopback1 scope 8
 ip pim send-rp-discovery Loopback1 scope 8
 ip msdp peer J.3.0.250 connect-source Loopback0 remote-as 4
 ip msdp sa-filter in J.3.0.250 list 124
 ip msdp sa-filter out J.3.0.250 list 124
 ip msdp peer J.3.0.204 connect-source Loopback0 remote-as 3
 ip msdp cache-sa-state
 !
 access-list 1 deny     224.0.1.39
```

continues

Example 5-1 *ISP3BB3 Configuration (Continued)*

```
access-list 1 deny     224.0.1.40
access-list 1 deny     239.0.0.0 0.255.255.255
access-list 1 permit any
access-list 30 deny    223.255.240.0 0.0.15.255
access-list 30 permit any
access-list 112 permit ip J.3.0.0 0.0.255.255 255.255.0.0 0.0.255.255
access-list 112 deny   ip any any
access-list 124 deny   ip any host 224.0.2.2
access-list 124 deny   ip any host 224.0.1.3
access-list 124 deny   ip any host 224.0.1.24
access-list 124 deny   ip any host 224.0.1.22
access-list 124 deny   ip any host 224.0.1.2
access-list 124 deny   ip any host 224.0.1.35
access-list 124 deny   ip any host 224.0.1.60
access-list 124 deny   ip any host 224.0.1.39
access-list 124 deny   ip any host 224.0.1.40
access-list 124 deny   ip any 239.0.0.0 0.255.255.255
access-list 124 deny   ip 10.0.0.0 0.255.255.255 any
access-list 124 deny   ip 127.0.0.0 0.255.255.255 any
access-list 124 deny   ip 172.16.0.0 0.15.255.255 any
access-list 124 deny   ip K.168.0.0 0.0.255.255 any
access-list 124 permit ip any any
snmp-server engineID local 0000000902000010F6FB0000
snmp-server community public RO
snmp-server community STSS RW
no snmp-server ifindex persist
snmp-server packetsize 2048
snmp-server contact sysadmin
snmp-server chassis-id ISP3BB3
no cdp run
route-map connected-bgp permit 10
 match ip address 112
 set ip next-hop J.3.0.203
 set origin igp
!
route-map redis-ospf permit 10
 match ip address 30
!
!
alias exec int_desc show int | include Description
alias exec cpu show proc cpu | include CPU
alias exec mem show mem free | include Processor
!
line con 0
 exec-timeout 0 0
 login authentication NOTACACS
 transport input none
line aux 0
line vty 0 4
 exec-timeout 0 0
 password lab
!
end
```

ISP3BB4

ISP3BB4 is a backbone router in ISP3. Figure 5-4 shows the topology of ISP3 and ISP3BB4's location in ISP3.

Figure 5-4 *ISP3BB4*

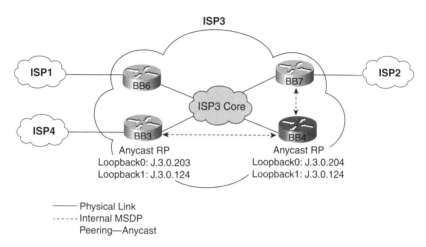

Device Characteristics for ISP3BB4

Table 5-2 lists the hardware and software device characteristics for ISP3BB4.

Table 5-2 *Hardware and Software Device Characteristics for ISP3BB4*

ISP3BB4	Device Characteristics
Host name	ISP3BB4
Chassis type	Cisco 7513 router
Physical interfaces	4 Ethernet/IEEE 802.3 1 ATM 1 Packet over SONET (POS)
Hardware components	Cisco RSP8 (R7000) processor 2 VIP2 controllers (4 Ethernet) (1 POS) 1 VIP2 R5K controllers (1 ATM)
Software loaded	Cisco IOS Release 12.0(11.5)S
Memory	Cisco RSP8 (R7000) processor: 256 MB

continues

Table 5-2 *Hardware and Software Device Characteristics for ISP3BB4 (Continued)*

ISP3BB4	Device Characteristics
IP addresses	Loopback0: J.3.0.204 255.255.255.255 Loopback1: J.3.0.124 255.255.255.255 Ethernet0/0/2: J.3.10.1 255.255.255.248 ATM1/0/0.114 point-to-point: J.3.0.10 255.255.255.252 ATM1/0/0.124 point-to-point: J.3.0.30 255.255.255.252 ATM1/0/0.134 point-to-point: J.3.0.46 255.255.255.252 ATM1/0/0.145 point-to-point: J.3.0.61 255.255.255.252 ATM1/0/0.146 point-to-point: J.3.0.65 255.255.255.252 ATM1/0/0.147 point-to-point: J.3.0.69 255.255.255.252

Configuration File for ISP3BB4

ISP3BB4 is a core router for ISP3. BGP and MBGP internal peering is configured to all other routers in ISP3 except for Route Reflector clients. For multicast, ISP3BB4 is configured as one of the two anycast RPs in ISP3. ISP3BB4 is also configured to have MSDP internal peering sessions with ISP3BB3 and ISP3BB7, with SA filters to block unwanted sources and prevent the unnecessary creation, forwarding, and caching of some well-known domain local sources. Additional filters are set up on the external AS connections to block administratively-scoped multicast and RP announce and discovery addresses.

Example 5-2 displays the show running-config privileged EXEC command output for host ISP3BB4.

Example 5-2 *ISP3BB4 Configuration*

```
ISP3BB4#show running-config
version 12.0
no service pad
service timestamps debug datetime localtime show-timezone
service timestamps log datetime localtime show-timezone
no service password-encryption
service udp-small-servers
service tcp-small-servers
!
hostname ISP3BB4
!
logging buffered 1000000 debugging
no logging console
enable password lab
!
clock timezone PST -8
clock summer-time PST recurring
ip subnet-zero
ip cef distributed
no ip domain-lookup
ip multicast-routing distributed
ip multicast multipath
!
```

Example 5-2 *ISP3BB4 Configuration (Continued)*

```
!
clns routing
!
!
interface Loopback0
 ip address J.3.0.204 255.255.255.255
 no ip directed-broadcast
 no ip route-cache
 no ip mroute-cache
!
interface Loopback1
 ip address J.3.0.124 255.255.255.255
 no ip directed-broadcast
 ip pim sparse-mode
 no ip route-cache
 no ip mroute-cache
!
interface Ethernet0/0/2
 description To ISP3DC
 ip address J.3.10.1 255.255.255.248
 no ip redirects
 no ip directed-broadcast
 ip pim sparse-mode
 ip route-cache distributed
!
interface ATM1/0/0
 description To ISP3BPX1, 2.4
 no ip address
 no ip directed-broadcast
 ip route-cache distributed
 atm sonet stm-1
 atm pvc 16 0 16 ilmi
 no atm enable-ilmi-trap
 no atm ilmi-keepalive
!
interface ATM1/0/0.114 point-to-point
 description To ISP3BB1
 ip address J.3.0.10 255.255.255.252
 no ip redirects
 no ip directed-broadcast
 no ip proxy-arp
 ip pim sparse-mode
 atm pvc 114 0 114 aal5snap
 no atm enable-ilmi-trap
 tag-switching ip
!
interface ATM1/0/0.124 point-to-point
 description To ISP3BB2
 ip address J.3.0.30 255.255.255.252
 no ip redirects
 no ip directed-broadcast
 no ip proxy-arp
 ip pim sparse-mode
 atm pvc 124 0 124 aal5snap
```

continues

Example 5-2 *ISP3BB4 Configuration (Continued)*

```
 no atm enable-ilmi-trap
 tag-switching ip
!
interface ATM1/0/0.134 point-to-point
 description To ISP3BB3
 ip address J.3.0.46 255.255.255.252
 no ip redirects
 no ip directed-broadcast
 no ip proxy-arp
 ip pim sparse-mode
 atm pvc 134 0 134 aal5snap
 no atm enable-ilmi-trap
 tag-switching ip
!
interface ATM1/0/0.145 point-to-point
 description To ISP3BB5
 ip address J.3.0.61 255.255.255.252
 no ip redirects
 no ip directed-broadcast
 no ip proxy-arp
 ip pim sparse-mode
 atm pvc 145 0 145 aal5snap
 no atm enable-ilmi-trap
 tag-switching ip
!
interface ATM1/0/0.146 point-to-point
 description To ISP3BB6
 ip address J.3.0.65 255.255.255.252
 no ip redirects
 no ip directed-broadcast
 no ip proxy-arp
 ip pim sparse-mode
 atm pvc 146 0 146 aal5snap
 no atm enable-ilmi-trap
 tag-switching ip
!
interface ATM1/0/0.147 point-to-point
 description To ISP3BB7
 ip address J.3.0.69 255.255.255.252
 no ip redirects
 no ip directed-broadcast
 no ip proxy-arp
 ip pim sparse-mode
 atm pvc 147 0 147 aal5snap
 no atm enable-ilmi-trap
 tag-switching ip
!
router ospf 3
 log-adjacency-changes
 network J.3.0.0 0.0.0.255 area 0
 network J.3.8.0 0.0.3.255 area 4
!
router isis
!
```

Example 5-2 *ISP3BB4 Configuration (Continued)*

```
router bgp 3
 no synchronization
 bgp cluster-id 3333
 redistribute connected route-map connected-bgp
 neighbor ISP3INTERNAL peer-group nlri unicast multicast
 neighbor ISP3INTERNAL remote-as 3
 neighbor ISP3INTERNAL update-source Loopback0
 neighbor J.3.0.201 peer-group ISP3INTERNAL
 neighbor J.3.0.202 peer-group ISP3INTERNAL
 neighbor J.3.0.203 peer-group ISP3INTERNAL
 neighbor J.3.0.205 peer-group ISP3INTERNAL
 neighbor J.3.0.206 remote-as 3
 neighbor J.3.0.206 update-source Loopback0
 neighbor J.3.0.206 route-reflector-client
 neighbor J.3.0.207 remote-as 3
 neighbor J.3.0.207 update-source Loopback0
 neighbor J.3.0.207 route-reflector-client
 neighbor J.3.0.208 peer-group ISP3INTERNAL
 neighbor J.3.0.208 shutdown
 neighbor J.3.0.209 peer-group ISP3INTERNAL
 neighbor J.3.0.209 shutdown
 neighbor J.3.0.240 peer-group ISP3INTERNAL
 neighbor J.3.0.241 peer-group ISP3INTERNAL
 no auto-summary
!
ip classless
ip pim rp-address J.3.0.124
ip pim accept-rp J.3.0.124
ip pim send-rp-announce Loopback1 scope 8
ip pim send-rp-discovery Loopback1 scope 8
ip msdp peer J.3.0.203 connect-source Loopback0
ip msdp peer J.3.0.207 connect-source Loopback0
ip msdp cache-sa-state
!
access-list 1 deny    224.0.1.39
access-list 1 deny    224.0.1.40
access-list 1 deny    239.0.0.0 0.255.255.255
access-list 1 permit any
access-list 30 deny   223.255.240.0 0.0.15.255
access-list 30 permit any
access-list 112 permit ip J.3.0.0 0.0.255.255 255.255.0.0 0.0.255.255
access-list 112 permit ip 209.1.0.0 0.0.255.255 255.255.0.0 0.0.255.255
access-list 112 deny   ip any any
access-list 124 deny   ip any 229.0.0.0 0.255.255.255
access-list 124 deny   ip any 239.0.0.0 0.255.255.255
access-list 124 permit ip any any
snmp-server engineID local 0000000902000010F6A40800
snmp-server community public RO
snmp-server community STSS RW
no snmp-server ifindex persist
snmp-server packetsize 2048
snmp-server contact sysadmin
snmp-server chassis-id ISP3BB4
```

continues

Example 5-2 *ISP3BB4 Configuration (Continued)*

```
route-map connected-bgp permit 10
 match ip address 112
 set ip next-hop J.3.0.204
 set origin igp
!
route-map redis-ospf permit 10
 match ip address 30
!
!
alias exec int_desc show int | include Description
alias exec cpu show proc cpu | include CPU
alias exec mem show mem free | include Processor
!
line con 0
 exec-timeout 0 0
 login authentication NOTACACS
 length 20
 transport input none
line aux 0
line vty 0 4
 exec-timeout 0 0
 password lab
 login authentication TACACS+
!
end
```

ISP3BB6

ISP3BB6 is a backbone router in ISP3. Figure 5-5 shows the topology of ISP3 and ISP3BB6's location in ISP3.

Figure 5-5 *ISP3BB6*

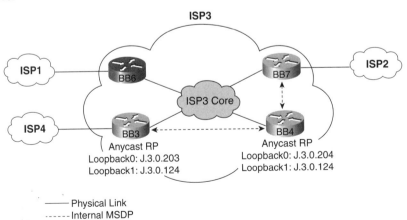

Device Characteristics for ISP3BB6

Table 5-3 lists the hardware and software device characteristics for ISP3BB6.

Table 5-3 *Hardware and Software Device Characteristics for ISP3BB6*

ISP3BB6	Device Characteristics
Host name	ISP3BB6
Chassis type	Cisco 7513 router
Physical interfaces	4 Ethernet/IEEE 802.3 1 Fast Ethernet/IEEE 802.3 22 Serial 2 ATM 3 Packet over SONET (POS)
Hardware components	Cisco RSP2 (R4700) processor 3 VIP2 controllers (4 Ethernet) 2 POS) 3 VIP2 R5K controllers (1 Fast Ethernet) (1 FDDI) (1 ATM) (1 POS)
Software loaded	Cisco IOS Release 12.0(11.5)S
Memory	Cisco RSP2 (R4700) processor: 128 MB
IP addresses	Loopback0: J.3.0.206 255.255.255.255 ATM1/0/0.116 point-to-point: J.3.0.18 255.255.255.252 ATM1/0/0.126 point-to-point: J.3.0.38 255.255.255.252 ATM1/0/0.136 point-to-point: J.3.0.54 255.255.255.252 ATM1/0/0.146 point-to-point: J.3.0.66 255.255.255.252 ATM1/0/0.156 point-to-point: J.3.0.74 255.255.255.252 ATM1/0/0.167 point-to-point: J.3.0.81 255.255.255.252 ATM8/0/0.267 point-to-point J.3.0.85 255.255.255.252 POS12/0/0: J.3.0.245 255.255.255.252

Configuration File for ISP3BB6

ISP3BB6, a core router for ISP3, has an external connection to ISP1BB6. BGP and MBGP internal peering is to only the Route Reflector servers. BGP and MBGP external peering is with ISP1BB6. For multicast, ISP3BB6 uses the anycast RP address of J.3.0.124 as its static RP address. Additional filters are set up on the external AS connections to block administratively-scoped multicast and RP announce and discovery addresses.

Example 5-3 displays the **show running-config** privileged EXEC command output for host ISP3BB6.

Example 5-3 *ISP3BB6 Configuration*

```
ISP3BB6#show running-config
version 12.0
service timestamps debug datetime localtime show-timezone
service timestamps log datetime localtime show-timezone
no service password-encryption
service udp-small-servers
service tcp-small-servers
!
hostname ISP3BB6
!
logging buffered 1000000 debugging
no logging console
enable password lab
!
clock timezone PST -8
clock summer-time PST recurring
ip subnet-zero
ip cef distributed
no ip domain-lookup
ip multicast-routing distributed
!
!
clns routing
!
!
controller T1 8/1/0
 clock source internal
 cablelength short 133
 channel-group 0 timeslots 1-24
!
controller T1 8/1/1
!
controller T1 8/1/2
!
controller T1 8/1/3
!
controller T1 8/1/4
!
controller T1 8/1/5
!
controller T1 8/1/6
!
controller T1 8/1/7
!
controller T1 9/0/0
 channel-group 0 timeslots 1-24
!
controller T1 9/0/1
!
```

Example 5-3 *ISP3BB6 Configuration (Continued)*

```
controller T1 9/0/2
!
controller T1 9/0/3
!
!
interface Loopback0
 ip address J.3.0.206 255.255.255.255
 no ip directed-broadcast
!
interface ATM1/0/0
 description To ISP3BPX1, 2.2
 no ip address
 no ip directed-broadcast
 ip route-cache distributed
 atm sonet stm-1
 atm pvc 16 0 16 ilmi
 no atm enable-ilmi-trap
 no atm ilmi-keepalive
!
interface ATM1/0/0.116 point-to-point
 description To ISP3BB1
 ip address J.3.0.18 255.255.255.252
 no ip redirects
 no ip directed-broadcast
 no ip proxy-arp
 ip pim sparse-mode
 no atm enable-ilmi-trap
 pvc BB1<-BB6 0/116
  encapsulation aal5snap
 !
 tag-switching ip
!
interface ATM1/0/0.126 point-to-point
 description To ISP3BB2
 ip address J.3.0.38 255.255.255.252
 no ip redirects
 no ip directed-broadcast
 no ip proxy-arp
 ip pim sparse-mode
 no atm enable-ilmi-trap
 pvc BB2<-BB6 0/126
  encapsulation aal5snap
 !
 tag-switching ip
!
interface ATM1/0/0.136 point-to-point
 description To ISP3BB3
 ip address J.3.0.54 255.255.255.252
 no ip redirects
 no ip directed-broadcast
 no ip proxy-arp
 ip pim sparse-mode
```

continues

Example 5-3 *ISP3BB6 Configuration (Continued)*

```
 no atm enable-ilmi-trap
 pvc BB3<-BB6 0/136
  encapsulation aal5snap
 !
 tag-switching ip
!
interface ATM1/0/0.146 point-to-point
 description To ISP3BB4
 ip address J.3.0.66 255.255.255.252
 no ip redirects
 no ip directed-broadcast
 no ip proxy-arp
 ip pim sparse-mode
 no atm enable-ilmi-trap
 pvc BB4<-BB6 0/146
  encapsulation aal5snap
 !
 tag-switching ip
!
interface ATM1/0/0.156 point-to-point
 description To ISP3BB5
 ip address J.3.0.74 255.255.255.252
 no ip redirects
 no ip directed-broadcast
 no ip proxy-arp
 ip pim sparse-mode
 no atm enable-ilmi-trap
 pvc BB5<-BB6 0/156
  encapsulation aal5snap
 !
 tag-switching ip
!
interface ATM1/0/0.167 point-to-point
 description To ISP3BB7
 ip address J.3.0.81 255.255.255.252
 no ip redirects
 no ip directed-broadcast
 no ip proxy-arp
 ip pim sparse-mode
 no atm enable-ilmi-trap
 pvc BB6<-BB7 0/167
  encapsulation aal5snap
 !
 tag-switching ip
!
interface ATM8/0/0
 description To ISP3BPX1, 10.1
 no ip address
 no ip directed-broadcast
 ip route-cache distributed
 load-interval 60
 atm pvc 16 0 16 ilmi
```

Example 5-3 *ISP3BB6 Configuration (Continued)*

```
  no atm enable-ilmi-trap
  no atm ilmi-keepalive
 !
 interface ATM8/0/0.267 point-to-point
  description To ISP3BB6
  ip address J.3.0.85 255.255.255.252
  no ip redirects
  no ip directed-broadcast
  no ip proxy-arp
  ip pim sparse-mode
  no atm enable-ilmi-trap
  pvc PARISPVC 0/267
   vbr-nrt 34000 1000 1000
   encapsulation aal5snap
  !
 !
 interface POS12/0/0
  description TO ISP1BB6, POS9/0/0
  ip address J.3.0.245 255.255.255.252
  no ip directed-broadcast
  ip pim bsr-border
  ip pim sparse-mode
  ip multicast boundary 1
  ip route-cache distributed
  ip mroute-cache distributed
  clock source internal
  pos scramble-atm
  pos flag c2 22
  no cdp enable
 !
 router ospf 3
  log-adjacency-changes
  network J.3.0.0 0.0.0.255 area 0
  network J.3.16.0 0.0.3.255 area 6
  maximum-paths 6
 !
 router bgp 3
  no synchronization
  redistribute connected route-map connected-bgp
  neighbor ISP3ISP1PEER peer-group nlri unicast multicast
  neighbor ISP3ISP1PEER remote-as 1
  neighbor J.3.0.204 remote-as 3 nlri unicast multicast
  neighbor J.3.0.204 update-source Loopback0
  neighbor J.3.0.205 remote-as 3 nlri unicast multicast
  neighbor J.3.0.205 update-source Loopback0
  neighbor J.3.0.246 peer-group ISP3ISP1PEER
  no auto-summary
 !
 ip classless
 ip route J.3.21.4 255.255.255.252 ATM8/0/0.267
 ip route J.3.22.8 255.255.255.248 ATM8/0/0.267
 ip pim rp-address J.3.0.124
```

continues

Example 5-3 *ISP3BB6 Configuration (Continued)*

```
ip pim accept-rp J.3.0.124
!
!
vc-class atm BackBone-PVCs
  abr 49862 24931
  encapsulation aal5snap
access-list 1 deny    224.0.1.39
access-list 1 deny    224.0.1.40
access-list 1 deny    239.0.0.0 0.255.255.255
access-list 1 permit any
access-list 30 deny    223.255.240.0 0.0.15.255
access-list 30 permit any
access-list 112 permit ip J.3.0.0 0.0.255.255 255.255.0.0 0.0.255.255
access-list 112 deny    ip any any
access-list 124 deny    ip any 229.0.0.0 0.255.255.255
access-list 124 deny    ip any 239.0.0.0 0.255.255.255
access-list 124 permit ip any any
snmp-server engineID local 0000000902000010F6A37800
snmp-server community public RO
snmp-server community RW RO
snmp-server community STSS RW
no snmp-server ifindex persist
snmp-server packetsize 2048
no cdp run
route-map connected-bgp permit 10
 match ip address 112
 set ip next-hop J.3.0.206
 set origin igp
!
route-map redis-ospf permit 10
 match ip address 30
!
!
alias exec int_desc show int | include Description
alias exec cpu show proc cpu | include CPU
alias exec mem show mem free | include Processor
!
line con 0
 exec-timeout 0 0
 login authentication NOTACACS
 transport input none
line aux 0
line vty 0 4
 exec-timeout 0 0
 password lab
!
end
```

ISP3BB7

ISP3BB7 is a backbone router in ISP3. Figure 5-6 shows the topology of ISP3 and ISP3BB7's location in ISP3.

Figure 5-6 *ISP3BB7*

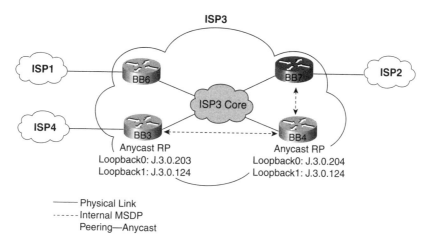

Device Characteristics for ISP3BB7

Table 5-4 lists the hardware and software device characteristics for ISP3BB7.

Table 5-4 *Hardware and Software Device Characteristics for ISP3BB7*

ISP3BB7	Device Characteristics
Host name	ISP3BB7
Chassis type	Cisco 7513 router
Physical interfaces	4 Ethernet/IEEE 802.3 2 Fast Ethernet/IEEE 802.3 1 ATM 3 Packet over SONET (POS)
Hardware components	Cisco RSP4 (R5000) processor 5 VIP2 controllers (2 Fast Ethernet) (4 Ethernet) (3 POS) 2 VIP2 R5K controllers (2 ATM)
Software loaded	Cisco IOS Release 12.0(11.5)S

continues

Table 5-4 *Hardware and Software Device Characteristics for ISP3BB7 (Continued)*

ISP3BB7	Device Characteristics
Memory	Cisco RSP4 (R5000) processor: 128 MB
IP addresses	Loopback0: J.3.0.207 255.255.255.255 Ethernet0/0/0: J.3.20.1 255.255.255.0 Ethernet0/0/2: J.3.22.1 255.255.255.248 Ethernet0/0/3: J.3.22.25 255.255.255.248 ATM1/0/0.117 point-to-point: J.3.0.22 255.255.255.252 ATM1/0/0.127 point-to-point: J.3.0.42 255.255.255.252 ATM1/0/0.137 point-to-point: J.3.0.58 255.255.255.252 ATM1/0/0.147 point-to-point: J.3.0.70 255.255.255.252 ATM1/0/0.157 point-to-point: J.3.0.78 255.255.255.252 ATM1/0/0.167 point-to-point: J.3.0.82 255.255.255.252 ATM8/0/0.267 point-to-point: J.3.0.86 255.255.255.252 POS12/0/0: J.2.0.246 255.255.255.252

Configuration File for ISP3BB7

ISP3BB7, a core router for ISP3, has an external connection to ISP2BB3. BGP and MBGP internal peering is to only the Route Reflector servers. BGP and MBGP external peering is with ISP2BB3. For multicast, ISP3BB7 uses the anycast RP address of J.3.0.124 as its static RP address. It is also configured to have an MSDP internal peering session with ISP3BB4 and an external peering session with ISP2BB3, with SA filters to block unwanted sources and prevent the unnecessary creation, forwarding, and caching of some well-known domain local sources.

Example 5-4 displays the **show running-config** privileged EXEC command output for host ISP3BB7.

Example 5-4 *ISP3BB7 Configuration*

```
ISP3BB7#show running-config
version 12.0
service timestamps debug datetime localtime show-timezone
service timestamps log datetime localtime show-timezone
no service password-encryption
service udp-small-servers
service tcp-small-servers
!
hostname ISP3BB7
!
logging buffered 1000000 debugging
no logging console
enable password lab
!
clock timezone PST -8
clock summer-time PST recurring
ip subnet-zero
ip cef distributed
```

Example 5-4 *ISP3BB7 Configuration (Continued)*

```
no ip domain-lookup
ip multicast-routing distributed
!
!
clns routing
!
!
interface Loopback0
 ip address J.3.0.207 255.255.255.255
 no ip directed-broadcast
 ip pim sparse-mode
!
interface Ethernet0/0/0
 description To RVT300, E7
 ip address J.3.20.1 255.255.255.0
 no ip directed-broadcast
 ip route-cache distributed
!
interface Ethernet0/0/2
 description To ISP3BB7CL1
 ip address J.3.22.1 255.255.255.248
 no ip directed-broadcast
 ip pim sparse-mode
 ip route-cache distributed
!
interface Ethernet0/0/3
 description To ISP3LINUX, MGEN
 ip address J.3.23.1 255.255.255.0 secondary
 ip address J.3.22.25 255.255.255.248
 no ip directed-broadcast
 ip pim sparse-mode
 ip route-cache distributed
 ip mroute-cache distributed
!
interface ATM1/0/0
 description TO ISP3BPX1, 2.1
 no ip address
 no ip directed-broadcast
 ip route-cache distributed
 load-interval 60
 atm sonet stm-1
 atm pvc 16 0 16 ilmi
 no atm enable-ilmi-trap
 no atm ilmi-keepalive
!
interface ATM1/0/0.117 point-to-point
 description To ISP3BB1
 ip address J.3.0.22 255.255.255.252
 no ip redirects
 no ip directed-broadcast
 no ip proxy-arp
 ip pim sparse-mode
 no atm enable-ilmi-trap
 pvc 0/117
```

continues

Example 5-4 *ISP3BB7 Configuration (Continued)*

```
  class-vc BackBone-PVCs
 !
 tag-switching ip
 !
 interface ATM1/0/0.127 point-to-point
  description To ISP3BB2
  ip address J.3.0.42 255.255.255.252
  no ip redirects
  no ip directed-broadcast
  no ip proxy-arp
  ip pim sparse-mode
  no atm enable-ilmi-trap
  pvc 0/127
   class-vc BackBone-PVCs
 !
 tag-switching ip
 !
 interface ATM1/0/0.137 point-to-point
  description To ISP3BB3
  ip address J.3.0.58 255.255.255.252
  no ip redirects
  no ip directed-broadcast
  no ip proxy-arp
  ip pim sparse-mode
  no atm enable-ilmi-trap
  pvc 0/137
   class-vc BackBone-PVCs
 !
 tag-switching ip
 !
 interface ATM1/0/0.147 point-to-point
  description To ISP3BB4
  ip address J.3.0.70 255.255.255.252
  no ip redirects
  no ip directed-broadcast
  no ip proxy-arp
  ip pim sparse-mode
  no atm enable-ilmi-trap
  pvc 0/147
   class-vc BackBone-PVCs
 !
 tag-switching ip
 !
 interface ATM1/0/0.157 point-to-point
  description To ISP3BB5
  ip address J.3.0.78 255.255.255.252
  no ip redirects
  no ip directed-broadcast
  no ip proxy-arp
  ip pim sparse-mode
  no atm enable-ilmi-trap
  pvc 0/157
   class-vc BackBone-PVCs
```

Example 5-4 *ISP3BB7 Configuration (Continued)*

```
!
tag-switching ip
!
interface ATM1/0/0.167 point-to-point
 description To ISP3BB6
 ip address J.3.0.82 255.255.255.252
 no ip redirects
 no ip directed-broadcast
 no ip proxy-arp
 ip pim sparse-mode
 no atm enable-ilmi-trap
 pvc 0/167
  class-vc BackBone-PVCs
!
tag-switching ip
!
interface ATM8/0/0
 description To ISP3BPX1, 9.1
 no ip address
 no ip directed-broadcast
 ip route-cache distributed
 load-interval 60
 atm framing cbitplcp
 atm pvc 16 0 16 ilmi
 no atm enable-ilmi-trap
 no atm ilmi-keepalive
!
interface ATM8/0/0.267 point-to-point
 description To ISP3BB7
 ip address J.3.0.86 255.255.255.252
 no ip redirects
 no ip directed-broadcast
 no ip proxy-arp
 ip pim sparse-mode
 no atm enable-ilmi-trap
 pvc PARISPVC 0/267
  vbr-nrt 34000 1000 1000
  encapsulation aal5snap
!
interface POS12/0/0
 description TO ISP2BB3, POS 0/0
 ip address J.2.0.246 255.255.255.252
 no ip directed-broadcast
 ip pim bsr-border
 ip pim sparse-mode
 ip multicast boundary 1
 ip route-cache distributed
 ip mroute-cache distributed
 clock source internal
!
router ospf 3
 log-adjacency-changes
 network J.3.0.0 0.0.0.255 area 0
```

continues

Example 5-4 *ISP3BB7 Configuration (Continued)*

```
 network J.3.20.0 0.0.3.255 area 7
!
router bgp 3
 no synchronization
 redistribute connected route-map connected-bgp
 neighbor ISP3ISP2PEER peer-group nlri unicast multicast
 neighbor ISP3ISP2PEER remote-as 2
 neighbor J.2.0.245 peer-group ISP3ISP2PEER
 neighbor J.3.0.204 remote-as 3 nlri unicast multicast
 neighbor J.3.0.204 update-source Loopback0
 neighbor J.3.0.205 remote-as 3 nlri unicast multicast
 neighbor J.3.0.205 update-source Loopback0
 no auto-summary
!
ip classless
ip route J.3.17.4 255.255.255.252 ATM8/0/0.267
ip route J.3.18.8 255.255.255.248 ATM8/0/0.267
ip route J.3.73.8 255.255.255.248 ATM1/0/0.127
ip pim rp-address J.3.0.124
ip msdp peer J.3.0.204 connect-source Loopback0
ip msdp peer J.2.0.204 connect-source Loopback0 remote-as 2
ip msdp sa-filter in J.2.0.204 list 124
ip msdp sa-filter out J.2.0.204 list 124
ip msdp cache-sa-state
ip msdp originator-id Loopback0
!
!
vc-class atm BackBone-PVCs
   abr 49862 24931
   encapsulation aal5snap
access-list 1 deny    224.0.1.39
access-list 1 deny    224.0.1.40
access-list 1 deny    239.0.0.0 0.255.255.255
access-list 1 permit any
access-list 30 deny   223.255.240.0 0.0.15.255
access-list 30 permit any
access-list 112 permit ip J.3.0.0 0.0.255.255 255.255.0.0 0.0.255.255
access-list 112 permit ip host J.2.0.245 host 0.0.0.0
access-list 112 deny   ip any any
access-list 124 deny   ip any host 224.0.2.2
access-list 124 deny   ip any host 224.0.1.3
access-list 124 deny   ip any host 224.0.1.24
access-list 124 deny   ip any host 224.0.1.22
access-list 124 deny   ip any host 224.0.1.2
access-list 124 deny   ip any host 224.0.1.35
access-list 124 deny   ip any host 224.0.1.60
access-list 124 deny   ip any host 224.0.1.39
access-list 124 deny   ip any host 224.0.1.40
access-list 124 deny   ip any 239.0.0.0 0.255.255.255
access-list 124 deny   ip 10.0.0.0 0.255.255.255 any
access-list 124 deny   ip 127.0.0.0 0.255.255.255 any
access-list 124 deny   ip 172.16.0.0 0.15.255.255 any
access-list 124 deny   ip K.168.0.0 0.0.255.255 any
access-list 124 permit ip any any
```

Example 5-4 *ISP3BB7 Configuration (Continued)*

```
snmp-server engineID local 00000009020000801CACF800
snmp-server community public RO
snmp-server community STSS RW
no snmp-server ifindex persist
snmp-server packetsize 2048
route-map connected-bgp permit 10
 match ip address 112
 set ip next-hop J.3.0.207
 set origin igp
!
route-map redis-ospf permit 10
 match ip address 30
!
!
alias exec int_desc show int | include Description
alias exec cpu show proc cpu | include CPU
alias exec mem show mem free | include Processor
!
line con 0
 exec-timeout 0 0
 login authentication NOTACACS
 transport input none
line aux 0
line vty 0 4
 exec-timeout 0 0
 password lab
!
end
```

ISP4BB3

ISP4BB3 is a backbone router in ISP4. Figure 5-7 shows the topology of ISP4 and ISP4BB3's location in ISP4.

Figure 5-7 *ISP4BB3*

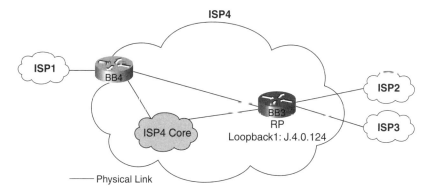

Device Characteristics for ISP4BB3

Table 5-5 lists the hardware and software device characteristics for ISP4BB3.

Table 5-5 *Hardware and Software Device Characteristics for ISP4BB3*

ISP4BB3	Device Characteristics
Host name	ISP4BB3
Chassis type	Cisco 7513 router
Physical interfaces	12 Ethernet/IEEE 802.3 1 Fast Ethernet/IEEE 802.3 4 High-Speed Serial Interface (HSSI) 1 FDDI 3 Packet over SONET (POS)
Hardware components	Cisco RSP4 (R5000) processor 3 VIP2 controllers (3 POS) 3 VIP2 R5K controllers (1 Fast Ethernet) (12 Ethernet) (4 HSSI) (1 FDDI)
Software loaded	Cisco IOS Release 12.0(11.5)S
Memory	Cisco RSP4 (R5000) processor: 256 MB
IP addresses	Loopback0: J.4.0.203 255.255.255.255 Loopback1: J.4.0.124 255.255.255.255 Ethernet0/0/2: J.4.6.1 255.255.255.248 Ethernet0/0/3: J.4.7.129 255.255.255.128 Hssi2/0/0: J.4.0.6 255.255.255.252 Ethernet2/1/0: J.4.7.9 255.255.255.248 POS5/0/0: J.2.0.250 255.255.255.252 Hssi10/1/0: J.4.0.25 255.255.255.252 Hssi10/1/1: J.4.0.17 255.255.255.252 POS12/0/0: J.3.0.250 255.255.255.252

Configuration File for ISP4BB3

ISP4BB3, a core router for ISP4, has an external connection to ISP2BB6 and ISP3BB3. BGP and MBGP internal peering is configured to all other routers in ISP4. BGP and MBGP external peering is with ISP2BB6 and ISP3BB3. For multicast, the router is configured to act as the RP for all of ISP4. Additionally, ISP4BB3 is configured to have MSDP external peering sessions with ISP1BB3, ISP2BB4, and ISP3BB3, with SA filters to block unwanted sources and prevent the unnecessary creation, forwarding, and caching of some well-known domain local sources.

Example 5-5 displays the **show running-config** privileged EXEC command output for host ISP4BB3.

Example 5-5 *ISP4BB3 Configuration*

```
ISP4BB3#show running-config
version 12.0
service timestamps debug uptime
service timestamps log datetime localtime show-timezone
no service password-encryption
service udp-small-servers
service tcp-small-servers
!
hostname ISP4BB3
!
logging buffered 1000000 debugging
no logging console
enable password lab
!
clock timezone PDT -8
ip subnet-zero
ip cef distributed
no ip domain-lookup
ip multicast-routing distributed
!
!
interface Loopback0
 description ISP4BB3 LOOPBACK 0
 ip address J.4.0.203 255.255.255.255
 no ip directed-broadcast
 ip pim sparse-mode
!
interface Loopback1
 description ISP4BB4 LOOPBACK1 FOR MULTICAST
 ip address J.4.0.124 255.255.255.255
 no ip directed-broadcast
 ip pim sparse-mode
!
interface Ethernet0/0/2
 description To ISP4BB3CL-1 & IPTV-SRVR 1
 ip address J.4.6.1 255.255.255.248
 no ip directed-broadcast
 ip pim sparse-mode
 ip route-cache distributed
 ip ospf cost 19
 ip mroute-cache distributed
 no cdp enable
!
interface Ethernet0/0/3
 description TO I4EBGP1
 ip address J.4.7.129 255.255.255.128
 no ip directed-broadcast
 ip route-cache distributed
 ip ospf cost 19
```

continues

Example 5-5 *ISP4BB3 Configuration (Continued)*

```
 no cdp enable
!
interface Hssi2/0/0
 description To ISP4BB1, HSSI 2/0/0
 ip address J.4.0.6 255.255.255.252
 no ip directed-broadcast
 ip pim sparse-mode
 ip mrm test-sender
 ip route-cache distributed
 ip ospf cost 13
 ip mroute-cache distributed
 hssi internal-clock
 no cdp enable
!
interface Hssi2/0/1
 description To ISP4BB1, HSSI 2/0/1
 ip address J.4.0.10 255.255.255.252
 no ip directed-broadcast
 ip route-cache distributed
 ip ospf cost 13
 hssi internal-clock
 no cdp enable
!
interface POS5/0/0
 description TO ISP2BB6, POS 0/0
 ip address J.2.0.250 255.255.255.252
 no ip directed-broadcast
 ip pim bsr-border
 ip pim sparse-mode
 ip multicast ttl-threshold 16
 ip multicast boundary 1
 ip route-cache distributed
 clock source internal
 no cdp enable
!
interface Hssi10/1/0
 description To ISP4BB4, HSSI 4/0/0
 ip address J.4.0.25 255.255.255.252
 no ip directed-broadcast
 ip pim sparse-mode
 ip route-cache distributed
 ip ospf cost 13
 ip mroute-cache distributed
 hssi internal-clock
 no cdp enable
!
interface Hssi10/1/1
 description To ISP4BB4, HSSI 2/1/0
 ip address J.4.0.17 255.255.255.252
 no ip directed-broadcast
 ip route-cache distributed
 ip ospf cost 13
```

Example 5-5 *ISP4BB3 Configuration (Continued)*

```
  hssi internal-clock
  no cdp enable
!
interface POS12/0/0
  description To ISP3BB3, POS 12/0/0
  ip address J.3.0.250 255.255.255.252
  no ip directed-broadcast
  ip pim bsr-border
  ip multicast ttl-threshold 16
  ip multicast boundary 1
  ip route-cache distributed
  ip ospf cost 7
  clock source internal
  pos scramble-atm
  pos flag c2 22
  no cdp enable
!
autonomous-system 4
!
router ospf 4
  log-adjacency-changes
  redistribute connected subnets route-map redis-ospf
  redistribute static subnets
  passive-interface Ethernet0/0/1
  passive-interface POS5/0/0
  passive-interface POS8/0/0
  passive-interface FastEthernet10/0/0
  passive-interface POS12/0/0
  network J.4.0.203 0.0.0.0 area 0
  network J.4.0.0 0.0.0.255 area 0
  network J.4.4.0 0.0.0.255 area 3
  network J.4.5.0 0.0.0.255 area 3
  network J.4.6.0 0.0.0.255 area 3
  network J.4.7.0 0.0.0.255 area 3
  maximum-paths 6
  default-information originate always
!
router bgp 4
  no synchronization
  network K.255.0.0 mask 255.255.0.0 route-map connected-bgp
  redistribute connected route-map connected-bgp
  neighbor ISP3ISP4PEER peer-group nlri unicast multicast
  neighbor I4EBGP1 peer-group
  neighbor ISP4ISP2PEER peer-group nlri unicast multicast
  neighbor ISP4ISP2PEER remote-as 2
  neighbor ISP4INTERNAL peer-group nlri unicast multicast
  neighbor ISP4INTERNAL remote-as 4
  neighbor ISP4INTERNAL update-source Loopback0
  neighbor J.2.0.249 peer-group ISP4ISP2PEER
  neighbor J.3.0.249 remote-as 3
  neighbor J.3.0.249 peer-group ISP3ISP4PEER
  neighbor J.4.0.201 peer-group ISP4INTERNAL
```

continues

Example 5-5 *ISP4BB3 Configuration (Continued)*

```
            neighbor J.4.0.202 peer-group ISP4INTERNAL
            neighbor J.4.0.204 peer-group ISP4INTERNAL
            neighbor J.4.7.130 remote-as 400
            neighbor J.4.7.130 peer-group I4EBGP1
            neighbor J.4.7.131 remote-as 401
            neighbor J.4.7.131 peer-group I4EBGP1
            neighbor J.4.7.132 remote-as 402
            neighbor J.4.7.132 peer-group I4EBGP1
            neighbor J.4.7.133 remote-as 403
            neighbor J.4.7.133 peer-group I4EBGP1
            neighbor J.4.7.134 remote-as 404
            neighbor J.4.7.134 peer-group I4EBGP1
            neighbor J.4.7.135 remote-as 405
            neighbor J.4.7.135 peer-group I4EBGP1
            neighbor J.4.7.136 remote-as 406
            neighbor J.4.7.136 peer-group I4EBGP1
            neighbor J.4.7.137 remote-as 407
            neighbor J.4.7.137 peer-group I4EBGP1
            neighbor J.4.7.138 remote-as 408
            neighbor J.4.7.138 peer-group I4EBGP1
            neighbor J.4.7.139 remote-as 409
            neighbor J.4.7.139 peer-group I4EBGP1
            neighbor J.4.7.140 remote-as 410
            neighbor J.4.7.140 peer-group I4EBGP1
            neighbor J.4.7.141 remote-as 411
            neighbor J.4.7.141 peer-group I4EBGP1
            neighbor J.4.7.142 remote-as 412
            neighbor J.4.7.142 peer-group I4EBGP1
            neighbor J.4.7.143 remote-as 413
            neighbor J.4.7.143 peer-group I4EBGP1
            neighbor J.4.7.144 remote-as 414
            neighbor J.4.7.144 peer-group I4EBGP1
            neighbor J.4.7.145 remote-as 415
            neighbor J.4.7.145 peer-group I4EBGP1
            neighbor J.4.7.146 remote-as 416
            neighbor J.4.7.146 peer-group I4EBGP1
            neighbor J.4.7.147 remote-as 417
            neighbor J.4.7.147 peer-group I4EBGP1
            neighbor J.4.7.148 remote-as 418
            neighbor J.4.7.148 peer-group I4EBGP1
            neighbor J.4.7.149 remote-as 419
            neighbor J.4.7.149 peer-group I4EBGP1
            neighbor J.4.7.150 remote-as 420
            neighbor J.4.7.150 peer-group I4EBGP1
            neighbor J.4.7.151 remote-as 421
            neighbor J.4.7.151 peer-group I4EBGP1
            neighbor J.4.7.152 remote-as 422
            neighbor J.4.7.152 peer-group I4EBGP1
            neighbor J.4.7.153 remote-as 423
            neighbor J.4.7.153 peer-group I4EBGP1
            neighbor J.4.7.154 remote-as 424
            neighbor J.4.7.154 peer-group I4EBGP1
```

Example 5-5 *ISP4BB3 Configuration (Continued)*

```
 neighbor J.4.7.155 remote-as 425
 neighbor J.4.7.155 peer-group I4EBGP1
 neighbor J.4.7.156 remote-as 426
 neighbor J.4.7.156 peer-group I4EBGP1
 neighbor J.4.7.157 remote-as 427
 neighbor J.4.7.157 peer-group I4EBGP1
 neighbor J.4.7.158 remote-as 428
 neighbor J.4.7.158 peer-group I4EBGP1
 neighbor J.4.7.159 remote-as 429
 neighbor J.4.7.159 peer-group I4EBGP1
 neighbor J.4.7.160 remote-as 430
 neighbor J.4.7.160 peer-group I4EBGP1
 neighbor J.4.7.161 remote-as 431
 neighbor J.4.7.161 peer-group I4EBGP1
 neighbor J.4.7.228 remote-as 490
 neighbor J.4.7.228 peer-group I4EBGP1
 neighbor J.4.7.229 remote-as 491
 neighbor J.4.7.229 peer-group I4EBGP1
 neighbor J.4.7.230 remote-as 492
 neighbor J.4.7.230 peer-group I4EBGP1
 no auto-summary
!
no ip classless
ip pim rp-address J.4.0.124
ip msdp peer J.3.0.249 connect-source Loopback0 remote-as 3
ip msdp sa-filter in J.3.0.249 list 124
ip msdp sa-filter out J.3.0.249 list 124
ip msdp peer J.2.0.204 connect-source Loopback0 remote-as 2
ip msdp sa-filter in J.2.0.204 list 124
ip msdp sa-filter out J.2.0.204 list 124
ip msdp peer J.1.0.203 connect-source Loopback0 remote-as 1
ip msdp sa-filter in J.1.0.203 list 124
ip msdp sa-filter out J.1.0.203 list 124
ip msdp cache-sa-state
!
!
ip prefix-list local-routes seq 5 permit 229.0.0.0/8
ip prefix-list local-routes seq 15 deny 0.0.0.0/0 le 32
access-list 1 deny    224.0.1.39
access-list 1 deny    224.0.1.40
access-list 1 deny    239.0.0.0 0.255.255.255
access-list 1 permit any
access-list 10 deny   224.0.1.39
access-list 10 deny   224.0.1.40
access-list 10 deny   239.0.0.0 0.255.255.255
access-list 10 permit 224.0.0.0 15.255.255.255
access-list 30 deny   223.255.240.0 0.0.15.255
access-list 30 permit any
access-list 112 permit ip J.4.0.0 0.0.255.255 255.255.0.0 0.0.255.255
access-list 112 permit ip K.255.0.0 0.0.255.255 255.255.0.0 0.0.255.255
access-list 112 deny   ip any any
access-list 124 deny    ip any host 224.0.2.2
```

continues

Example 5-5 *ISP4BB3 Configuration (Continued)*

```
access-list 124 deny   ip any host 224.0.1.3
access-list 124 deny   ip any host 224.0.1.24
access-list 124 deny   ip any host 224.0.1.22
access-list 124 deny   ip any host 224.0.1.2
access-list 124 deny   ip any host 224.0.1.35
access-list 124 deny   ip any host 224.0.1.60
access-list 124 deny   ip any host 224.0.1.39
access-list 124 deny   ip any host 224.0.1.40
access-list 124 deny   ip any 239.0.0.0 0.255.255.255
access-list 124 deny   ip 10.0.0.0 0.255.255.255 any
access-list 124 deny   ip 127.0.0.0 0.255.255.255 any
access-list 124 deny   ip 172.16.0.0 0.15.255.255 any
access-list 124 deny   ip K.168.0.0 0.0.255.255 any
access-list 124 permit ip any any
snmp-server engineID local 00000009020000801CF87800
snmp-server community public RO
snmp-server community STSS RW
no snmp-server ifindex persist
snmp-server packetsize 2048
no cdp run
route-map connected-bgp permit 10
 match ip address 112
 set ip next-hop J.4.0.203
 set origin igp
!
route-map local-routes permit 20
 match ip address prefix-list local-routes
!
route-map redis-ospf permit 10
 match ip address 30
!
!
line con 0
 exec-timeout 0 0
 login authentication NOTACACS
 length 30
 transport input none
line aux 0
line vty 0 4
 exec-timeout 0 0
 password lab
 login authentication NOTACACS
!
end
```

ISP4BB4

ISP4BB4 is a backbone router in ISP4. Figure 5-8 shows the topology of ISP4 and ISP4BB4's location in ISP4.

Figure 5-8 *ISP4BB4*

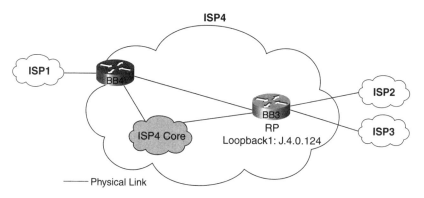

Device Characteristics for ISP4BB4

Table 5-6 lists the hardware and software device characteristics for ISP4BB4.

Table 5-6 *Hardware and Software Device Characteristics for ISP4BB4*

ISP4BB4	Device Characteristics
Host name	ISP4BB4
Chassis type	Cisco 7513 router
Physical interfaces	12 Ethernet/IEEE 802.3 2 Fast Ethernet/IEEE 802.3 4 High-Speed Serial Interface (HSSI) 1 FDDI 3 Packet over SONET (POS)
Hardware components	Cisco RSP2 (R4600) processor 1 Ethernet Interface Processor (EIP) controller (4 Ethernet) 4 VIP2 controllers (1 Fast Ethernet) (8 Ethernet) (1 FDDI) (2 POS) 3 VIP2 R5K controllers (1 Fast Ethernet) (4 HSSI) (1 POS)
Software loaded	Cisco IOS Release 12.0(11.5)S
Memory	Cisco RSP2 (R4600) processor: 128 MB

continues

Table 5-6 *Hardware and Software Device Characteristics for ISP4BB4 (Continued)*

ISP4BB4	Device Characteristics
IP addresses	Loopback0: J.4.0.204 255.255.255.255 Ethernet0/0/3: J.4.10.1 255.255.255.248 Ethernet1/0: J.4.10.9 255.255.255.248 Hssi4/0/0: J.4.0.26 255.255.255.252 FastEthernet4/1/0: J.4.11.1 255.255.255.128 POS11/0/0: J.4.0.30 255.255.255.252 POS12/0/0: J.4.0.33 255.255.255.252

Configuration File for ISP4BB4

ISP4BB4, a core router for ISP4, has an external connection to ISP1BB3. BGP and MBGP internal peering is configured to all other routers in ISP4. ISP4BB4 also has an external BGP and MBGP peering to ISP1BB3. For multicast, the router is statically configured to use ISP4BB3 as its RP.

Example 5-6 displays the **show running-config** privileged EXEC command output for host ISP4BB4.

Example 5-6 *ISP4BB4 Configuration*

```
ISP4BB4#show running-config
version 12.0
service timestamps debug uptime
service timestamps log datetime localtime show-timezone
no service password-encryption
service udp-small-servers
service tcp-small-servers
!
hostname ISP4BB4
!
logging buffered 1000000 debugging
aaa new-model
aaa authentication login NOTACACS enable
enable password lab
!
clock timezone PDT -8
ip subnet-zero
ip cef distributed
no ip domain-lookup
ip multicast-routing distributed
!
interface Loopback0
 description ISP4BB4 LOOPBACK 0
 ip address J.4.0.204 255.255.255.255
 ip directed-broadcast
 ip pim sparse-mode
!
```

Example 5-6 *ISP4BB4 Configuration (Continued)*

```
interface Ethernet0/0/3
 description To ISP4BB4CL-1
 ip address J.4.10.1 255.255.255.248
 no ip directed-broadcast
 ip pim sparse-mode
 ip route-cache distributed
 ip ospf cost 19
 ip mroute-cache distributed
 no cdp enable
!
interface Ethernet1/0
 description To IPTV RCVR-5
 ip address J.4.10.9 255.255.255.248
 no ip directed-broadcast
 ip pim sparse-mode
 ip ospf cost 19
 no cdp enable
!
interface Hssi4/0/0
 description To ISP4BB3, HSSI 10/1/0
 ip address J.4.0.26 255.255.255.252
 no ip directed-broadcast
 ip pim sparse-mode
 ip route-cache distributed
 ip ospf cost 13
 ip mroute-cache distributed
 hssi internal-clock
 no cdp enable
!
interface FastEthernet4/1/0
 ip address J.4.11.1 255.255.255.128
 no ip directed-broadcast
 ip pim sparse-mode
 ip route-cache distributed
 ip ospf cost 11
 ip mroute-cache distributed
 full-duplex
 no cdp enable
!
interface POS11/0/0
 description To ISP4BB2, POS 2/0/0
 ip address J.4.0.30 255.255.255.252
 no ip directed-broadcast
 ip pim sparse-mode
 ip route-cache distributed
 ip ospf cost 7
 ip mroute-cache distributed
 clock source internal
 no cdp enable
!
interface POS12/0/0
 description To ISP1BB3, POS 9/0/0
```

continues

Example 5-6 *ISP4BB4 Configuration (Continued)*

```
  ip address J.4.0.33 255.255.255.252
  no ip directed-broadcast
  ip pim bsr-border
  ip pim sparse-mode
  ip multicast boundary 10
  ip route-cache distributed
  ip ospf cost 7
  clock source internal
  no cdp enable
 !
 autonomous-system 4
 !
 router ospf 4
  log-adjacency-changes
  redistribute connected subnets route-map redis-ospf
  passive-interface Ethernet0/0/1
  passive-interface FastEthernet10/0/0
  network J.4.0.204 0.0.0.0 area 0
  network J.4.0.0 0.0.0.255 area 0
  network J.4.8.0 0.0.0.255 area 4
  network J.4.9.0 0.0.0.255 area 4
  network J.4.10.0 0.0.0.255 area 4
  network J.4.11.0 0.0.0.255 area 4
  network J.4.16.0 0.0.0.255 area 7
  maximum-paths 6
 !
 router bgp 4
  no synchronization
  network K.255.0.0 mask 255.255.0.0 route-map connected-bgp
  redistribute connected route-map connected-bgp
  neighbor ISP4INTERNAL peer-group nlri unicast multicast
  neighbor ISP4INTERNAL remote-as 4
  neighbor ISP4INTERNAL update-source Loopback0
  neighbor ISP4ISP1PEER peer-group nlri unicast multicast
  neighbor ISP4ISP1PEER remote-as 1
  neighbor J.4.0.34 peer-group ISP4ISP1PEER
  neighbor J.4.0.201 peer-group ISP4INTERNAL
  neighbor J.4.0.202 peer-group ISP4INTERNAL
  neighbor J.4.0.203 peer-group ISP4INTERNAL
  no auto-summary
 !
 no ip classless
 ip pim rp-address J.4.0.124
 !
 access-list 10 deny    224.0.1.39
 access-list 10 deny    224.0.1.40
 access-list 10 deny    239.0.0.0 0.255.255.255
 access-list 10 permit any
 access-list 30 deny    223.255.240.0 0.0.15.255
 access-list 30 permit any
 access-list 112 permit ip J.4.0.0 0.0.255.255 255.255.0.0 0.0.255.255
 access-list 112 permit ip K.255.0.0 0.0.255.255 255.255.0.0 0.0.255.255
```

Example 5-6 *ISP4BB4 Configuration (Continued)*

```
access-list 112 deny   ip any any
snmp-server engineID local 00000009020000602FAA4D00
snmp-server community public RO
snmp-server community STSS RW
no snmp-server ifindex persist
snmp-server packetsize 2048
route-map connected-bgp permit 10
 match ip address 112
 set ip next-hop J.4.0.204
 set origin igp
!
route-map redis-ospf permit 10
 match ip address 30
!
line con 0
 exec-timeout 0 0
 login authentication NOTACACS
 length 30
 transport input none
line aux 0
line vty 0 4
 exec-timeout 0 0
 password lab
 login authentication NOTACACS
!
end
```

PART III

Interdomain Multicast with SSM

Chapter 6 Implementing Interdomain Multicast Using SSM

Chapter 7 Device Characteristics and Configuration Files for Implementing Interdomain Multicast Using SSM

This chapter covers the following topics:

- Initial Interdomain Network Topology
- Understanding SSM
- Possible Solutions for Implementing SSM
- Proposed Solution: URD Host Signaling
- Implementing URD Host Signaling

CHAPTER 6

Implementing Interdomain Multicast Using SSM

The current IP multicast infrastructure in the Internet and many enterprise intranets is based on the Protocol Independent Multicast sparse mode (PIM-SM) protocol and Multicast Source Discovery Protocol (MSDP). These protocols are reliable, extensive, and efficient. However, they are bound to the complexity and functionality limitations of the Internet Standard Multicast (ISM) service model. For example, with ISM, the network must maintain knowledge about which hosts in the network are actively sending multicast traffic. With Source Specific Multicast (SSM), receivers provide this information through the source addresses relayed to the last hop routers by Internet Group Management Protocol Version 3 (IGMPv3), IGMP Version 3 lite (IGMP v3lite), or URL Rendezvous Directory (URD).

SSM is an incremental response to the issues associated with ISM and is intended to coexist in the network with the protocols developed for ISM. In general, SSM provides a more advantageous IP multicast service.

This chapter describes how an Internet service provider (ISP) customer within an interdomain multicast network implements SSM in its network using URD. This chapter begins by introducing the initial interdomain ISP topology and describing basic SSM operations (including SSM IP address range). There are three ways to implement SSM in an interdomain environment: using IGMPv3 host signaling, using IGMP v3lite host signaling, and using URD host signaling. Each of these possibilities is briefly described. This chapter then presents and discusses the recommended implementation solution: SSM using URD host signaling. This discussion includes benefits and ramifications of implementing SSM using URD host signaling, necessary prerequisites, and implementation process steps. This chapter concludes with a list of recommended and related documents.

The SSM solution presented in this chapter is based on an actual customer situation. This solution was tested and verified in a lab environment and has been deployed in the field. Alternative ways to implement SSM, such as with IGMPv3 and IGMP v3lite host signaling, are discussed but were not implemented in our lab environment.

The scope of this chapter is to describe basic design and deployment of SSM using URD. It does not discuss in detail the general operation of the protocols associated with developing interdomain multicast networks such as PIM-SM. For more information about PIM-SM, refer to Chapter 1, "IP Multicast Technology Overview."

Initial Interdomain Network Topology

The SSM network scenario used in this chapter is based on the hypothetical interdomain ISP network scenario described in Chapter 2, "Implementing Interdomain Multicast Using MSDP." Figure 6-1 shows the logical connections of the initial interdomain multicast network topology. Each ISP in Figure 6-1 has established Border Gateway Protocol (BGP) peering and its own autonomous system (AS). The design of each ISP multicast network topology depends on the individual requirements of the ISP.

Figure 6-1 *Logical Connections of the Initial Interdomain Multicast Network Topology*

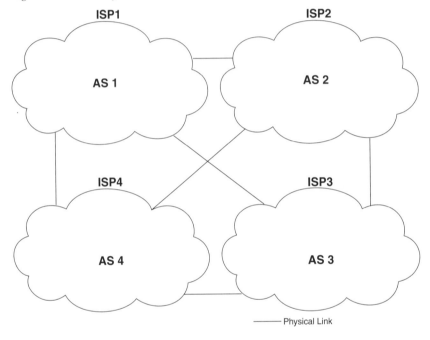

NOTE The solution presented in this document is based on a hypothetical interdomain ISP environment. All the IP addresses and configuration in this document are provided for illustrative purposes only.

Understanding SSM

SSM is a datagram delivery model that best supports one-to-many applications, also known as Internet broadcast applications. SSM is a core networking technology for the Cisco implementation of IP multicast solutions targeted for applications such as audio and video broadcasting.

To run SSM with IGMPv3, SSM must be supported in the Cisco IOS router, in the host where the application is running, and in the application itself. IGMP v3lite and URD, two Cisco-developed transition solutions, enable the immediate development and deployment of SSM services, without the need to wait for the availability of full IGMPv3 support in host operating systems and SSM receiver applications. IGMPv3, IGMP v3lite, and URD interoperate with each other so that both IGMP v3lite and URD can easily be used as transitional solutions toward full IGMPv3 support in hosts.

This section covers the following topics:

- Differences Between SSM and ISM
- SSM IP Address Range
- SSM Operations

Differences between SSM and ISM

The Internet Standard Multicast (ISM) service is described in RFC 1112, "Host Extensions for IP Multicasting." This service consists of the delivery of IP datagrams from any source to a group of receivers called the *multicast host group*. Datagram traffic for the multicast host group consists of datagrams with an arbitrary IP unicast source address S and the multicast group address G as the IP destination address. Systems receive this traffic when they become members of the host group. Membership in a host group simply requires signaling the host group through IGMP Version 1, 2, or 3.

In SSM, delivery of datagrams is based on (S, G) channels. Traffic for one (S, G) channel consists of datagrams with an IP unicast source address S and the multicast group address G as the IP destination address. Systems receive this traffic when they become members of the (S, G) channel rather than the host group. No signaling is required to become a source in either SSM or ISM. However, in SSM, receivers must subscribe or unsubscribe to (S, G) channels to receive or stop receiving traffic from specific sources. In other words, in SSM, receivers can receive traffic only from (S, G) channels to which they are subscribed. In ISM, receivers need not know the IP addresses of sources from which they receive their traffic. The proposed standard approach for channel subscription signaling uses IGMP INCLUDE mode membership reports, which are supported only in IGMPv3.

SSM IP Address Range

SSM can coexist with ISM service by applying the SSM delivery model to a configured subset of the IP multicast group address range. The Internet Assigned Numbers Authority (IANA) has reserved the address range 232.0.0.0 through 232.255.255.255 for SSM applications and protocols. Cisco IOS software allows SSM configuration for an arbitrary subset of the IP multicast address range from 224.0.0.0 through 239.255.255.255. When an SSM range is defined, existing IP multicast receiver applications will not receive any traffic when they try to use addresses in the SSM range unless the application is modified to use explicit (S, G) channel subscription or is SSM-enabled through URD.

SSM Operations

An established network in which IP multicast service is based on PIM-SM can support SSM services. You can also deploy SSM alone in a network without the full range of protocols that are required for interdomain PIM-SM (for example, MSDP, Auto-RP, or bootstrap router [BSR]) if only SSM service is needed. However, multiprotocol BGP might be required (and Cisco recommends its use) to maintain IP multicast connectivity if multiple autonomous systems are deployed in a network.

If SSM is deployed in a network already configured for PIM-SM (Cisco IOS Software Release 12.0 or later is recommended), only the last hop routers must be upgraded to a Cisco IOS Software Release 12.1(5)T or later that supports SSM. Routers that are not directly connected to receivers can run Cisco IOS Software Release 12.0 or later releases. In general, non-last hop routers must run only PIM-SM in the SSM range and might need additional access control configuration to suppress MSDP signalling, registering, or PIM-SM shared tree operations from occurring within the SSM range.

In Cisco IOS Software Release 12.1(3)T and later releases, you enable the SSM operation mode by configuring the SSM range through the **ip pim ssm** global configuration command. This configuration has the following effects:

- For groups within the SSM range, (S, G) channel subscriptions are accepted through IGMPv3 INCLUDE mode membership reports, IGMP v3lite, or URD. Each of these methods must be configured on a per-interface basis. IGMP v3lite and URD (S, G) channel subscriptions are ignored for groups outside the SSM range.

- PIM operations within the SSM range of addresses change to PIM source-specific mode (PIM-SSM). PIM-SSM, the routing protocol that supports the implementation of SSM, is derived from PIM-SM. In PIM-SSM mode, only PIM (S, G) join and prune messages are generated by the router, and no (S, G) rendezvous point tree (RPT) or (*, G) RPT messages are generated. Incoming messages related to RPT operations are ignored or rejected, and incoming PIM register messages are immediately answered with register-stop messages. PIM-SSM is backward-compatible with PIM-SM, unless the router is a last hop router. Routers that are not last hop routers can run PIM-SM for SSM groups (for example, if they do not yet support SSM).

- No MSDP Source-Active (SA) messages within the SSM range will be accepted, generated, or forwarded.

Possible Solutions for Implementing SSM

The following sections discuss three possible solutions for implementing SSM with Cisco IOS software:

- Solution 1: IGMPv3 Host Signaling
- Solution 2: IGMP v3lite Host Signaling
- Solution 3: URD Host Signaling

Solution 1: IGMPv3 Host Signaling

IGMPv3 is the third version of the Internet Engineering Task Force (IETF) standards track protocol used by hosts to signal membership to last hop routers of multicast groups. IGMPv3 introduces the ability for hosts to signal group membership with filtering capabilities with respect to sources, which is required for SSM. A host can either signal that it wants to receive traffic from all sources sending to a group except for some specific sources (called EXCLUDE mode), or that it wants to receive traffic only from some specific sources sending to the group (called INCLUDE mode).

IGMPv3 can operate with both ISM and SSM. In ISM, the last hop router accepts both EXCLUDE and INCLUDE mode reports. In SSM, the last hop router accepts only INCLUDE mode reports, but ignores EXCLUDE mode reports. For more information on IGMPv3, refer to the Cisco IOS Software Release 12.1(5)T IGMP Version 3 feature module.

Solution 2: IGMP v3lite Host Signaling

IGMP v3lite is a Cisco-developed transitional solution that enables you to write and run SSM applications on hosts that do not yet support IGMPv3 in their operating system kernel. IGMP v3lite allows immediate development of SSM receiver applications and switches to IGMPv3 as soon as it becomes available.

You must compile applications with the Host Side IGMP Library (HSIL) for IGMP v3lite. This software provides a subset of the IGMPv3 applications programming interface (API) that is required to write SSM-aware applications. HSIL was developed for Cisco by Talarian and is available on the following web site:

    www.talarianmulticast.com/cgi-bin/igmpdownld

One part of the HSIL is a client library linked to the SSM application. It provides the SSM subset of the IGMPv3 API to the SSM application. If possible, the library checks whether the operating system kernel supports IGMPv3. If it does, the API calls are passed through to the kernel. If the kernel does not support IGMPv3, the library uses the IGMP v3lite mechanism.

When using the IGMP v3lite mechanism, the library tells the operating system kernel to join to the whole multicast group. Joining to the whole group is the only method for the application to receive traffic for that multicast group (if the operating system kernel supports only IGMPv1 or IGMPv2). In addition, the library signals the (S, G) channel subscriptions to an IGMP v3lite server process, which is also part of the HSIL. A server process is needed because multiple SSM applications might be on the same host. This server process sends IGMP v3lite-specific (S, G) channel subscriptions to the last hop Cisco IOS router, which must be enabled for IGMP v3lite. The Cisco IOS router sees both the IGMPv1 or IGMPv2 group membership reports from the operating system kernel and the (S, G) channel subscription from the HSIL server process. If the router sees both of these messages, it will interpret them as an SSM (S, G) channel subscription and join to the channel through PIM-SSM.

NOTE Refer to the documentation accompanying the HSIL software for more information about how to use IGMP v3lite with your application.

Solution 3: URD Host Signaling

URD is a Cisco-developed transitional solution that enables the deployment of SSM with existing IP multicast receiver applications that do not support IGMPv3. The software on the end-user systems running the application do not need to be updated. URD is a content provider solution in which receiver applications can be started or controlled through a web browser.

The next section explains URD Host Signaling in more detail.

Proposed Solution: URD Host Signaling

The company in this proposed solution implemented URD because it wanted to immediately deploy SSM services with existing IP multicast receiver applications that did not support IGMPv3. The company did not want to upgrade any software on its end-user systems.

This section addresses the following issues pertaining to this URD Host Signaling scenario:

- Strategy
- Network Topology
- Benefits
- Ramifications
- How URD Host Signaling Works

Strategy

This proposed solution's strategy assumes that IP multicast using MSDP is already deployed in the ISP's autonomous system and that IP multicast connectivity exists between ISPs.

The following strategy deploys SSM with URD:

- Determine an IP multicast address range to run SSM. The suggested default range is from 232.0.0.0 through 232.255.255.255.
- Disable rendezvous point (RP) and MSDP peers from processing this SSM address range as ISM services.
- Configure edge devices to process URD host reports.

Network Topology

Figure 6-2 shows the logical connections of the SSM network topology. As demonstrated in Figure 6-2, the IPTV server is the SSM source and is located within ISP2. (The URD web server also happens to be located within ISP2, but the URD web server could have been located in any of the ISPs. Because its location is not critical, the URD web server has been omitted from the diagram.) The IPTV client is the SSM/URD client. The SSM/URD client is located within the customer network ISP1AC1. The audio and video streams use the group addresses 232.0.2.1 and 232.0.2.2. Within this topology, please note that any existing RPs or MSDP peers have disabled processing of the SSM range.

Figure 6-2 *Logical Connections of the Initial SSM Network Topology*

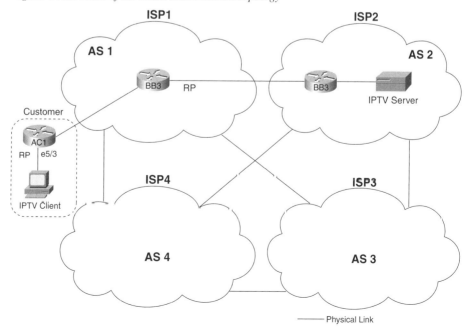

Benefits

Deploying SSM in a network provides the following benefits:

- IP multicast address management is not required
- Denial-of-service attacks from unwanted sources are inhibited
- Easy to install and manage
- Ideal for Internet broadcast applications

The sections that follow address these benefits at greater length.

IP Multicast Address Management Is Not Required

In the ISM service, applications must acquire a unique IP multicast group address because traffic distribution is based only on the IP multicast group address used. If two applications with different sources and receivers use the same IP multicast group address, receivers of both applications will receive traffic from the senders of both applications. Even though the receivers, if programmed appropriately, can filter out the unwanted traffic, this situation would cause unacceptable levels of unwanted traffic.

Allocating a unique IP multicast group address for an application is still a problem. Most short-lived applications use mechanisms like Session Description Protocol (SDP) and Session Announcement Protocol (SAP) to obtain a random address, but this solution does not work well given the rising number of applications in the Internet. The best current solution for long-lived applications is GLOP Addressing, which is described in Chapter 1. GLOP Addressing strategy was originally meant to be a temporary solution until a coherent multicasting address allocation scheme was devised. The GLOP Addressing solution suffers from the restriction that each autonomous system is limited to only 255 usable IP multicast addresses. SSM does not rely on a unique group address because the combination of the source and group is always unique. If you use SSM, multicast addressing is no longer an issue for interdomain multicast.

In SSM, traffic from each source is forwarded between routers in the network independent of traffic from other sources, so different sources can reuse multicast group addresses in the SSM range.

Denial-of-Service Attacks from Unwanted Sources Are Inhibited

In SSM, multicast traffic from each individual source is transported across the network only if it was requested (through IGMPv3, IGMP v3lite, or URD memberships) from a receiver. In contrast, ISM forwards traffic from any active source sending a multicast group to all receivers requesting that multicast group. In Internet broadcast applications, this ISM behavior is undesirable because it allows unwanted sources to easily disturb the actual Internet broadcast source by sending traffic to the same multicast group. This denial-of-service attack depletes bandwidth at the receiver side with unwanted traffic and disrupts the reception of the Internet broadcast. In SSM, because traffic is transported across the network only when it is requested, simply sending traffic to a multicast group does not cause this type of denial-of-service attack.

Easy to Install and Manage

SSM is easy to install and provision in a network because it does not require the network to maintain which active sources are sending to multicast groups. This requirement exists in ISM (with IGMPv1, IGMPv2, or IGMPv3).

The current standard solutions for ISM service are PIM-SM and MSDP. Rendezvous point (RP) management in PIM-SM (including the necessity for Auto-RP or BSR) and MSDP are required only for the network to learn about active sources. This management is not necessary in SSM, making SSM easier to install and manage, and easier to operationally scale in deployment. Another factor that contributes to SSM's easy installation is that it can leverage preexisting PIM-SM networks and requires only the upgrade of last hop routers to support IGMPv3, IGMP v3lite, or URD.

Ideal for Internet Broadcast Applications

The three benefits previously described make SSM ideal for Internet broadcast-style applications for the following reasons:

- The ability to provide Internet broadcast services through SSM without the need for unique IP multicast addresses allows content providers to easily offer their services (IP multicast address allocation has been a serious problem for content providers).
- The prevention of denial-of-service attacks is an important factor for Internet broadcast services because, with their exposure to a large number of receivers, they are the most common targets for such attacks.
- The ease of installation and operation of SSM makes it ideal for network operators, especially in those cases where content needs to be forwarded between multiple independent PIM domains (because there is no need to manage MSDP for SSM between PIM domains).

Ramifications

Deploying SSM in a network has the following ramifications:

- Legacy applications within the SSM range restrictions
- IGMP v3lite and URD require a Cisco last hop router
- Address management restrictions
- State maintenance limitations

The sections that follow address these ramifications at greater length.

Legacy Applications Within the SSM Range Restrictions

Existing applications in a network predating SSM will not work within the SSM range unless they are modified to support (S, G) channel subscriptions or are enabled through URD. Therefore, enabling SSM in a network might cause problems for existing applications if they use addresses within the designated SSM range. An example of this problem would be the failure of sources and receivers to communicate because the PIM-SM network would no longer use the RP to introduce sources and receivers. Receivers learn about sources through the RP in PIM-SM. SSM does not use this in-band mechanism. Applications using SSM address ranges must use an out-of-band method to notify receivers that the source is active.

IGMP v3lite and URD Require a Cisco Last Hop Router

The IETF is standardizing SSM and IGMPv3 solutions. However, Cisco developed IGMP v3lite and URD. For IGMP v3lite and URD to operate properly for a host, the last hop router toward that host must be a Cisco IOS router with IGMP v3lite or URD enabled.

NOTE An application using the HSIL does not require a Cisco last hop router if the host has kernel support for IGMPv3, because the HSIL will use the kernel IGMPv3 instead of IGMP v3lite. IGMPv3 is standard in Windows XP and is also available for FreeBSD. IGMP v3lite is currently available for all Windows operating systems (Windows 95, 98, 2000, NT, ME, and XP).

Address Management Restrictions

Address management is still necessary to some degree when SSM is used with Layer 2 switching mechanisms. Cisco Group Management Protocol (CGMP), IGMP Snooping, and Router-Port Group Management Protocol (RGMP) currently support only group-specific filtering, not (S, G) channel-specific filtering. If different receivers in a switched network request different (S, G) channels that share the same group, they will not benefit from these existing mechanisms. Instead, both receivers will receive all (S, G) channel traffic and filter out the unwanted traffic on input. SSM's ability to reuse group addresses in the SSM range for many independent applications can lead to less-than-expected traffic filtering in a switched network. Follow the recommendations set forth in the IETF drafts for SSM to use random IP addresses out of the SSM range. This minimizes the chance for reuse of a single address within the SSM range between different applications. For example, even with SSM, an application service providing a set of television channels should use a different group for each television (S, G) channel. This setup guarantees that multiple receivers on different channels within the same application service never experience traffic aliasing in networks that include Layer 2 switches.

State Maintenance Limitations

In PIM-SSM, the last hop router will periodically send (S, G) join messages if appropriate (S, G) subscriptions are on the interfaces. As long as receivers send (S, G) subscriptions, the shortest path tree (SPT) state from the receivers to the source will be maintained, even if the source does not send traffic for longer periods of time than in normal PIM-SM (or even if the source has never been active).

This case differs from PIM-SM, where (S, G) state is maintained only if the source is sending traffic and receivers are joining the group. If a source stops sending traffic for more than 3 minutes in PIM-SM, the (S, G) state will be deleted and reestablished only after packets from the source arrive again through the RPT. Because no mechanism in PIM-SSM notifies a receiver that a source is active, the network must maintain the (S, G) state in PIM-SSM as long as receivers are requesting receipt of that channel.

How URD Host Signalling Works

URD operates by passing a special URL from the web browser to the last hop router. This URL is called a *URD intercept URL*. A URD intercept URL is encoded with the (S, G) channel subscription and has a format that allows the last hop router to easily intercept it. The router recognizes the URD intercept URL because it is on the well-known TCP port 465.

As soon as the last hop router intercepts an (S, G) channel subscription encoded in a URD intercept URL and sees an IGMP group membership report for the same multicast group from the receiver application, the last hop router will use PIM-SSM to join toward the (S, G) channel as long as the application maintains the membership for the multicast group G. The URD intercept URL is needed only initially to provide the last hop router with the address of the sources to join to.

A URD intercept URL has the following syntax:

```
webserver:465/path?group=group&source=source1&...source=sourceN&
```

The *webserver* string is the name or IP address to which the URL is targeted. This target need not be the IP address of an existing web server, except for situations where the web server wants to recognize that the last hop router failed to support the URD mechanism. The number 465 indicates the URD port. Port 465 is reserved for Cisco by the IANA for the URD mechanism. No other applications can use this port.

When a host's browser encounters a URD intercept URL, it tries to open a TCP connection to the web server on port 465. If the last hop router is enabled for URD on the interface where the router receives the TCP packets from the host, it will intercept all packets for TCP connections destined to port 465 independent of the actual destination address of the TCP connection (that is, independent of the address of the web server). Once intercepted, the last hop router will "speak" a simple subset of HTTP on this TCP connection, emulating a web server.

The only HTTP request that the last hop router will understand and reply to is the following GET request:

```
GET argument HTTP/1.0
argument = /path?group=group&source=source1&...source=sourceN&
```

When the router receives a GET request, it tries to parse the argument according to the preceding syntax to derive one or more (S, G) channel memberships. The *path* string of the argument is anything up to, but not including, the first question mark. The router ignores this string. The *group* and *source1* through *sourceN* strings are the IP addresses or fully qualified domain names of the channels for which this argument is a subscription request. If the argument matches the syntax shown, the router interprets the argument to be subscriptions for the channels (*source1*, *group*) through (*sourceN*, *group*).

The router will accept the channel subscriptions if the following conditions are met:

- The multicast group's IP address is within the SSM range.
- The IP address of the host that originated the TCP connection is directly connected to the router.

If the channel subscription is accepted, the router will respond to the TCP connection with the following HTML page format:

```
HTTP/1.1 200 OK
Server:cisco IOS
Content-Type:text/html
<html>
<body>
Retrieved URL string successfully
</body>
</html>
```

If an error condition occurs, the <body> part of the returned HTML page will carry an appropriate error message. The HTML page is a by-product of the URD mechanism. Depending on how the web pages carrying a URD intercept URL are designed, this returned text can be displayed to the user or be sized so that the actual returned HTML page is invisible.

The primary effect of the URD mechanism is that the router "remembers" received channel subscriptions and matches them against IGMP group membership reports received by the host. The router will remember a URD (S, G) channel subscription for up to three minutes without a matching IGMP group membership report. When the router sees that it has received both an IGMP group membership report for a multicast group G and a URD (S, G) channel subscription for the same group G, it will join the (S, G) channel through PIM-SSM. The router then continues to join to the (S, G) channel based on only the presence of a continuing IGMP membership from the host. One initial URD channel subscription is all that needs to be added through a web page to enable SSM with URD.

If the last hop router from the receiver host is not enabled for URD, it will not intercept the HTTP connection toward the web server on port 465. This situation results in a TCP connection to port 465 on the web server. If no further provisions on the Web server are taken, the user might see a notice (for example, "Connection refused") in the area of the web page reserved for displaying the URD intercept URL (if the web page was designed to show this output). You can also let the web server "listen" to requests on port 465 and install a Common Gateway Interface (CGI) script to allow the web server to know if a channel subscription failed (for example, to subsequently return more complex error descriptions to the user).

Because the router returns a Content-Type of text and HTML, the best way to include the URD intercept URL into a web page is to use a frame. By defining the size of the frame, you can also hide the URD intercept URL on the displayed page.

By default, URD is disabled on all interfaces. When URD is configured on an interface using the **ip urd** interface configuration command, it is active only for IP multicast addresses in the SSM range.

Implementing URD Host Signaling

The following sections describe how an ISP customer within an interdomain multicast network implemented SSM in its network using URD. This section covers the following topics:

- Prerequisite
- Implementation Process Steps

Prerequisite

The prerequisite for deploying SSM using URD is to configure interdomain multicast using the following configuration tasks:

- Configure MBGP to exchange multicast routing information.
- Configure multicast borders appropriately.

For more information on how to perform these configuration tasks, refer to Chapter 2.

Implementation Process Steps

The following steps were used to configure SSM using URD on the devices shown in Figure 6-2. For more information about the commands used to configure SSM using URD, please refer to Appendix A, "IP Multicast Command Summary." For more information about how each device in the ISP was configured, please refer to Chapter 7, "Device Characteristics and Configuration Files for Implementing Interdomain Multicast Using SSM."

The multicast solutions in this document were tested with valid IP addresses. Normally, when a configuration file is published, the valid IP addresses are replaced with IP addresses specified in RFC 1918, "Address Allocation for Private Networks." Because the range of available IP addresses was insufficient to span the range of IP addresses used in this solution, the first octet of the valid IP addresses was replaced with a variable. In the example configurations provided in the following sections, the first octet of these reserved IP addresses has been replaced with the letter J or the letter K for privacy reasons. The letter J always represents one unique number, and the letter K always represents a unique number that is different from J.

The example configurations are intended for illustrative purposes only. The letters J and K must be replaced with valid numbers when these IP addresses are configured in an actual network.

NOTE The example configurations provided in the following sections use highlighted text to indicate pertinent configuration commands used for deploying the IP multicast solutions described in this document.

Use the following steps to configure SSM using URD on the devices shown in Figure 6-2:

Step 1 Select and enable the SSM range in the ISP.

The following sample configuration shows how to select and enable the SSM range in ISP1:

```
ip pim ssm
```

Step 2 Configure filters on the RP for PIM-SM and MSDP traffic in the SSM address range.

The following sample configuration shows how to configure filters on the RP (ISP1BB3 router) for PIM-SM and MSDP traffic in the SSM address range:

```
ip msdp sa-filter in J.4.0.203 list 124
ip msdp sa-filter out J.4.0.203 list 124
```

The following access list is configured on the ISP1BB3 router:

```
access-list 124 deny    ip any host 224.0.2.2
access-list 124 deny    ip any host 224.0.1.3
access-list 124 deny    ip any host 224.0.1.24
access-list 124 deny    ip any host 224.0.1.22
access-list 124 deny    ip any host 224.0.1.2
access-list 124 deny    ip any host 224.0.1.35
access-list 124 deny    ip any host 224.0.1.60
access-list 124 deny    ip any host 224.0.1.39
access-list 124 deny    ip any host 224.0.1.40
access-list 124 deny    ip any 239.0.0.0 0.255.255.255
access-list 124 deny    ip 10.0.0.0 0.255.255.255 any
```

Implementing URD Host Signaling

```
access-list 124 deny    ip 127.0.0.0 0.255.255.255 any
access-list 124 deny    ip 172.16.0.0 0.15.255.255 any
access-list 124 deny    ip 192.168.0.0 0.0.255.255 any
access-list 124 deny    ip any 232.0.0.0 0.255.255.255
```

Step 3 Configure URD on user interfaces.

The following sample configuration shows how to configure URD on Ethernet5/3 on the ISP1AC1 router. The **ip urd** interface configuration command enables interception of TCP packets sent to the reserved URD port 465 on an interface and the processing of URD channel subscription reports.

```
ISP1AC1# configure terminal
Enter configuration commands, one per line.  End with CNTL/Z.
ISP1AC1(config)# interface Ethernet 5/3
ISP1AC1(config-if)# ip urd
ISP1AC1(config-if)#
```

Step 4 Verify that URD clients can connect to a source. (Optional)

(a) Enable debug output and attempt to connect to a source:

```
ISP1AC1# debug ip igmp 232.0.2.1
ISP1AC1# debug ip igmp 232.0.2.2
ISP1AC1# debug ip urd
ISP1AC1# debug ip mrouting


Mar  7 14:17:37 PST:URD:Intercepted TCP SYN packet from K.250.1.41,
0:772431754(ack:seq)
Mar  7 14:17:37 PST:URD:Intercepted TCP ACK packet from K.250.1.41,
48154099:772431755(ack:seq)
Mar  7 14:17:37 PST:URD:Data intercepted from K.250.1.41, offset 5
Mar  7 14:17:37 PST:URD:Enqueued string:'/cgi-bin/
error.html?group=232.0.2.2&port=22306&source=J.2.11.6&lifet'
Mar  7 14:17:37 PST:URD:Dequeued URD packet, len:137
Mar  7 14:17:37 PST:URD:String:/cgi-bin/
error.html?group=232.0.2.2&port=22306&source=J.2.11.6&lifetim
e=7200&group=232.0.2.1&port=49254&source=J.2.11.6&lifetime=7200
Mar  7 14:17:37 PST:URD:Matched token:group
Mar  7 14:17:37 PST:URD:Parsed value:232.0.2.2
Mar  7 14:17:37 PST:URD:Matched token:source
Mar  7 14:17:37 PST:URD:Parsed value:J.2.11.6
Mar  7 14:17:37 PST:URD:Matched token:lifetime
Mar  7 14:17:37 PST:URD:Parsed value:7200
Mar  7 14:17:37 PST:URD:Matched token:group
Mar  7 14:17:37 PST:URD:Parsed value:232.0.2.1
Mar  7 14:17:37 PST:URD:Matched token:source
Mar  7 14:17:37 PST:URD:Parsed value:J.2.11.6
Mar  7 14:17:37 PST:URD:Matched token:lifetime
Mar  7 14:17:37 PST:URD:Parsed value:7200
```

Chapter 6: Implementing Interdomain Multicast Using SSM

```
Mar 7 14:17:37 PST:URD:Creating IGMP source state for group 232.0.2.2
Mar 7 14:17:37 PST:IGMP:Setting source flags 18 on (J.2.11.6,232.0.2.2)

Mar 7 14:17:37 PST:URD:Creating IGMP source state for group 232.0.2.1
Mar 7 14:17:38 PST:MRT:Create (J.2.11.6/32, 232.0.2.1), RPF
  FastEthernet3/0/K.250.1.1, PC 0x609E5CA0
Mar 7 14:17:38 PST:MRT:Add/Update Ethernet5/3/232.0.2.1 to the olist of
  (J.2.11.6, 232.0.2.1), Forward state
Mar 7 14:17:38 PST:MRT:Create (K.250.1.41/32, 232.0.2.1), RPF
  Ethernet5/3/0.0.0.0, PC 0x609F25FC

Mar 7 14:17:39 PST:IGMP:Received v2 Report on Ethernet5/3 from
  K.250.1.41 for 232.0.2.2
Mar 7 14:17:39 PST:MRT:Create (J.2.11.6/32, 232.0.2.2), RPF
  FastEthernet3/0/K.250.1.1, PC 0x609E5CA0
Mar 7 14:17:39 PST:MRT:Add/Update Ethernet5/3/232.0.2.2 to the olist of
  (J.2.11.6, 232.0.2.2), Forward state
Mar 7 14:17:39 PST:MRT:Create (K.250.1.41/32, 232.0.2.2), RPF
  Ethernet5/3/0.0.0.0, PC 0x609F25FC
```

(b) Verify that SSM flags are set:

```
ISP1AC1# show ip mroute

IP Multicast Routing Table
Flags:D - Dense, S - Sparse, B - Bidir Group, s - SSM Group, C -
Connected,
       L - Local, P - Pruned, R - RP-bit set, F - Register flag,
       T - SPT-bit set, J - Join SPT, M - MSDP created entry,
       X - Proxy Join Timer Running, A - Advertised via MSDP, U - URD,
       I - Received Source Specific Host Report
Outgoing interface flags:H - Hardware switched
Timers:Uptime/Expires
Interface state:Interface, Next-Hop or VCD, State/Mode

(*, 224.0.1.40), 00:01:55/00:00:00, RP K.250.0.201, flags:SJCL
  Incoming interface:Null, RPF nbr 0.0.0.0
  Outgoing interface list:
    Loopback0, Forward/Sparse, 00:01:55/00:02:59

(J.2.11.6, 232.0.2.2), 00:00:45/00:02:59, flags:sCTUI
  Incoming interface:FastEthernet3/0, RPF nbr K.250.1.1
  Outgoing interface list:
    Ethernet5/3, Forward/Sparse, 00:00:16/00:02:46

(K.250.1.41, 232.0.2.2), 00:00:45/00:02:14, flags:sPCT
  Incoming interface:Ethernet5/3, RPF nbr 0.0.0.0
  Outgoing interface list:Null
```

Summary

This chapter described how an ISP customer within an interdomain multicast network implemented SSM in its network using URD. The initial topology was introduced and SSM basics—including SSM IP address range and SSM operation—were discussed. URD Host Signaling was identified as being the best solution for implementing SSM. URD was described and implementation steps were presented.

Related Documents

- *Changes in MBGP Commands Between 12.0S and 12.0T/12.1*, Cisco Application Note (www.cisco.com/warp/public/cc/pd/iosw/prodlit/mcb12_an.htm)
- *Cisco IOS IP and IP Routing Command Reference*, Release 12.1 (www.cisco.com/univercd/cc/td/doc/product/software/ios121/121cgcr/ip_r/index.htm)
- *Cisco IOS IP and IP Routing Configuration Guide*, Release 12.1 (www.cisco.com/univercd/cc/td/doc/product/software/ios121/121cgcr/ip_c/index.htm)
- Cisco IOS Software IP Multicast Group External Homepage (ftpeng.cisco.com/ipmulticast/index.html)
- Cisco IOS Software Multicast Services Web Page (www.cisco.com/go/ipmulticast)
- *Gaining New Efficiencies in Multicast Service Delivery*, Cisco Beyond Basic IP Newsletter V1.36 (www.cisco.com/warp/public/779/servpro/promotions/bbip/volume_01_issue36.htm)
- *Source Specific Multicast with IGMPv3, IGMP v3lite, and URD*, Cisco IOS Software Release 12.1(5)T feature module (www.cisco.com/univercd/cc/td/doc/product/software/ios121/121newft/121t/121t5/dtssm5t.htm)
- *IGMP Version 3*, Cisco IOS Software Release 12.1(5)T feature module (www.cisco.com/univercd/cc/td/doc/product/software/ios121/121newft/121t/121t5/dtigmpv3.htm)
- *IP Multicast Technology Overview*, Cisco white paper (www.cisco.com/univercd/cc/td/doc/cisintwk/intsolns/mcst_sol/mcst_ovr.htm)
- *Multicast Source Discovery Protocol SA Filter Recommendations*, Cisco Tech Note (www.cisco.com/warp/public/105/49.html)
- *Multiprotocol BGP Extensions for IP Multicast*, Cisco IOS Software Release 12.0(7)T feature module (www.cisco.com/univercd/cc/td/doc/product/software/ios120/120newft/120t/120t7/mbgp.htm)
- RFC 1112, *Host extensions for IP multicasting*, S. Deering
- RFC 2770, *GLOP Addressing in 233/8*, D. Meyer, P. Lothberg

This chapter includes the device characteristics and configuration files for the following host names in ISP1 and ISP2 as described in Chapter 6, "Implementing Interdomain Multicast Using SSM":

- ISP1AC1
- ISP2BB3
- ISP1BB3

CHAPTER 7

Device Characteristics and Configuration Files for Implementing Interdomain Multicast Using SSM

This chapter provides the characteristics and configuration files for the devices associated with ISP1 and ISP2 as described in Chapter 6. Figure 7-1 shows the logical connections of the SSM network topology. As shown in the figure, the IPTV server is the Source Specific Multicast (SSM) source and is located within ISP2. (The URL Rendezvous Directory (URD) Web server is also located within ISP2, but the URD Web server could have been located in any of the ISPs. Because its location is not critical, it has been omitted from the diagram.) The IPTV client is the SSM/URD client. The SSM/URD client is located within the customer network ISP1AC1.

Figure 7-1 *Logical Connections of the SSM Network Topology*

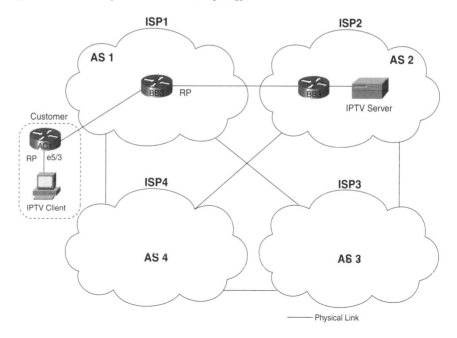

The multicast solutions in this document were tested with valid IP addresses. Normally, when a configuration file is published, the valid IP addresses are replaced with IP addresses as specified in RFC 1918, "Address Allocation for Private Networks." Because the range of available IP addresses was insufficient to span the range of IP addresses used in this solution, the first octet of the valid IP addresses was replaced with a variable. In the example configurations provided in the following sections, the first octet of these reserved IP addresses has been replaced with the letter J or the letter K for privacy reasons. The letter J always represents one unique number and the letter K always represents a unique number that is different from J.

The example configurations are intended for illustrative purposes only. The letters J and K must be replaced with valid numbers when these IP addresses are configured in an actual network.

NOTE The example configurations provided in the following sections use highlighted text to indicate pertinent configuration commands that are used to deploy the IP multicast solutions described in this chapter.

ISP1AC1

ISP1AC1 is an access/customer router (AC) for the POP in ISP1. Figure 7-2 shows the topology of ISP1 and ISP1AC1's location in ISP1. Figure 7-3 shows ISP1AC1's relative position within the SSM solution.

Figure 7-2 *ISP1AC1 Location in ISP1*

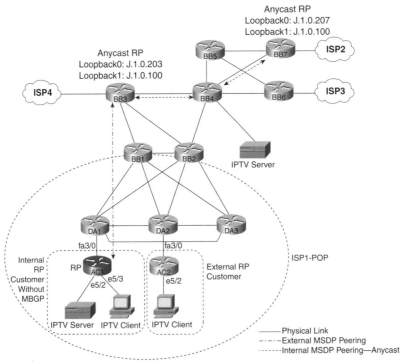

Figure 7-3 *ISP1AC1 Relative Location Within the SSM Solution*

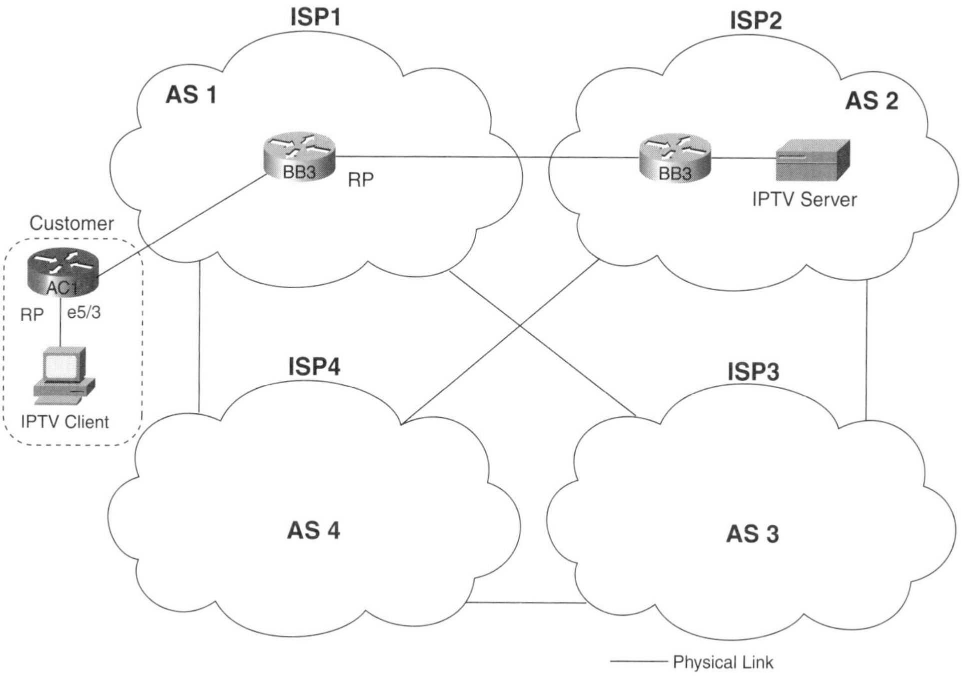

Device Characteristics for ISP1AC1

Table 7-1 lists the hardware and software device characteristics for ISP1AC1.

Table 7-1 *Hardware and Software Device Characteristics for ISP1AC1*

ISP1AC1	Device Characteristics
Host name	ISP1AC1
Chassis type	Cisco 7206VXR router
Physical interfaces	8 Ethernet/IEEE 802.3 3 Fast Ethernet/IEEE 802.3
Hardware components	Cisco 7206VXR (NPE300) processor
Software loaded	Cisco IOS Release 12.1(5)T
Memory	Cisco 7206VXR (NPE300) processor (revision D): 40 MB

continues

Table 7-1 *Hardware and Software Device Characteristics for ISP1AC1 (Continued)*

ISP1AC1	Device Characteristics
IP addresses	Loopback0: K.250.0.201 255.255.255.255 FastEthernet3/0: K.250.1.2 255.255.255.248 Ethernet5/2: K.250.1.33 255.255.255.248 Ethernet5/3: K.250.1.41 255.255.255.248

Configuration File for ISP1AC1

ISP1AC1 is an AC router for the POP in ISP1. Routing is achieved via a default route. For multicast, ISP1AC1 acts as an rendezvous point (RP) for any customers connecting to it. ISP1AC1 also learns about other sources by having an internal MSDP peering session with ISP1BB3, with SA filters to block unwanted sources and prevent the unnecessary creation, forwarding, and caching of some well-known domain local sources. For SSM, the router uses the default SSM range of 232.0.0.0 through 232.255.255.255. The customer attached to Ethernet5/3 uses URD for host signaling.

Example 7-1 *ISP1AC1 Configuration*

```
ISP1CA1#show running-config
!
version 12.1
service timestamps debug datetime localtime show-timezone
service timestamps log datetime localtime show-timezone
!
hostname ISP1AC1
!
logging buffered 1000000 debugging
logging rate-limit console 10 except errors
aaa new-model
aaa authentication login default group tacacs+ enable
aaa authentication login NOTACACS enable
aaa accounting commands 15 default start-stop group tacacs+
aaa accounting system default start-stop group tacacs+
enable password lab
!
clock timezone PST -8
clock summer-time PST recurring
ip subnet-zero
ip cef
!
!
ip multicast-routing
call rsvp-sync
!
!
interface Loopback0
 ip address K.250.0.201 255.255.255.255
 ip pim sparse-mode
!
interface FastEthernet3/0
 description To ISP1DA1, FA0/1/0
```

Example 7-1 *ISP1AC1 Configuration (Continued)*

```
  ip address K.250.1.2 255.255.255.248
  ip pim bsr-border
  ip pim sparse-mode
  ip multicast boundary 1
  duplex full
!
interface Ethernet5/2
 description TO ISP1AC1IPTV
 ip address K.250.1.33 255.255.255.248
 ip pim sparse-mode
 duplex half
!
interface Ethernet5/3
 description TO ISP1AC1CL1
 ip address K.250.1.41 255.255.255.248
 ip pim sparse-mode
 ip urd
 duplex half
!
ip classless
ip route 0.0.0.0 0.0.0.0 K.250.1.1
no ip http server
ip pim rp-address K.250.0.201
ip pim ssm default
ip msdp peer J.1.0.203 connect-source FastEthernet3/0
ip msdp sa-filter in J.1.0.203 list 124
ip msdp sa-filter out J.1.0.203 list 124
ip msdp cache-sa-state
ip msdp redistribute list 124
!
access-list 1 deny     224.0.1.39
access-list 1 deny     224.0.1.40
access-list 1 deny     239.0.0.0 0.255.255.255
access-list 1 permit any
access-list 124 deny    ip any host 224.0.2.2
access-list 124 deny    ip any host 224.0.1.3
access-list 124 deny    ip any host 224.0.1.24
access-list 124 deny    ip any host 224.0.1.22
access-list 124 deny    ip any host 224.0.1.2
access-list 124 deny    ip any host 224.0.1.35
access-list 124 deny    ip any host 224.0.1.60
access-list 124 deny    ip any host 224.0.1.39
access-list 124 deny    ip any host 224.0.1.40
access-list 124 deny    ip any 239.0.0.0 0.255.255.255
access-list 124 deny    ip 10.0.0.0 0.255.255.255 any
access-list 124 deny    ip 127.0.0.0 0.255.255.255 any
access-list 124 deny    ip 172.16.0.0 0.15.255.255 any
access-list 124 deny    ip 192.168.0.0 0.0.255.255 any
access-list 124 deny    ip any 232.0.0.0 0.255.255.255
access-list 124 permit ip any any
snmp-server engineID local 00000009020000024ADFB800
snmp-server community public RO
snmp-server community STSS RW
snmp-server packetsize 2048
```

continues

Example 7-1 *ISP1AC1 Configuration (Continued)*

```
snmp-server contact sysadmin
snmp-server chassis-id ISP1AC1
!
tacacs-server host 223.255.254.254 key cisco12345
tacacs-server key cisco12345
!
alias exec int_desc show int | include Description
alias exec cpu show proc cpu | include CPU
alias exec mem show mem free | include Processor
!
line con 0
 exec-timeout 0 0
 login authentication NOTACACS
 transport input none
line aux 0
 exec-timeout 0 0
line vty 0 4
 exec-timeout 0 0
 password lab
line vty 5 15
!
ntp clock-period 17180286
ntp update-calendar
ntp server 223.255.254.254 version 1
end
```

ISP2BB3

ISP2BB3 is a backbone router in ISP2. Figure 7-4 shows the topology of ISP2 and ISP2BB3's location in ISP2. Figure 7-5 shows ISP2BB3's relative position within the SSM solution.

Figure 7-4 *ISP2BB3 Location in ISP2*

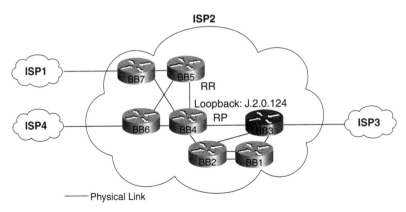

ISP2BB3   261

Figure 7-5 *ISP2BB3 Relative Location Within the SSM Solution*

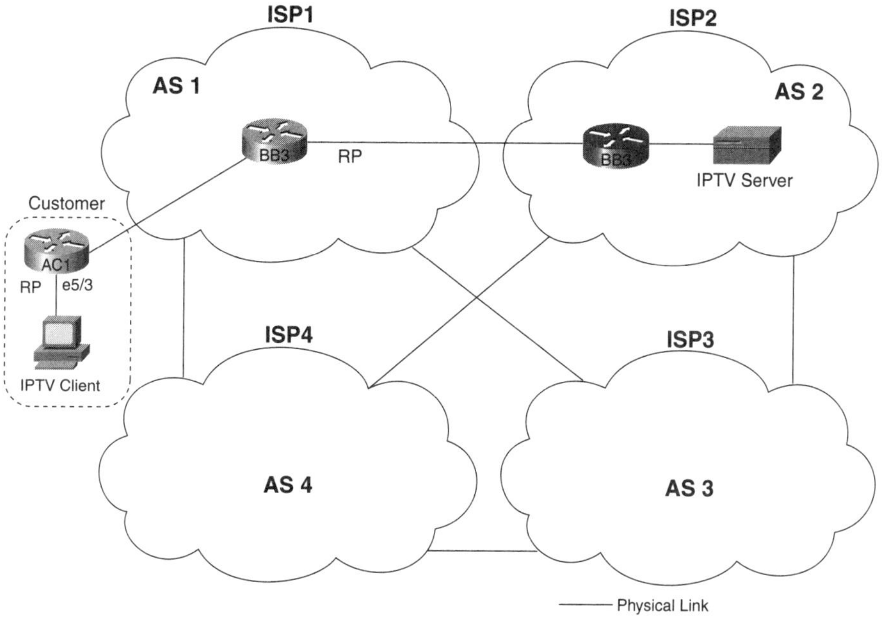

Device Characteristics for ISP2BB3

Table 7-2 lists the hardware and software device characteristics for ISP2BB3.

Table 7-2 *Hardware and Software Device Characteristics for ISP2BB3*

ISP2BB3	Device Characteristics
Host name	ISP2BB3
Chassis type	Cisco 12008 Gigabit Switch Router (GSR)
Physical interfaces	1 Ethernet/IEEE 802.3 1 Gigabit Ethernet/IEEE 802.3 7 Packet over SONET (POS)
Hardware components	Cisco 12008/GRP (R5000) processor (revision 0x01) 1 Route Processor card 1 clock scheduler card 3 switch fabric cards 1 four-port OC-3 POS controller (4 POS) 3 OC-48 POS E.D. controllers (3 POS) 1 single-port Gigabit Ethernet/IEEE 802.3z controller (1 Gigabit Ethernet)

continues

Table 7-2 *Hardware and Software Device Characteristics for ISP2BB3 (Continued)*

ISP2BB3	Device Characteristics
Software loaded	Cisco IOS Release 12.0(13)S2
Memory	Cisco 12008/GRP (R5000) processor (revision 0X01): 128 MB
IP addresses	Loopback0: J.2.0.203 255.255.255.255 POS0/0: J.2.0.245 255.255.255.252 POS0/1: J.2.182.1 255.255.255.240 POS0/2: J.2.192.1 255.255.255.240 POS1/0: J.2.0.14 255.255.255.252 POS2/0: J.2.0.22 255.255.255.252 POS4/0: J.2.0.33 255.255.255.252 GigabitEthernet6/1.330: J.2.11.1 255.255.255.248 GigabitEthernet6/1.340: J.2.12.1 255.255.255.0

Configuration File for ISP2BB3

ISP2BB3 is a core router for ISP2. For multicast, the router is statically configured to use ISP2BB4 as its RP. An SSM source is directly connected to this router.

Example 7-2 *ISP2BB3 Configuration*

```
ISP2BB3#show running-config
version 12.0
service timestamps debug datetime localtime show-timezone
service timestamps log datetime localtime show-timezone
!
hostname ISP2BB3
!
aaa new-model
aaa authentication login default tacacs+ enable
aaa authentication login NOTACACS enable
aaa accounting exec default start-stop tacacs+
aaa accounting commands 0 default start-stop tacacs+
aaa accounting commands 15 default start-stop tacacs+
enable password lab
!
clock timezone PDT -8
clock summer-time PDT recurring
!
!
ip subnet-zero
ip domain-name isp2.com
ip name-server J.4.7.10
ip multicast-routing distributed
clns routing
!
!
interface Loopback0
 ip address J.2.0.203 255.255.255.255
 no ip directed-broadcast
```

Example 7-2 *ISP2BB3 Configuration (Continued)*

```
 ip pim sparse-mode
 ip router isis
 ip mroute-cache distributed
!
interface POS0/0
 description TO ISP3BB7, POS12/0/0
 ip address J.2.0.245 255.255.255.252
 no ip directed-broadcast
 ip pim bsr-border
 ip pim sparse-mode
 ip multicast boundary 1
 ip router isis
 ip mroute-cache distributed
 crc 16
 clock source internal
!
interface POS0/1
ip address J.2.182.1 255.255.255.240
 no ip directed-broadcast
 ip router isis
 no ip mroute-cache
 no keepalive
 crc 16
 clock source internal
!
interface POS0/2
ip address J.2.192.1 255.255.255.240
 no ip directed-broadcast
 ip router isis
 no ip mroute-cache
 no keepalive
 crc 16
 clock source internal
!
interface POS1/0
 description TO ISP2BB1/0, POS 3/0
 ip address J.2.0.14 255.255.255.252
 ip pim sparse-mode
 ip router isis
 ip mroute-cache distributed
 load-interval 30
 crc 32
 clock source internal
!
interface POS2/0
 description TO ISP2BB2, POS0/0
 ip address J.2.0.22 255.255.255.252
 ip pim sparse-mode
 ip router isis
 ip mroute-cache distributed
 crc 32
 clock source internal
!
```

continues

Example 7-2 *ISP2BB3 Configuration (Continued)*

```
interface POS4/0
 ip address J.2.0.33 255.255.255.252
 ip pim sparse-mode
 ip router isis
 ip mroute-cache distributed
 crc 32
 clock source internal
!
interface GigabitEthernet6/0
 no ip address
 no ip directed-broadcast
 no negotiation auto
!
interface GigabitEthernet6/1.330
 description To Client/Server
 encapsulation dot1Q 330
 ip address J.2.11.1 255.255.255.248
 ip pim sparse-mode
 ip router isis
!
interface GigabitEthernet6/1.340
 description OPEN
 encapsulation dot1Q 340
 ip address J.2.12.1 255.255.255.0
 ip pim sparse-mode
 ip router isis
!
interface GigabitEthernet6/1.350
 encapsulation dot1Q 350
 ip pim sparse-mode
!
router isis
 net 49.0002.0000.0000.0003.00
 is-type level-1
!
router bgp 2
 no synchronization
 redistribute connected
 neighbor ISP2INTERNAL peer-group nlri unicast multicast
 neighbor ISP2INTERNAL remote-as 2
 neighbor ISP2INTERNAL update-source Loopback0
 neighbor ISP2INTERNAL route-map connected-bgp out
 neighbor ISP2ISP3PEER peer-group nlri unicast multicast
 neighbor ISP2ISP3PEER remote-as 3
 neighbor J.2.0.201 peer-group ISP2INTERNAL
 neighbor J.2.0.202 peer-group ISP2INTERNAL
 neighbor J.2.0.204 peer-group ISP2INTERNAL
 neighbor J.2.0.205 peer-group ISP2INTERNAL
 neighbor J.2.0.206 peer-group ISP2INTERNAL
 neighbor J.2.0.207 peer-group ISP2INTERNAL
 neighbor J.2.0.208 peer-group ISP2INTERNAL
 neighbor J.2.0.246 peer-group ISP2ISP3PEER
 no auto-summary
```

Example 7-2 *ISP2BB3 Configuration (Continued)*

```
!
no ip classless
ip http server
ip http authentication local
ip pim rp-address J.2.0.124
ip pim accept-register list no-ssm-range
!
!
ip access-list extended no-ssm-range
 deny ip any 232.0.0.0 0.255.255.255
 permit ip any any
logging trap emergencies
access-list 1 deny    224.0.1.39
access-list 1 deny    224.0.1.40
access-list 1 deny    239.0.0.0 0.255.255.255
access-list 1 permit any
access-list 10 permit J.2.11.1
access-list 20 permit J.2.11.9
access-list 69 permit J.2.11.0 0.0.0.255
access-list 69 deny    any
access-list 112 deny ip 223.0.0.0 0.255.255.255 255.255.0.0 0.0.255.255
access-list 112 permit ip any any
access-list 124 deny    ip any 229.0.0.0 0.255.255.255
access-list 124 deny    ip any 239.0.0.0 0.255.255.255
access-list 124 permit ip any any
snmp-server engineID local 000000009020000101F453CC0
snmp-server community public RO
snmp-server community STSS RW
snmp-server contact sysadmin
snmp-server chassis-id ISP2BB3
route-map connected-bgp permit 10
 match ip address 112
 set ip next-hop J.2.0.203
 set origin igp
!
tacacs-server host 223.255.254.254
tacacs-server key cisco12345
!
!
line con 0
 exec-timeout 0 0
 login authentication NOTACACS
 transport input none
line aux 0
lino vty 0 4
 exec-timeout 0 0
 password lab
!
ntp clock-period 17180140
ntp update-calendar
ntp server 223.255.254.254 version 1
end
```

ISP1BB3

ISP1BB3 is a backbone router in ISP1. Figure 7-6 shows the topology of ISP1 and ISP1BB3's location in ISP1. Figure 7-7 shows ISP1BB3's relative position within the SSM solution.

Figure 7-6 *ISP1BB3 Location in ISP1*

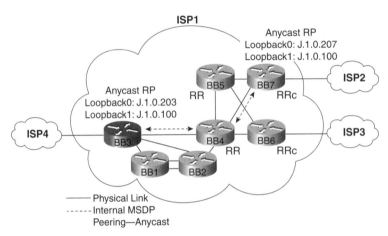

Figure 7-7 *ISP1BB3 Relative Location Within the SSM Solution*

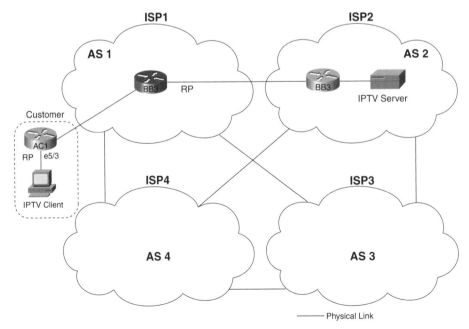

Device Characteristics for ISP1BB3

Table 7-3 lists the hardware and software device characteristics for ISP1BB3.

Table 7-3 *Hardware and Software Device Characteristics for ISP2BB3*

ISP1BB3	Device Characteristics
Host name	ISP1BB3
Chassis type	Cisco 7513 router
Physical interfaces	4 Ethernet/IEEE 802.3 1 Fast Ethernet/IEEE 802.3 5 Packet over SONET (POS)
Hardware components	Cisco Route/Switch Processor Version 2 (RSP2) (R4700) 6 Versatile Interface Processor Version 2 (VIP2) controllers (1 Fast Ethernet) (4 Ethernet) (5 POS)
Software loaded	Cisco IOS Release 12.1(5)T
Memory	Cisco RSP2 (R4700) processor: 128 MB
IP addresses	Loopback0: J.1.0.203 255.255.255.255 Loopback1: J.1.0.100 255.255.255.255 Ethernet0/0/2: J.1.6.1 255.255.255.248 FastEthernet0/1/0: J.1.99.1 255.255.255.248 POS1/0/0: J.1.0.2 255.255.255.252 POS1/1/0: J.1.0.14 255.255.255.252 POS3/0/0: J.1.0.17 255.255.255.252 POS8/1/0: J.4.0.34 255.255.255.252

Configuration File for ISP1BB3

ISP1BB3 is a core router for ISP1. For multicast, ISP1BB3 is configured as one of the two anycast RPs in ISP1. Accept-register filters are set up so that the RP will not allow any source on the SSM range to register. Additional filters keep the RP from announcing or accepting any source in the SSM range.

Example 7-3 *ISP1BB3 Configuration*

```
ISP1BB3#show running-config
!
version 12.1
service timestamps debug datetime localtime
service timestamps log datetime localtime
service udp-small-servers
service tcp-small-servers
!
hostname ISP1BB3
!
```

continues

Example 7-3 *ISP1BB3 Configuration (Continued)*

```
logging buffered 10000 debugging
logging rate-limit console 10 except errors
no logging console
aaa new-model
aaa group server tacacs+ E2EST
  server 223.255.254.254
!
aaa authentication login default group E2EST enable
aaa authentication login NOTACACS enable
aaa accounting exec default start-stop group E2EST
aaa accounting commands 0 default start-stop group E2EST
aaa accounting commands 15 default start-stop group E2EST
aaa accounting system default start-stop group E2EST
enable password lab
!
clock timezone PDT -8
clock summer-time PDT recurring
ip subnet-zero
ip cef distributed
ip domain-name isp1.com
ip host tftpserv 223.255.254.254
ip name-server J.4.7.10
!
ip multicast-routing distributed
clns routing
no tag-switching advertise-tags
no tag-switching ip
!
!
interface Loopback0
 ip address J.1.0.203 255.255.255.255
 ip directed-broadcast
 ip router isis
 ip pim sparse-mode
!
interface Loopback1
 ip address J.1.0.100 255.255.255.255
 ip router isis
 ip pim sparse-mode
!
interface Ethernet0/0/2
 description TO ISP1BB3CL1
 ip address J.1.6.1 255.255.255.248
 ip router isis
 ip pim sparse-mode
 ip route-cache distributed
 ip mroute-cache distributed
 ip urd
 load-interval 30
!
interface FastEthernet0/1/0
 description to isp1bb3ce FA1
 ip address J.1.99.1 255.255.255.248
```

Example 7-3 *ISP1BB3 Configuration (Continued)*

```
  ip router isis
  ip pim sparse-mode
  ip route-cache distributed
  ip mroute-cache distributed
  no keepalive
  full-duplex
 !
 interface POS1/0/0
  description TO ISP1BB1, POS 1/2
  ip address J.1.0.2 255.255.255.252
  ip router isis
  ip pim sparse-mode
  ip route-cache distributed
  ip mroute-cache distributed
  clock source internal
 !
 interface POS1/1/0
  description TO ISP1BB2, POS 2/0
  ip address J.1.0.14 255.255.255.252
  ip router isis
  ip pim sparse-mode
  ip route-cache distributed
  ip mroute-cache distributed
  clock source internal
 !
 interface POS3/0/0
  description TO ISP1BB4, POS 2/0/0
  ip address J.1.0.17 255.255.255.252
  ip router isis
  ip pim sparse-mode
  ip route-cache distributed
  ip mroute-cache distributed
  clock source internal
 !
 interface POS8/1/0
  description TO ISP4BB4, POS 12/0/0
  ip address J.4.0.34 255.255.255.252
  ip router isis
  ip pim bsr-border
  ip pim sparse-mode
  ip multicast boundary 10
  ip route-cache distributed
  ip mroute-cache distributed
  clock source internal
 !
 router isis
  net 49.0001.0000.0000.0003.00
  is-type level-1
 !
 router bgp 1
  no synchronization
  bgp log-neighbor-changes
  redistribute connected
```

continues

Example 7-3 *ISP1BB3 Configuration (Continued)*

```
 neighbor ISP1INTERNAL peer-group
 neighbor ISP1INTERNAL remote-as 1
 neighbor ISP1INTERNAL update-source Loopback0
 neighbor ISP1INTERNAL route-map connected-bgp out
 neighbor ISP4ISP1PEER peer-group
 neighbor ISP4ISP1PEER remote-as 4
 neighbor J.1.0.200 peer-group ISP1INTERNAL
 neighbor J.1.0.201 peer-group ISP1INTERNAL
 neighbor J.1.0.202 peer-group ISP1INTERNAL
 neighbor J.1.0.204 peer-group ISP1INTERNAL
 neighbor J.1.0.205 peer-group ISP1INTERNAL
 neighbor J.1.0.208 peer-group ISP1INTERNAL
 neighbor J.1.0.209 peer-group ISP1INTERNAL
 neighbor J.1.0.210 peer-group ISP1INTERNAL
 neighbor J.4.0.33 peer-group ISP4ISP1PEER
 no auto-summary
 !
 address-family ipv4 multicast
 redistribute connected route-map connected-bgp
 neighbor ISP1INTERNAL activate
 neighbor ISP4ISP1PEER activate
 neighbor J.1.0.200 activate
 neighbor J.1.0.201 activate
 neighbor J.1.0.202 activate
 neighbor J.1.0.204 activate
 neighbor J.1.0.205 activate
 neighbor J.1.0.208 activate
 neighbor J.1.0.209 activate
 neighbor J.1.0.210 activate
 neighbor J.4.0.33 activate
 exit-address-family
 !
 no ip classless
 ip http server
 ip pim rp-address J.1.0.100
 ip pim accept-register list no-ssm-range
 ip msdp peer K.250.1.2 connect-source Loopback0
 ip msdp sa-filter in K.250.1.2 list 124
 ip msdp sa-filter out K.250.1.2 list 124
 ip msdp peer J.4.0.203 connect-source Loopback0 remote-as 4
 ip msdp sa-filter in J.4.0.203 list 124
 ip msdp sa-filter out J.4.0.203 list 124
 ip msdp sa-request J.4.0.203
 ip msdp peer J.1.0.204 connect-source Loopback0
 ip msdp sa-filter in J.1.0.204 list msdp-nono-list
 ip msdp sa-request J.1.0.204
 ip msdp cache-sa-state
 ip msdp redistribute list msdp-nono-list
 ip msdp originator-id Loopback0
 !
 !
 ip access-list extended msdp-nono-list
   deny   ip any 232.0.0.0 0.255.255.255
   permit ip any any
 ip access-list extended no-ssm-range
```

Example 7-3 *ISP1BB3 Configuration (Continued)*

```
  deny   ip any 232.0.0.0 0.255.255.255
  permit ip any any
logging K.50.0.2
access-list 10 deny    224.0.1.39
access-list 10 deny    224.0.1.40
access-list 10 deny    239.0.0.0 0.255.255.255
access-list 10 permit  any
access-list 22 permit  232.0.0.0 0.255.255.255
access-list 22 deny    any
access-list 112 deny   ip 223.0.0.0 0.255.255.255 255.255.0.0 0.0.255.255
access-list 112 permit ip any any
access-list 124 deny   ip any host 224.0.2.2
access-list 124 deny   ip any host 224.0.1.3
access-list 124 deny   ip any host 224.0.1.24
access-list 124 deny   ip any host 224.0.1.22
access-list 124 deny   ip any host 224.0.1.2
access-list 124 deny   ip any host 224.0.1.35
access-list 124 deny   ip any host 224.0.1.60
access-list 124 deny   ip any host 224.0.1.39
access-list 124 deny   ip any host 224.0.1.40
access-list 124 deny   ip any 239.0.0.0 0.255.255.255
access-list 124 deny   ip 10.0.0.0 0.255.255.255 any
access-list 124 deny   ip 127.0.0.0 0.255.255.255 any
access-list 124 deny   ip 172.16.0.0 0.15.255.255 any
access-list 124 deny   ip K.168.0.0 0.0.255.255 any
access-list 124 deny   ip 232.0.0.0 0.255.255.255 any
access-list 124 permit ip any any
route-map connected-bgp permit 10
 match ip address 112
 set origin igp
!
snmp-server engineID local 00000009020000100DDEE000
snmp-server community public RO
snmp-server community STSS RW
snmp-server packetsize 2048
snmp-server contact sysadmin
snmp-server chassis-id ISP1BB3
!
tacacs-server host 223.255.254.254
tacacs-server key cisco12345
!
line con 0
 exec-timeout 0 0
 login authentication NOTACACS
 length 40
 transport input none
line aux 0
line vty 0 4
 exec-timeout 0 0
 password lab
!
ntp clock-period 17180261
ntp update-calendar
ntp server 223.255.254.254 version 1
end
```

APPENDIX A

IP Multicast Command Summary

This appendix summarizes all of the Cisco IOS commands used in the interdomain multicast solutions discussed in this book. For more detailed information on these commands, go to the Cisco IOS Software Configuration site:

www.cisco.com/univercd/cc/td/doc/product/software/index.htm

In this appendix, command descriptions use the following conventions:

- **Boldface** applied to commands and keywords that are entered literally as shown.
- *Italics* applied to arguments for which you supply values.
- Vertical bars (|) separate alternative, mutually exclusive elements.
- Square brackets [] indicate optional elements.
- Braces { } indicate a required choice.
- Braces within square brackets [{ }] indicate a required choice within an optional element.

address-family ipv4 Command

Purpose: To enter address family configuration mode for configuring routing sessions, such as Border Gateway Protocol (BGP), that use standard IP Version 4 (IPv4) address prefixes, use the **address-family ipv4** router configuration command. To disable address family configuration mode, use the **no** form of this command.

```
address-family ipv4 [multicast | unicast | vrf vrf-name]
```

```
no address-family ipv4 [multicast | unicast | vrf vrf-name]
```

Syntax Description:

Parameter	Description
multicast	(Optional) Specifies IPv4 multicast address prefixes.
unicast	(Optional) Specifies IPv4 unicast address prefixes.
vrf *vrf-name*	(Optional) Specifies the name of the virtual routing and forwarding (VRF) instance to associate with subsequent IPv4 address family configuration mode commands.

debug ip igmp Command

Purpose: To display Internet Group Management Protocol (IGMP) packets received and sent, and IGMP host-related events, use the **debug ip igmp** privileged EXEC command. To disable debugging output, use the **no** form of this command.

    debug ip igmp

    no debug ip igmp

Syntax Description:

This command has no arguments or keywords.

debug ip mrouting Command

Purpose: To display changes to the IP multicast routing table, use the **debug ip mrouting** privileged EXEC command. To disable debugging output, use the **no** form of this command.

    debug ip mrouting [group]

    no debug ip mrouting [group]

Syntax Description:

Parameter	Description
group	(Optional) Group name or address to monitor the packet activity of a single group.

debug ip urd Command

Purpose: To display debug messages for URL Rendezvous Directory (URD) channel subscription report processing, use the **debug ip urd** EXEC command. To disable debugging of URD reports, use the **no** form of this command.

    debug ip urd [hostname | ip-address]

    no debug ip urd

Syntax Description:

Parameter	Description
hostname	(Optional) The Domain Name System (DNS) name
ip-address	(Optional) The IP address

ip cgmp Command

Purpose: To enable Cisco Group Management Protocol (CGMP) on an interface of a router connected to a Catalyst 5000 switch, use the **ip cgmp** interface configuration command. To disable CGMP routing, use the **no** form of this command.

    ip cgmp [proxy]

    no ip cgmp

Syntax Description:

Parameter	Description
proxy	(Optional) Enables CGMP and the CGMP proxy function.

ip igmp v3lite Command

Purpose: To enable acceptance and processing of Internet Group Management Protocol Version 3 lite (IGMP v3lite) membership reports on an interface, use the **ip igmp v3lite** interface configuration command. To disable IGMP v3lite, use the **no** form of this command.

    ip igmp v3lite

    no ip igmp v3lite

Syntax Description:

This command has no arguments or keywords.

ip igmp version Command

Purpose: To configure which version of Internet Group Management Protocol (IGMP) the router uses, use the **ip igmp version** interface configuration command. To restore the default value, use the **no** form of this command.

    ip igmp version {1 | 2 | 3}

    no ip igmp version

Syntax Description:

Parameter	Description
1	IGMP Version 1
2	IGMP Version 2
3	IGMP Version 3

ip mrm Command

Purpose: To configure an interface to operate as a Test Sender, Test Receiver, or both, for Multicast Routing Monitor (MRM), use the **ip mrm** interface configuration command. To remove the interface as a Test Sender or Test Receiver, use the **no** form of this command.

    ip mrm {test-sender | test-receiver | test-sender-receiver}

    no ip mrm {test-sender | test-receiver | test-sender-receiver}

Syntax Description:

Parameter	Description
test-sender	Configures the interface to be a Test Sender.
test-receiver	Configures the interface to be a Test Receiver.
test-sender-receiver	Configures the interface to be both a Test Sender and Test Receiver (for different groups).

ip mrm manager Command

Purpose: To identify a test by name and place the router in manager configuration mode, use the **ip mrm manager** global configuration command. To remove the test, use the **no** form of this command.

    ip mrm manager test-name

    no ip mrm manager test-name

Syntax Description:

Parameter	Description
test-name	Name of the group of MRM test parameters that follow.

ip mroute-cache Command

Purpose: To configure IP multicast fast switching or multicast distributed switching (MDS), use the **ip mroute-cache** command in interface configuration mode. To disable either of these features, use the **no** form of this command.

    ip mroute-cache [distributed]

    no ip mroute-cache [distributed]

Syntax Description:

Parameter	Description
distributed	(Optional) Enables MDS on the interface. In the case of the Route/Switch Processor (RSP), this keyword is optional; if omitted, fast switching occurs. On the Gigabit Switch Router (GSR), this keyword is required because the GSR does only distributed switching.

ip msdp cache-sa-state Command

Purpose: To have the router create Source-Active (SA) state, use the **ip msdp cache-sa-state** global configuration command.

```
ip msdp cache-sa-state
```

Syntax Description:

This command has no arguments or keywords.

ip msdp originator-id Command

To allow a Multicast Source Discovery Protocol (MSDP) speaker that originates a Source-Active (SA) message to use the IP address of the interface as the rendezvous point (RP) address in the SA message, use the **ip msdp originator-id** global configuration command. To prevent the RP address from being derived in this way, use the **no** form of this command.

```
ip msdp originator-id type number
```

```
no ip msdp originator-id type number
```

Syntax Description:

Parameter	Description
type number	Interface type and number on the local router, whose IP address is used as the RP address in SA messages.

ip msdp peer Command

Purpose: To configure a Multicast Source Discovery Protocol (MSDP) peer, use the **ip msdp peer** global configuration command. To remove the peer relationship, use the **no** form of this command.

```
ip msdp peer {peer-name | peer-address} [connect-source type number] [remote-as as-number]
```

```
no ip msdp peer {peer-name | peer-address}
```

Syntax Description:

Parameter	Description
peer-name	peer-address	Domain Name System (DNS) name or IP address of the router that is to be the MSDP peer.
connect-source type number	(Optional) Interface type and number whose primary address becomes the source IP address for the TCP connection. This interface is on the router being configured.

continues

Continued

remote-as *as-number*	(Optional) Autonomous system number of the MSDP peer used for display purposes only.
	There are cases where a peer might appear to be in another autonomous system (other than the one in which it really resides) when you have an MSDP peer session but do not have a Border Gateway Protocol (BGP) peer session with that peer. In this case, if the peer's prefix is injected by another autonomous system, it is displayed as the autonomous system number of the peer (and is misleading).

ip msdp redistribute Command

Purpose: To configure which (S, G) entries from the multicast routing table are advertised in SA messages originated to Multicast Source Discovery Protocol (MSDP) peers, use the **ip msdp redistribute** global configuration command. To remove the filter, use the **no** form of this command.

```
ip msdp redistribute [list access-list] [asn as-access-list] [route-map map-name]
```

```
no ip msdp redistribute
```

Syntax Description:

Parameter	Description
list *access-list*	(Optional) Standard or extended IP access list number or name that controls which local sources are advertised and to which groups they send.
asn *as-access-list*	(Optional) Standard or extended IP access list number in the range from 1 to 199. This access list number must also be configured in the **ip as-path** global configuration command.
route-map *map-name*	(Optional) Defines the route map.

ip msdp sa-filter in Command

Purpose: To configure an incoming filter list for SA messages received from the specified Multicast Source Discovery Protocol (MSDP) peer, use the **ip msdp sa-filter in** global configuration command. To remove the filter, use the **no** form of this command.

```
ip msdp sa-filter in {peer-address | peer-name} [list access-list] [route-map map-name]
```

```
no ip msdp sa-filter in {peer-address | peer-name} [list access-list] [route-map map-name]
```

Syntax Description:

Parameter	Description
peer-address | *peer-name*	IP address or name of the MSDP peer from which the SA messages are filtered.
list *access-list*	(Optional) IP access list number or name. If no access list is specified, all source/group pairs from the peer are filtered.
route-map *map-name*	(Optional) Route map name. Only those SA messages that meet the match criteria in the route map *map-name* argument pass from the specified MSDP peer. If all match criteria are true, a **permit** keyword from the route map will pass routes through the filter. A **deny** keyword will filter routes.

ip msdp sa-filter out Command

Purpose: To configure an outgoing filter list for SA messages sent to the specified Multicast Source Discovery Protocol (MSDP) peer, use the **ip msdp sa-filter out** global configuration command. To remove the filter, use the **no** form of this command.

```
ip msdp sa-filter out {peer-address | peer-name} [list access-list] [route-map map-name]
```

```
no ip msdp sa-filter out {peer-address | peer-name} [list access-list] [route-map map-name]
```

Syntax Description:

Parameter	Description
peer-address | *peer-name*	IP address or Domain Name System (DNS) name of the MSDP peer to which the SA messages are filtered.
list *access-list*	(Optional) Extended IP access list number or name. If no access list is specified, all source/group pairs are filtered. Only those SA messages that pass the extended access list pass to the specified MSDP peer. If both the **list** and the **route-map** keywords are used, all conditions must be true to pass any (S, G) pairs in outgoing SA messages.
route-map *map-name*	(Optional) Route map name. Only those SA messages that meet the match criteria in the route map *map-name* argument pass to the specified MSDP peer. If all match criteria are true, a **permit** keyword from the route map will pass routes through the filter. A **deny** keyword will filter routes.

ip multicast boundary Command

Purpose: To configure an administratively scoped boundary, use the **ip multicast boundary** interface configuration command. To remove the boundary, use the **no** form of this command.

    ip multicast boundary access-list

    no ip multicast boundary

Syntax Description:

Parameter	Description
access-list	Number or name identifying an access list that controls the range of group addresses affected by the boundary.

ip multicast multipath Command

Purpose: To enable IP multicast traffic load splitting across multiple equal-cost paths, use the **ip multicast multipath** global configuration command. To disable this configuration, use the **no** form of this command.

    ip multicast multipath

    no ip multicast multipath

Syntax Description:

This command has no arguments or keywords.

ip multicast-routing Command

Purpose: To enable IP multicast routing, use the **ip multicast-routing** command in global configuration mode. To disable IP multicast routing, use the **no** form of this command.

    ip multicast-routing [distributed]

    no ip multicast-routing

Syntax Description:

Parameter	Description
distributed	(Optional) Enables multicast distributed switching (MDS).

ip pim Command

Purpose: To enable Protocol Independent Multicast (PIM) on an interface, use the **ip pim** interface configuration command. To disable PIM on the interface, use the **no** form of this command.

```
ip pim {sparse-mode | sparse-dense-mode | dense-mode [proxy-register {list access
    list | route-map map-name}]}
```

```
no ip pim
```

Syntax Description:

Parameter	Description
sparse-mode	Enables sparse mode of operation.
sparse-dense-mode	Treats interface in either sparse mode or dense mode of operation, depending on which mode the multicast group operates in.
dense-mode	Enables dense mode of operation.
proxy-register	(Optional) Enables proxy registering on the interface of a designated router (DR) (leading toward the bordering dense mode region) for multicast traffic from sources not connected to the DR.
list *access-list*	(Optional) Defines the extended access list number or name.
route-map *map-name*	(Optional) Defines the route map.

ip pim accept-register Command

Purpose: To configure a candidate rendezvous point (RP) router to filter PIM register messages, use the **ip pim accept-register** global configuration command. To disable this configuration, use the **no** form of this command.

```
ip pim accept-register {list access-list | route-map map-name}
```

```
no ip pim accept-register {list access-list | route-map map-name}
```

Syntax Description:

Parameter	Description
list *access-list*	Defines the extended access list number or name.
route-map *map-name*	Defines the route map.

ip pim accept-rp Command

Purpose: To configure a router to accept join or prune messages destined for a specified RP and for a specific list of groups, use the **ip pim accept-rp** global configuration command. To remove that check, use the **no** form of this command.

    ip pim accept-rp {rp-address | auto-rp} [access-list]

    no ip pim accept-rp {rp-address | auto-rp} [access-list]

Syntax Description:

Parameter	Description
rp-address	Address of the RP allowed to send join messages to groups in the range specified by the group access list.
auto-rp	Accepts join and register messages only for RPs in the Auto-RP cache.
access-list	(Optional) Access list number or name that defines which groups are subject to the check.

ip pim bsr-border Command

Purpose: To prevent bootstrap router (BSR) messages from being sent or received through an interface, use the **ip pim bsr-border** interface configuration command. To disable this configuration, use the **no** form of this command.

    ip pim bsr-border

    no ip pim bsr-border

Syntax Description:

This command has no arguments or keywords.

ip pim rp-address Command

To configure the address of a PIM RP for a particular group, use the **ip pim rp-address** global configuration command. To remove an RP address, use the **no** form of this command.

    ip pim rp-address rp-address [access-list] [override] [bidir]

    no ip pim rp-address

Syntax Description:

Parameter	Description
rp-address	IP address of a router to be a PIM RP. This is a unicast IP address in four-part, dotted notation.
access-list	(Optional) Access list number or name that defines for which multicast groups the RP should be used.
override	(Optional) Indicates that, if there is a conflict, the RP configured with this command prevails over the RP learned by Auto-RP.
bidir	(Optional) Indicates that the multicast groups specified by the *access-list* argument should operate in bidirectional mode. If the command is configured without this option, the groups specified will operate in PIM sparse mode (PIM-SM).

ip pim send-rp-announce Command

Purpose: To use Auto-RP to configure groups for which the router acts as an RP, use the **ip pim send-rp-announce** global configuration command. To deconfigure this router as an RP, use the **no** form of this command.

```
ip pim send-rp-announce type number scope ttl-value [group-list access-list]
   [interval seconds] [bidir]
```

```
no ip pim send-rp-announce
```

Syntax Description:

Parameter	Description
type number	Interface type and number that identify the RP address.
scope *ttl-value*	Time-to-live (TTL) value that limits the number of Auto-RP announcements.
group-list *access-list*	(Optional) Standard IP access list number or name that defines the group prefixes advertised in association with the RP address. The access list name cannot contain a space or quotation mark and must begin with an alphabetic character to avoid confusion with numbered access lists.
interval *seconds*	(Optional) Specifies the interval between RP announcements (in seconds). The total hold time of the RP announcements is automatically set to three times the value of the interval. The default interval is 60 seconds.
bidir	(Optional) Indicates that the multicast groups specified by the *access-list* argument should operate in bi-directional mode. If the command is configured without this option, the groups specified will operate in Protocol Independent Multicast sparse mode (PIM-SM).

ip pim send-rp-discovery Command

Purpose: To configure the router to be anRP mapping agent, use the **ip pim send-rp-discovery** global configuration command. To restore the default value, use the **no** form of this command.

```
ip pim send-rp-discovery scope ttl-value
```

```
no ip pim send-rp-discovery
```

Syntax Description:

Parameter	Description
scope *ttl-value*	Time-to-live (TTL) value in the IP header that keeps the discovery messages within this number of hops.

ip pim spt-threshold Command

Purpose: To configure when a PIM leaf router should join the shortest path source tree for the specified group, use the **ip pim spt-threshold** global configuration command. To restore the default value, use the **no** form of this command.

```
ip pim spt-threshold {kbps | infinity} [group-list access-list]
```

```
no ip pim spt-threshold
```

Syntax Description:

Parameter	Description
kbps	Traffic rate (in kbps)
infinity	Causes all sources for the specified group to use the shared tree.
group-list *access-list*	(Optional) Indicates which groups the threshold applies to. Must be an IP standard access list number or name. If the value is 0 or is omitted, the threshold applies to all groups.

ip pim ssm Command

To define the Source Specific Multicast (SSM) range of IP multicast addresses, use the **ip pim ssm** global configuration command. To disable the SSM range, use the **no** form of this command.

```
ip pim ssm {default | range access-list}
```

```
no ip pim ssm
```

Syntax Description:

Parameter	Description
default	(Optional) Defines the SSM range access list to 232/8.
range access-list	(Optional) Standard IP access list number or name defining the SSM range.

ip urd Command

Purpose: To enable interception of TCP packets sent to the reserved URL Rendezvous Directory (URD) port 659 on an interface and URD channel subscription report processing, use the **ip urd** interface configuration command. To disable URD on an interface, use the **no** form of this command.

```
ip urd

no ip urd
```

Syntax Description:

This command has no arguments or keywords.

manager Command

Purpose: To specify that an interface is the Manager for Multicast Routing Monitor (MRM) and to specify the multicast group address to which the Test Receiver will listen, use the **manager** manager configuration command. To remove the Manager or group address, use the **no** form of this command.

```
manager type number group ip-address

no manager type number group ip-address
```

Syntax Description:

Parameter	Description
type number	Interface type and number of the Manager. The IP address associated with this interface is the Manager's source address.
group ip address	IP multicast group address to which the Test Receiver will listen.

match nlri Command

Purpose: To match a unicast or multicast Routing Information Base (RIB) entry, use the **match nlri** route-map configuration command. To remove a path list entry, use the **no** form of this command.

```
match nlri {unicast | multicast | unicast multicast}

no match nlri {unicast | multicast | unicast multicast}
```

Syntax Description:

Parameter	Description
unicast	Matches unicast Network Layer Reachability Information (NLRI) from incoming update messages or an RIB for outgoing filters being processed for a route map.
multicast	Matches a multicast NLRI from incoming update messages or an RIB for outgoing filters being processed for a route map.
unicast multicast	This default setting matches either a unicast or multicast NLRI from incoming update messages or an RIB for outgoing filters being processed for a route map.

neighbor activate Command

Purpose: To enable the exchange of information with a neighboring router, use the **neighbor activate** command in address family configuration or router configuration mode. To disable the exchange of an address with a neighboring router, use the **no** form of this command.

```
neighbor {ip-address | peer-group-name} activate

no neighbor {ip-address | peer-group-name} activate
```

Syntax Description:

Parameter	Description
ip-address	IP address of the neighboring router.
peer-group-name	Name of BGP peer group.

neighbor default-originate Command

Purpose: To allow a Border Gateway Protocol (BGP) speaker (the local router) to send the default route 0.0.0.0 to a neighbor for use as a default route, use the **neighbor default-originate** command in address family or router configuration mode. To send no route as a default, use the **no** form of this command.

```
neighbor {ip-address | peer-group-name} default-originate [route-map map-name]

no neighbor {ip-address | peer-group-name} default-originate [route-map map-name]
```

Syntax Description:

Parameter	Description
ip-address	IP address of the neighbor.
peer-group-name	Name of a BGP peer group.
route-map *map-name*	(Optional) Name of the route map. The route map allows route 0.0.0.0 to be injected conditionally.

neighbor peer-group (creating) Command

Purpose: To create a BGP peer group, use the **neighbor peer-group** router configuration command. To remove the peer group and all of its members, use the **no** form of this command.

```
neighbor peer-group-name peer-group [nlri {unicast | multicast | unicast multicast}]
```

```
no neighbor peer-group-name peer-group [nlri {unicast | multicast | unicast multicast}]
```

Syntax Description:

Parameter	Description
peer-group-name	Name of the BGP peer group.
nlri unicast	(Optional) Only unicast Network Layer Reachability Information (NLRI) will be sent to the neighbor. This is the default value.
nlri multicast	(Optional) Only multicast NLRI will be sent to the neighbor.
nlri unicast multicast	(Optional) Both unicast and multicast NLRI will be sent to the neighbor.

neighbor remote-as Command

Purpose: To add an entry to the BGP neighbor table, use the **neighbor remote-as** router configuration command. To remove an entry from the table, use the **no** form of this command.

```
neighbor {ip-address | peer-group-name} remote-as number [nlri {unicast | multicast | unicast multicast}]
```

```
no neighbor {ip-address | peer-group-name} remote-as number [nlri {unicast | multicast | unicast multicast}]
```

Syntax Description:

Parameter	Description
ip-address	IP address of the neighboring router.
peer-group-name	Name of the BGP peer group.
number	Autonomous system to which the neighbor belongs.
nlri unicast	(Optional) Only unicast NLRI will be sent to the neighbor. Unicast NLRI is sent in conventional BGP encoding. If no NLRI designation is specified, **nlri unicast** is the default value.
nlri multicast	(Optional) Only multicast NLRI will be sent to the neighbor.
nlri unicast multicast	(Optional) Both unicast and multicast NLRI will be sent to the neighbor.

neighbor route-map Command

Purpose: To apply a route map to incoming or outgoing routes, use the **neighbor route-map** command in address family or router configuration mode. To remove a route map, use the **no** form of this command.

```
neighbor {ip-address | peer-group-name} route-map map-name {in | out}
```

```
no neighbor {ip-address | peer-group-name} route-map map-name {in | out}
```

Syntax Description:

Parameter	Description
ip-address	IP address of the neighbor.
peer-group-name	Name of a BGP or multiprotocol BGP peer group.
map-name	Name of a route map.
in	Applies route map to incoming routes.
out	Applies route map to outgoing routes.

network (BGP) Command

Purpose: To specify the list of networks for the BGP routing process, use this form of the **network** router configuration command. To remove an entry, use the **no** form of this command.

```
network network-number [mask network-mask] [nlri {unicast | multicast | unicast multicast}]
```

```
no network network-number [mask network-mask] [nlri {unicast | multicast | unicast multicast}]
```

Syntax Description:

Parameter	Description
network-number	Network that BGP will advertise.
mask	(Optional) Network or subnetwork mask.
network-mask	(Optional) Network mask address.
nlri unicast	(Optional) The specified network is injected into the unicast RIB only. NLRI unicast is the default value if no NLRI designation is specified.
nlri multicast	(Optional) The specified network is injected into the multicast RIB only.
nlri unicast multicast	(Optional) The specified network is injected into both the unicast and multicast RIBs.

receivers Command

Purpose: To establish Test Receivers for MRM, use the **receivers** command in manager configuration mode. To restore the default values, use the **no** form of this command.

```
receivers {access-list} [sender-list {access-list} [packet-delay]] [window seconds]
   [report-delay seconds] [loss percentage] [no-join] [monitor | poll]
```

```
no receivers {access-list} [sender-list {access-list} [packet-delay]] [window
   seconds] [report-delay seconds] [loss percentage] [no-join] [monitor | poll]
```

Syntax Description:

Parameter	Description
access-list	IP named or numbered access list that establishes the Test Receivers. Only these Test Receivers are subject to the other keywords and arguments specified in this command.
sender-list access-list	(Optional) Specifies the sources that the Test Receiver should monitor. If the named or numbered access list matches any access list specified in the **senders** command, the associated **packet-delay** milliseconds keyword and argument of that **senders** command are used in this command. Otherwise, the packet-delay argument is required in this **receivers** command.
packet-delay	(Optional) Specifies the delay between test packets (in milliseconds). If the **sender-list** access list matches any access list specified in the **senders** command, the associated **packet-delay** milliseconds keyword and argument of that **senders** command are used in the **receivers** command. Otherwise, the packet-delay argument is required in this **receivers** command.

continues

Continued

window *seconds*	(Optional) Test period duration (in seconds). This is a sliding window of time in which packet count is collected so the loss percentage can be calculated. The default is 5 seconds.
report-delay *seconds*	(Optional) Delay (in seconds) between staggered status reports from multiple Test Receivers to the Manager. The delay prevents multiple receivers from sending status reports to the Manager at the same time for the same failure. Receiver 1 sends status, *seconds* later Receiver 2 sends status, *seconds* later Receiver 3 sends status, and so on. This value is relevant only if multiple Test Receivers exist. The default is 1 second.
loss *percentage*	(Optional) Threshold percentage of packet loss required before a status report is triggered. The default is 0 percent, which means that a status report is sent for any packet loss. (This value is not applied to packet duplication; a fault report is sent for any duplicated packets.)
no-join	(Optional) Specifies that the Test Receiver does not join the monitored group. The default is that the Test Receiver joins the monitored group.
monitor | **poll**	(Optional) Specifies whether the Test Receiver monitors the test group or polls for receiver statistics. The **monitor** keyword means that the Test Receiver reports only if the test criteria are met. The **poll** keyword means that the Test Receiver sends status reports regularly, whether or not test criteria are met. The default is the **monitor** keyword.

redistribute (IP) Command

Purpose: To redistribute routes from one routing domain to another routing domain, use the **redistribute** command in router configuration mode. To disable redistribution, use the **no** form of this command.

```
redistribute protocol [process-id] {level-1 | level-1-2 | level-2} [as-number]
   [metric metric-value] [metric-type type-value] [match {internal | external 1 |
   external 2}] [tag tag-value] [route-map map-tag] [weight number-value] [subnets]

no redistribute protocol [process-id] {level-1 | level-1-2 | level-2} [as-number]
   [metric metric-value] [metric-type type-value] [match {internal | external 1 |
   external 2}] [tag tag-value] [route-map map-tag] [weight number-value] [subnets]
```

Syntax Description:

Parameter	Description
protocol	Source protocol from which routes are being redistributed. It can be one of the following keywords: **bgp**, **connected**, **egp**, **igrp**, **isis**, **ospf**, **static** [**ip**], or **rip**.
	Use the **static** [**ip**] keyword to redistribute IP static routes. Use the optional **ip** keyword when redistributing into the Intermediate System-to-Intermediate System (IS-IS) protocol.
	The **connected** keyword refers to routes that are established automatically by virtue of having enabled IP on an interface. For routing protocols such as Open Shortest Path First (OSPF) and IS-IS, these routes will be redistributed as external to the autonomous system.
process-id	(Optional) For the **bgp**, **egp**, or **igrp** keyword, this 16-bit decimal number is an autonomous system number.
	For the **isis** keyword, this is an optional tag value that defines a meaningful name for a routing process. You can specify only one IS-IS process per router. Creating a name for a routing process means that you use names when configuring routing.
	For the **ospf** keyword, this is an appropriate OSPF process ID from which routes are to be redistributed. This identifies the routing process. This value takes the form of a nonzero decimal number.
	For the **rip** keyword, no *process ID* value is needed.
level-1	Specifies that, for IS-IS, Level 1 routes are redistributed into other IP routing protocols independently.
level-1-2	Specifies that, for IS-IS, both Level 1 and Level 2 routes are redistributed into other IP routing protocols.
level-2	Specifies that, for IS-IS, Level 2 routes are redistributed into other IP routing protocols independently.
as-number	(Optional) Autonomous number system for the redistributed route
metric *metric-value*	(Optional) Metric used for the redistributed route. If a value is not specified for this option and no value is specified using the **default-metric** command, the default metric value is 0. Use a value consistent with the destination protocol.

continues

Continued

metric-type *type-value*	(Optional) For OSPF, the external link type associated with the default route advertised into the OSPF routing domain. It can be one of two values: **1**—Type 1 external route **2**—Type 2 external route If a **metric-type** is not specified, the Cisco IOS software adopts a Type 2 external route. For IS-IS, it can be one of two values: **internal**—IS-IS metric that is less than 63. **external**—IS-IS metric that is greater than 64 but less than 128. The default is **internal**.
match {**internal** | **external 1** | **external 2**}	(Optional) For the criteria by which OSPF routes are redistributed into other routing domains. It can be one of the following: **internal**—Routes that are internal to a specific autonomous system. **external 1**—Routes that are external to the autonomous system, but are imported into OSPF as Type 1 external routes. **external 2**—Routes that are external to the autonomous system, but are imported into OSPF as Type 2 external routes.
tag *tag-value*	(Optional) 32-bit decimal value attached to each external route. This is not used by OSPF itself. It may be used to communicate information between Autonomous System Boundary Routers (ASBRs). If none is specified, the remote autonomous system number is used for routes from Border Gateway Protocol (BGP) and Exterior Gateway Protocol (EGP); for other protocols, zero (0) is used.
route-map	(Optional) Route map that should be interrogated to filter the importation of routes from this source routing protocol to the current routing protocol. If not specified, all routes are redistributed. If this keyword is specified, but no route map tags are listed, no routes will be imported.
map-tag	(Optional) Identifier of a configured route map
weight *number-value*	(Optional) Network weight when redistributing into BGP. An integer from 0 to 65,535.
subnets	(Optional) For redistributing routes into OSPF, defines the scope of redistribution for the specified protocol.

senders Command

Purpose: To configure Test Sender parameters used inMRM, use the **senders** manager configuration command. To restore the default values, use the **no** form of this command.

```
senders {access-list} [packet-delay milliseconds] [rtp | udp] [target-only | all-
    multicasts | all-test-senders] [proxy_src]
```

```
no senders {access-list} [packet-delay milliseconds] [rtp | udp] [target-only | all-
    multicasts | all-test-senders] [proxy_src]
```

Syntax Description:

Parameter	Description
access-list	IP named or numbered access list that defines which Test Senders are involved in the test and to which Test Senders these parameters apply.
packet-delay *milliseconds*	(Optional) Specifies the delay between test packets (in milliseconds). The default is 200 milliseconds, which results in 5 packets per second.
rtp | udp	(Optional) Encapsulation of test packets, either Real-Time Transport Protocol (RTP)-encapsulated or User Datagram Protocol (UDP)-encapsulated. The default is RTP-encapsulated.
target-only	(Optional) Specifies that test packets be sent out on the targeted interface only (that is, the interface with the IP address that is specified in the Test Sender request target field). By default, test packets are sent as described in the **all-multicasts** keyword.
all-multicasts	(Optional) Specifies that the test packets be sent out on all interfaces that are enabled with IP multicast. This is the default way that test packets are sent.
all-test-senders	(Optional) Specifies that test packets be sent out on all interfaces that have test-sender mode enabled. By default, test packets are sent as described in the **all-multicasts** keyword.
proxy_src	(Optional) Source IP address for which the Test Sender will proxy test packets. Use this if you want to test a specific source to determine whether the multicast distribution tree is working.

set nlri Command

Purpose: To inject a route into the unicast or multicast RIB, use the **set nlri** route-map configuration command. To remove the set instruction, use the **no** form of this command.

```
set nlri {unicast | multicast}
```

```
no set nlri {unicast | multicast}
```

Syntax Description:

Parameter	Description
unicast	Injects a route that passes the match criteria into the unicast RIB.
multicast	Injects a route that passes the match criteria into the multicast RIB.

show ip bgp ipv4 multicast summary Command

Purpose: To display a summary of IP Version 4 (IPv4) multicast database-related information, use the **show ip bgp ipv4 multicast summary** EXEC command.

```
show ip bgp ipv4 multicast summary
```

Syntax Description:

This command has no arguments or keywords.

show ip bgp neighbors Command

Purpose: To display information about the TCP and BGP connections to neighbors, use the **show ip bgp neighbors** EXEC command.

```
show ip bgp neighbors [neighbor-address] [received-routes | routes | advertised-routes
    | {paths regexp} | dampened-routes]
```

Syntax Description:

Parameter	Description
neighbor-address	(Optional) Address of the neighbor whose routes have been learned. If this argument is omitted, all neighbors are displayed.
received-routes	(Optional) Displays all received routes (both accepted and rejected) from the specified neighbor.
routes	(Optional) Displays all routes that are received and accepted. This is a subset of the output from the **received-routes** keyword.
advertised-routes	(Optional) Displays all routes that the router has advertised to the neighbor.
paths *regexp*	(Optional) Regular expression that is used to match the paths received.
dampened-routes	(Optional) Displays the dampened routes to the neighbor at the IP address specified.

show ip igmp groups Command

Purpose: To display the multicast groups with receivers that are directly connected to the router and were learned through Internet Group Management Protocol (IGMP), use the **show ip igmp groups** EXEC command.

    show ip igmp groups [group-name | group-address | type number] [detail]

Syntax Description:

Parameter	Description
group-name	(Optional) Name of the multicast group, as defined in the Domain Name System (DNS) hosts table.
group-address	(Optional) Address of the multicast group. This multicast IP address appears in four-part, dotted notation.
type	(Optional) Interface type
number	(Optional) Interface number
detail	(Optional) Provides a detailed description of the sources known through IGMPv3, IGMP v3lite, or URD.

show ip mbgp summary Command

Purpose: To display a summary of multicast RIB-related information, use the **show ip mbgp summary** EXEC command.

    show ip mbgp summary

Syntax Description:

This command has no arguments or keywords.

show ip mroute Command

Purpose: To display the contents of the IP multicast routing table, use the **show ip mroute** EXEC command.

    show ip mroute [group-address | group-name] [source-address | source-name] [type
       number] [summary] [count] [active kbps]

Syntax Description:

Parameter	Description
group-address	group-name	(Optional) IP address or name multicast group, as defined in the DNS hosts table.

continues

Continued

source-address | *source-name*	(Optional) IP address or name of a multicast source.
type number	(Optional) Interface type and number
summary	(Optional) Displays a one-line, abbreviated summary of each entry in the IP multicast routing table.
count	(Optional) Displays group and source statistics, including number of packets, packets per second, average packet size, and bytes per second.
active *kbps*	(Optional) Displays the rate that active sources are sending to multicast groups. Active sources are those sending at the *kbps* value or higher. The *kbps* argument defaults to 4 kbps.

show ip msdp peer Command

Purpose: To display detailed information about the Multicast Source Discovery Protocol (MSDP) peer, use the **show ip msdp peer** EXEC command.

```
show ip msdp peer [peer-address | peer-name]
```

Syntax Description:

Parameter	Description
peer-address | *peer-name*	(Optional) Address or name of the MSDP peer for which information is displayed.

show ip msdp sa-cache Command

Purpose: To display (S, G) state learned from MSDP peers, use the **show ip msdp sa-cache** EXEC command.

```
show ip msdp sa-cache [group-address | source-address | group-name | source-name]
    [group-address | source-address | group-name | source-name] [as-number]
```

Syntax Description:

Parameter	Description
group-address | *source-address* | *group-name* | *source-name*	(Optional) Group address, source address, group name, or source name of the group or source about which (S, G) information is displayed. If two addresses or names are specified, an (S, G) entry corresponding to those addresses is displayed. If only one group address is specified, all sources for that group are displayed. If no options are specified, the entire SA cache is displayed.
as-number	(Optional) Only state originated by the autonomous system number specified is displayed.

INDEX

A

AC routers
    interdomain multicast configuration, 256–259
        example, 142–149
address scoping, 9
addresses, IP multicast, 7
    Class D, 7
    globally scoped addresses, 8
    GLOP addresses, 8
    Layer 2, 9
    limited scope addresses, 8
    reserved link local addresses, 7
    source specific addresses, 8
address-family ipv4 command, 273
administratively scoped addresses, 8
Anycast RP, 29–31
application-level multicast, 5
AS (autonomous system)
    address scoping, 9
    GLOP addressing, 8
ASICs (application-specific integrated circuits), 18
assignment of IP multicast addresses, 7
    globally scoped addresses, 8
    GLOP addresses, 8
    limited scope addresses, 8
    reserved link local addresses, 7
    source specific multicast addresses, 8

B

backbone routers
    interdomain multicast configuration, 197–233, 260–271
        characteristics, 153–154, 160–161, 168, 175, 180, 185, 189
        configuration file, 154–193
        example configuration, 93–127
BGP peering address, setting for Anycast RP, 31
bidirectional shared trees, 26
Bidir-PIM (Bidirectional PIM), 26–27

C

caching SA messages, 86
CGMP (Cisco Group Management Protocol), 16–17

characteristics of backbone routers, interdomain multicast deployment, 153–154, 160–161, 168, 175, 180, 185, 189
Class D IP multicast addresses, 7
    mapping to MAC addresses, 10
commands
    address-family ipv4, 273
    debug ip igmp, 274
    debug ip mrouting, 274
    debug ip urd, 274
    ip cgmp, 275
    ip igmp v3lite, 275
    ip igmp version, 275
    ip mrm, 276
    ip mrm manager, 276
    ip mroute-cache, 276
    ip msdp cache-sa-state, 277
    ip msdp originator-id, 277
    ip msdp peer, 277–278
    ip msdp redistribute, 278
    ip msdp sa-filter in, 278
    ip msdp sa-filter out, 279
    ip multicast boundary, 280
    ip multicast multipath, 280
    ip multicast-routing, 280
    ip pim, 281
    ip pim accept-register, 281
    ip pim accept-rp, 282
    ip pim bsr-border, 282
    ip pim rp-address, 282–283
    ip pim send-rp-announce, 283
    ip pim send-rp-discovery, 284
    ip pim spt-threshold, 284
    ip pim ssm, 284
    ip urd, 285
    manager, 285
    match nlri, 285
    neighbor activate, 286
    neighbor default-originate, 286–287
    neighbor peer-group, 287
    neighbor remote-as, 287–288
    neighbor route-map, 288
    network, 288
    receivers, 289
    redistribute, 290, 292
    senders, 293
    set nlri, 293
    show ip bgp ipv4 multicast summary, 294
    show ip bgp neighbors, 294
    show ip igmp groups, 295
    show ip mbgp summary, 295

show ip mroute, 295
show ip msdp peer, 296
show ip msdp sa-cache, 296
comparing
    shared and source trees, 21–22
    SSM and ISM, 239
configuration files, interdomain multicast backbone router deployment, 154–193
configuring
    MBGP
        peering sessions, 42–44, 76–84
        verifying multicast routing, 45
    MSDP peering sessions, 79–81, 85
    multicast borders, 46–47, 81–82, 87
    SA caching, 46, 74, 86
    SA filters, 45–46, 85
    SSM operation mode, 240

D

DA routers, interdomain multicast implementation, 128–142
datagram delivery with SSM, 239
debug ip igmp command, 274
debug ip mrouting command, 274
debug ip urd command, 274
denial-of-service attacks, preventing with SSM, 244
dense mode (PIM), 24
deploying
    interdomain multicast, 38, 42–47
        AC routers, example configuration, 142–149
        backbone routers, characteristics, 153–154, 160–161, 168, 175, 180, 185, 189
        backbone routers, configuration files, 154–193
        backbone routers, example configuration, 93–127
        connecting customers to infrastructure, 48
        DA routers, example configuration, 129–141
        MBGP configuration, 76–79, 82–84
        medium-scale ISPs, 59–75
        MSDP configuration, 79–81, 85
        multicast border configuration, 81–82, 87
        prerequisites, 38–39
        SA caching configuration, 86
        SA filter configuration, 85
        small-scale ISPs, 52–58
    intradomain multicast, 40
        global multicast configuration, 40
        in small-scale ISPs, 49–52
        interface configuration, 41
        RP configuration, 42
        RP selection, 42
        small-scale ISPs, 49–52
    SSM
        ramifications, 245–247
        requirements, 240
devices
    AC routers , interdomain multicast configuration, 142–149, 256–259
    backbone routers
        characteristics, 153–154, 160–161, 168, 175, 180, 185, 189
        configuration file, 154–193
        interdomain multicast configuration, 93–127, 197–233, 260–271
    DA routers, interdomain multicast implementation, 129–141
    icons, xix
distribution trees, shared trees
    bidirectional, 26
    unidirectional (PIM-SM), 25

E

efficiency of IP multicast, 5
establishing
    interdomain multicast strategy, 42–47
        connecting customers to infrastructure, 48
    intradomain multicast strategy, 40
        global multicast configuration, 40
        interface configuration, 41
        RP configuration, 42
        RP selection, 42
Ethernet
    mapping Class D multicast addresses to MAC addresses, 10
    switched backbone segments, 18
example configurations
    interdomain multicast
        AC routers 142–149, 256–259
        backbone routers, 93–127, 260–271
        DA routers, 128–142
        medium-scale ISP implementation, 59–75
        small-scale ISP implementation, 52–58
    intradomain multicast, small-scale ISP implementation, 49–52
examples
    of Anycast RP, 31
    of IP multicast, 6
EXCLUDE mode (IGMPv3), 15

F-G-H-I

fast switching, interface configuration, 41
field definitions
    IGMPv3 query messages, 14
    IGMPv3 report messages, 8–9, 15
filtering SA messages, 45–46, 85
forcing Router ID on Anycast RP, 31

globally scoped addresses, 8
GLOP addresses, 8
    IP address management, 244

IANA (Internet Assigned Numbers Authority), 7–8
    globally scoped addresses, 8
    GLOP addresses, 8
    limited scope addresses, 8
    reserved link local addresses, 7
    source specific multicast addresses, 8
icons
    network connections, xx
    peripheral devices, xix
IGMP (Internet Group Management Protocol), 11
    snooping, 17
    version 1, 11
    version 2, 12
    version 3
        EXCLUDE mode, 15
        host signaling, implementing SSM with Cisco IOS software, 241
        INCLUDE mode, 15
        source filtering, 13
IGMP v3lite host signaling, implementing SSM with Cisco IOS software, 241–242
implementing
    interdomain multicast, 38, 42–47
        AC router configuration, 142–149
        backbone router characteristics, 153–154, 160–161, 168, 175, 180, 185, 189
        backbone router configuration, 93–127, 154–193
        DA router configuration, 128–142
        multicast border configuration, 81–82, 87
        SA caching configuration, 86
        SA filter configuration, 85
        connecting customers to infrastructure, 48
        MBGP peering sessions, 76–84
        medium-scale ISPs, 59–75
        MSDP peering sessions, 79–81, 85
        prerequisites, 38–39
        small-scale ISPs, 52–58

    with SSM, 237–238
    intradomain multicast, 40
        global multicast configuration, 40
        in small-scale ISPs, 49–52
        interface configuration, 41
        RP configuration, 42
        RP selection, 42
    SSM
        IGMP v3lite host signaling, 241–242
        IGMPv3 host signaling, 241
        URD host signaling, 242–252
INCLUDE mode (IGMPv3), 15
installing SSM, 245
interdomain multicast
    connecting customers to infrastructure, 48
    implementing, 42–47
    prerequisites, 38–39

    MBGP, 27
    MSDP, 28
        AC routers, example configuration, 142–149
        Anycast RP, 29–31
        backbone router characteristics, 197–233
        backbone routers, example configuration, 93–127
        DA routers, example configuration, 128–142
    SSM, 32, 237
        benefits of, 244
        device characteristics, 256–271
        ramifications of using, 245
        topology, 238
intradomain multicast
    Bidir-PIM, 26–27
    global multicast configuration, 40
    IGMP, 11
        version 1, 11
        version 2, 12
        version 3, 13–15
    implementing, 40
    interface configuration, 41
    multicast distribution trees, 19
        shared trees, 20
        source trees, 19–20
    multicast forwarding, 22
        RPF, 22–23
    PGM, 27
    PIM, 24
        dense mode, 24
        sparse mode, 24–25
    RP configuration, 42
    RP selection, 42

IP addresses

IP addresses
- managing with SSM, 244
- reserved SSM range, 239

ip cgmp command, 275
ip igmp v3lite command, 275
ip igmp version command, 275
ip mrm command, 276
ip mrm manager command, 276
ip mroute-cache command, 276
ip msdp cache-sa-state command, 277
ip msdp originator-id command, 277
ip msdp peer command, 45, 277–278
ip msdp redistribute command, 278
ip msdp sa-filter in command, 278
ip msdp sa-filter out command, 279
IP multicast
- addresses, 7
  - Class D, 7
  - globally scoped addresses, 8
  - GLOP addresses, 8
  - Layer 2, 9
  - limited scope addresses, 8
  - reserved link local addresses, 7
  - source specific multicast addresses, 8
- Class D addresses, mapping to MAC addresses, 10
- efficiency of, 5
- example, 6
- forwarding, 22
  - RPF, 22–23
- groups, 6
- interdomain multicast
  - MBGP, 27
  - MSDP, 28–31
  - SSM, 32
- intradomain multicast
  - Bidir-PIM, 26–27
  - PGM, 27
  - PIM, 24–25
- Layer 2 switching environments, 16
  - CGMP, 16–17
  - IGMP snooping, 17
  - RGMP, 18

ip multicast boundary command, 280
ip multicast multipath command, 280
ip multicast-routing command, 280
ip pim accept-register command, 281
ip pim accept-rp command, 282
ip pim bsr-border command, 282
ip pim command, 281
ip pim rp-address command, 282–283
ip pim send-rp-announce command, 283
ip pim send-rp-discovery command, 284
ip pim spt-threshold command, 284
ip pim ssm command, 284
ip urd command, 285
ISM (Internet Standard Multicast), comparing with SSM, 239
ISPs
- interdomain multicast
  - connecting customers to infrastructure, 48
  - implementing, 38–39, 42–47
  - medium scale ISPs, 59–75
  - small-scale ISPs, 52–58
- intradomain multicast
  - global multicast configuration, 40
  - implementing, 40
  - interface configuration, 41
  - RP configuration, 42
  - RP selection, 42
  - small-scale ISPs, 49-52

J-K-L

LANs
- Ethernet
  - mapping Class D multicast addresses to MAC addresses, 10
  - switched backbone segments, 18
  - IP multicast, broadcast bit, 9
- Layer 2 switching, multicast, 16
  - addresses, 9
  - CGMP, 16–17
  - IGMP snooping, 17
  - RGMP, 18
- leave group messages (IGMPv2), 12
- limited scope addresses, 8

M

manager command, 285
managing IP addresses with SSM, 244
mapping Class D addresses to MAC addresses, 10
match nlri command, 285
MBGP (Multiprotocol Border Gateway Protocol), 27
- multicast routing, verifying, 45
- peering sessions, configuring, 42–44, 76, 82–84
medium-scale ISPs, interdomain multicast example configuration, 59–75
membership, IGMPv3 multicast groups, 15

memory requirements, shared tree-only environments, 22
messages
    IGMPv2, leave group, 12
    IGMPv3 query messages, field definitions, 14
    IGMPv3 report messages, field definitions, 8–9, 15
    SA
        caching, 86
        filtering, 45–46, 85
MSDP (Multicast Source Discovery Protocol), 28
    AC routers, example configuration, 142–149
    Anycast RP, 29–30
        forcing Router ID, 31
    backbone routers, example configuration, 93–127
    DA routers, example configuration, 128–142
    implementing interdomain multicast, backbone router characteristics, 197–233
    peering sessions, 28
        configuring, 79–81, 85
        verifying, 46
multicast
    application-level, 5
    borders
        configuring, 46–47
        interdomain multicast configuration, 81–82, 87
    distribution trees, 19
        shared trees, 20
        source trees, 19–20
    forwarding, 22
        RPF, 22–23
    groups, 6
    host groups, 239
    interdomain
        backbone router characteristics, 153–154, 160–161, 168, 175, 180, 185, 189
        backbone router configuration file, 154–193
        Bidir-PIM, 26–27
        connecting customers to infrastructure, 48
        implementing, 38–39, 42–47
        implementing with SSM, 237–238
    intradomain
        global multicast configuration, 40
        IGMP, 11–15
        implementing, 40
        interface configuration, 41
        PGM, 27
        PIM, 24–25
        RP configuration, 42
        RP selection, 42

Layer 2 switching environments, 16
    CGMP, 16–17
    IGMP snooping, 17
    RGMP, 18

N–O

neighbor activate command, 286
neighbor default-originate command, 286–287
neighbor peer-group command, 287
neighbor remote-as command, 287–288
neighbor route-map command, 288
network command, 288
network connections, icons for, xx
operation of URD host signaling, 247–249

P-Q

packets, IGMPv3 queries, 13
peering sessions
    MBGP, configuring, 42–44, 76–84
    MSDP, 28
        configuring, 79–81, 85
        verifying, 46, 86–87
PGM (Pragmatic General Multicast), 27
PIM (Protocol Independent Multicast), 24
    See also Bidir-PIM
    dense mode, 24
    sparse mode, 24–25
prerequisites for implementing URD host signaling, 249
preventing denial-of-service attacks with SSM, 244

query messages (IGMPv3), 13
    field definitions, 14

R

ramifications of deploying SSM, 245–247
receivers command, 289
redistribute command, 290–292
report messages (IGMPv3), field definitions, 8–9, 15
requirements for SSM operation, 240
reserved address range (SSM), 239
reserved link local addresses, 7

RFCs
    online reference, 40
    RFC 1112 "*Host Extensions for IP Multicasting*", 7
RGMP (Router-Port Group Management Protocol), 18
RPs (rendezvous points), 20
    Anycast RP, 30–31
    configuring, 42
RPF (Reverse Path Forwarding), 22
    RPF check, 23

S-T

SA caching
    configuring, 46, 86
    enabling, 74
SA messages, filtering, 45–46, 85
senders command, 293
set nlri command, 293
shared trees, 20
    bidirectional, 26
    unidirectional (PIM-SM), 25
    versus source trees, 21–22
show ip bgp ipv4 multicast summary command, 294
show ip bgp neighbors command, 294
show ip igmp groups command, 295
show ip mbgp summary command, 295
show ip mroute command, 295
show ip msdp peer command, 296
show ip msdp sa-cache command, 296
small-scale ISPs
    interdomain multicast, example configuration, 52–58
    intradomain multicast, example configuration, 49–52
source filtering, 13
source specific multicast addresses, 8
source trees, 19–20
    unidirecitonal (PIM-SM), 25
    versus shared trees, 21–22
sparse mode (PIM), 24–25
SSM (Source Specific Multicast), 32
    address management, 246
    broadcast applications, 245
    comparing with ISM, 239
    datagram delivery, 239
    description, 238
    IGMP v3lite host signaling, 241–242
    IGMPv3 host signaling, 241
    implementing interdomain multicast, 237
    device characteristics, 256–260, 263–271
    topology, 238
    installation, 245
    IP address management, 244
    IP address range, 239
    legacy application support, 246
    operational requirements, 240
    prevention of denial-of-service attacks, 244
    ramification of deploying, 245–247
    state maintenance limitations, 247
    URD host signaling, 242
        deployment strategy, 243
        implementing, 249–252
        network topology, 243–245
        operation, 247–249
state maintenance limitations with SSM, 247
STP (shortest path tree), 19
switching, IP multicast handling, 16
    CGMP, 16–17
    IGMP snooping, 17
    RGMP, 18
syntax, URD intercept URLs, 247

U

unidirectional shared trees, PIM-SM, 25
URD host signaling, implementing SSM with Cisco IOS software, 242, 249–252
    deployment strategy, 243
    network topology, 243–245
    operation, 247–249
    prerequisites, 249
URD intercept URL, 247–249
URLs
    RFC online reference, 40
    URD intercept URLs, 247–249

V-W-X-Y-Z

verifying
    MBGP multicast routing, 45
    MDSP peering sessions, 46
    MSDP peering sessions, 86–87
wildcard notation, shared trees, 21

Hey, you've got enough worries.
Don't let IT training be one of them.

Get on the fast track to IT training at InformIT,
your total Information Technology training network.

 | **www.informit.com** | **Cisco Press**

- Hundreds of timely articles on dozens of topics ■ Discounts on IT books from all our publishing partners, including Sams Publishing ■ Free, unabridged books from the InformIT Free Library ■ "Expert Q&A"—our live, online chat with IT experts ■ Faster, easier certification and training from our Web- or classroom-based training programs ■ Current IT news ■ Software downloads
- Career-enhancing resources

InformIT is a registered trademark of Pearson. Copyright ©2001 by Pearson.
Copyright ©2001 by Sams Publishing.

Train with authorized Cisco Learning Partners.

Discover all that's possible on the Internet.

One of the biggest challenges facing networking professionals is how to stay current with today's ever-changing technologies in the global Internet economy. Nobody understands this better than Cisco Learning Partners, the only companies that deliver training developed by Cisco Systems.

Just go to **cisco.com/go/training**. You'll find more than 120 Cisco Learning Partners in over 90 countries worldwide.* Only Cisco Learning Partners have instructors that are certified by Cisco to provide recommended training on Cisco networks and to prepare you for certifications.

To get ahead in this world, you first have to be able to keep up. Insist on training that is developed and authorized by Cisco, as indicated by the Cisco Learning Partner or Cisco Learning Solutions Partner logo.

Visit **cisco.com/go/training** today.

Copyright © 2001 Cisco Systems, Inc. All rights reserved. Empowering the Internet Generation is a service mark, and Cisco, Cisco Systems, and the Cisco Systems logo are registered trademarks of Cisco Systems, Inc. or its affiliates in the U.S. and certain other countries. *Valid as of December 15, 2000.

CISCO SYSTEMS

Cisco Press

CCNA® #640-607
Knowledge needed.
Experience required.

Learn.
Understand the concepts

Experience.
Apply your knowledge through hands-on labs

Prepare.
Get into exam mode

Practice.
Confirm your readiness—and practice, practice, practice!

**Cisco Certification is serious business.
Invest wisely.**

Go to ciscopress.com/ccna to find out more about these and other Cisco Press books and software products

Cisco Press CCNA Solutions

Interconnecting Cisco Network Devices
Cisco Systems, Edited by Steve McQuerry, CCIE
1-57870-111-2 • **AVAILABLE NOW**

Based on the Cisco-recommended CCNA training course taught worldwide, this is the official Coursebook from Cisco Systems that teaches you how to configure Cisco switches and routers in multiprotocol internetworks. This book provides you with the knowledge needed to identify and recommend the best Cisco solutions for small- to medium-sized businesses. Prepare for CCNA exam #640-607 while learning the fundamentals of setting up, configuring, maintaining, and troubleshooting Cisco networks.

CCNA Practical Studies
Gary Heap, CCIE, and Lynn Maynes, CCIE
1-58720-046-5 • **AVAILABLE NOW**

You learned the concepts Cisco says a CCNA should know, but can you put those concepts into practice? Gain critical hands-on experience with *CCNA Practical Studies*. This title provides practice scenarios that you can experiment with on lab equipment, a networking simulator, or a remote-access networking lab. It is the only practical lab book recommended by Cisco Systems for CCNA preparation.

Cisco CCNA Exam #640-607 Flash Card Practice Kit
Eric Rivard
1-58720-048-1 • **AVAILABLE NOW**

CCNA test time is rapidly approaching. You learned the concepts, you have the experience to put them into practice, and now you want to practice, practice, practice until exam time. *Cisco CCNA Exam #640-607 Flash Card Practice Kit* is an essential final-stage study tool with more than 350 flash cards for memory retention, 550 practice exam questions to verify your knowledge, and 54 study sheets for review of complex topics. Flash cards come in print and electronic formats, including PC, Palm® OS, and Pocket PC for optimal flexibility.

ciscopress.com

Cisco Press CCNA Solutions

Cisco CCNA #640-607 Preparation Library
Wendell Odom, CCIE; Steven McQuerry, CCIE; Cisco Systems
1-58705-093-5 • **AVAILABLE NOW**

The *Cisco CCNA #640-607 Preparation Library* is a comprehensive study package that combines the Cisco-recommended CCNA Coursebooks—*Interconnecting Cisco Network Devices* and *Internetworking Technologies Handbook*, Third Edition, with Cisco *CCNA Exam #640-607 Certification Guide* to form a value-priced library for CCNA preparation. Learn what you need to know, prepare for the exam, and succeed.

Cisco CCNA Exam #640-607 Certification Guide
Wendell Odom, CCIE
1-58720-055-4 • **AVAILABLE NOW**

A comprehensive late-stage study tool for CCNA #640-607 preparation, this new edition is completely updated to include technology advancements and new learning elements. Key updates and additions include hands-on lab exercises; updates to LAN, subnetting, and Frame Relay sections; "Credit" sections highlighting content that is beyond the scope of the exam but critical for you to know in your daily job; and a subnetting appendix. The accompanying CD-ROM includes a comprehensive CCNA #640-607 test bank of practice exam questions.

ciscopress.com

Cisco Press
Learning is serious business.
Invest wisely.

Cisco Press

For the latest on Cisco Press resources and Certification and Training guides, or for information on publishing opportunities, **visit www.ciscopress.com**.

CCIE Professional Development

Cisco OSPF Command and Configuration Handbook
William R. Parkhurst Ph.D., CCIE
1-58705-071-4 • AVAILABLE NOW

This title is a complete OSPF command reference—invaluable for network designers, engineers, and architects. It provides configuration, troubleshooting, and verification scenarios for every possible OSPF command supported by Cisco IOS Software and groups commands by area of implementation. This CCIE preparation source provides clear and concise commentary on the initial release, purpose, syntax, and usage of each OSPF command. Constructed as a portable field guide with easily navigable content so you can quickly find the information you need when you need it.

Cisco BGP-4 Command and Configuration Handbook
William R. Parkhurst, Ph. D., CCIE
1-58705-017-X • AVAILABLE NOW

Cisco BGP-4 Command and Configuration Handbook is a clear, concise, and complete source of documentation for all Cisco IOS Software BGP-4 commands. If you are preparing for the CCIE exam, this book can be used as a laboratory guide to learn the purpose and proper use of every BGP command. If you are a network designer, this book can be used as a ready reference for any BGP command.

Routing TCP/IP, Volume I
Jeff Doyle, CCIE
1-57870-041-8 • AVAILABLE NOW

This book takes the reader from a basic understanding of routers and routing protocols through a detailed examination of each of the IP interior routing protocols. Learn techniques for designing networks that maximize the efficiency of the protocol being used. Exercises and review questions provide core study for the CCIE Routing and Switching exam.

Routing TCP/IP, Volume II
Jeff Doyle, CCIE, and Jennifer DeHaven Carroll, CCIE
1-57870-089-2 • AVAILABLE NOW

Routing TCP/IP, Volume II, provides you with the expertise necessary to understand and implement BGP-4, multicast routing, NAT, IPv6, and effective router management techniques. Designed not only to help you walk away from the CCIE lab exam with the coveted certification, this book also helps you to develop the knowledge and skills essential to a CCIE.

Cisco Press Solutions

Developing IP Multicast Networks, Volume I
Beau Williamson, CCIE
1-57870-077-9 • **AVAILABLE NOW**

This book provides a solid foundation of IP multicast concepts and explains how to design and deploy the networks that will support appplications such as audio and video conferencing, distance-learning, and data replication. Includes an in-depth discussion of the PIM protocol used in Cisco routers and detailed coverage of the rules that control the creation and maintenance of Cisco mroute state entries.

Internet Routing Architectures, Second Edition
Sam Halabi
1-57870-233-X • **AVAILABLE NOW**

The BGP bible! Updated from the best-selling first edition. Explore the ins and outs of interdomain routing network designs and discover current perspectives on internetworking routing architectures. Includes detailed, updated coverage of the defacto interdomain routing protocol BGP and provides numerous, comprehensive configurations of BGP's attributes and various routing policies. A great resource for any organization that needs to build an efficient, reliable enterprise network accessing the Internet.

Cisco Secure PIX® Firewalls
David W. Chapman Jr. and Andy Fox, Editors
1-58705-035-8 • **AVAILABLE NOW**

Learn from the official Coursebook based on the instructor-led training course, *Cisco Secure PIX Firewall Advanced*. This book teaches you the skills needed to describe, configure, verify, and manage the PIX Firewall product family and the Cisco IOS Firewall feature set. Coverage includes not only basic installation details but also how to enable more advanced features and access control. The only book that concentrates solely on PIX Firewall implementation, *Cisco Secure PIX Firewalls* also includes configuration techniques, security management details, and real-life examples of firewall security implementation.